Land Use

Land Use

David Rhind and Ray Hudson

Methuen

London and New York

First published in 1980 by
Methuen & Co. Ltd
11 New Fetter Lane, London EC4P 4EE

Published in the USA by
Methuen & Co.
in association with Methuen, Inc.
733 Third Avenue, New York, NY 10017

Printed in the United States of America

British Library Cataloguing in Publication Data

Rhind, David William
  Land use.
  1. Land use
  I. Title   II. Hudson, Raymond
  III. University paperbacks
  333.7   HD111   80–40477
ISBN 0–416–71780–2
ISBN 0–416–71790–X Pbk (University paperbacks)

Contents

Part 5

Preface

It is perhaps rare to be able to identify the precise moment at which a particular decision was taken which, however elliptically, eventually led to the writing of a book. In this case, however, we retain a vivid memory of that moment. In the course of running a field trip for first year undergraduates to Alnwick in 1975, we designed a project on urban land use. Musing on the desirability of being able to collect detailed land use data not merely for one but for a whole series of towns, we chanced across a report in *The Times* concerning the establishment of the Job Creation Programme by the Manpower Services Commission. Could we get them to provide the financial resources to enable us to mount a survey to collect such comparative data? It transpired that we could and, as a result, a considerable slice of both our lives for the next three years was given over to organizing the Durham and Northumberland Land Use Surveys: we take this opportunity to record our gratitude to the one hundred or so staff employed at various times on these surveys for the high standards which they maintained throughout. Above all, we wish to record our thanks to Professor W.B. Fisher who, as Honorary Secretary of the Durham Research Trust, facilitated the running of these projects. As a consequence of the efforts of our staff, we found ourselves in possession of very detailed data for the use of individual properties in the urban areas of the counties of Durham and Northumberland, to which we subsequently added similar data for Tyne and Wear County (by courtesy of the Tyne and Wear County Council) and are adding data for Cleveland County. John Hanna and Mandy Lane contributed greatly in the analyses of these data, some of which are included in this book.

A consequence of directing these surveys was that we both became increasingly interested in more general issues to do with land use which, in turn, stimulated us to write this book. It is written primarily as an introduction for an Honours degree undergraduate audience, intended to open up the rich variety of information and concepts related to the study of the use of land. While it does contain some original material from our own joint and individual research, it largely involves the bringing together and synthesis of a wide variety of existing work pertaining to land use studies and is organized around the basic theme of 'how can we order land use data?' – necessarily encompassing all the various inter-related stages of data capture, interpretation, modelling and theorizing. It seemed to us that such a synthesis was not only intrinsically desirable but posed a stimulating intellectual challenge: whether we have succeeded we must leave to others to judge.

Acknowledgements and thanks are due to the following people who have, at one time or another, discussed aspects of land use or related matters with us: Dr J. Anderson, Dr M. Anderson, Dr R. Best, Dr P. Carter, Dr A. Champion, Dr A. Coleman, Professor J. T. Coppock, Dr N. J. Cox, Mr N. Dotchin, Dr I. S. Evans, Dr S. Guptill, Ms C. Hallam, Dr B. Harley, Dr R. Harris, Dr M. Jackson, Dr R. Kain, Ms A. Kemp, Dr S. Openshaw, Mrs B. Rose, Mr T. F. Smith, Mr J. Spicer and staff of the Tyne and Wear Joint Information System, Dr J. Townsend, Mr T. C. Waugh, Dr J. Wray.

Drs Best and Coleman, Professor Coppock, Dr Harris and Mr Smith kindly commented on drafts of some material. Their contributions are particularly appreciated.

The diagrams were drawn by Mr A. Corner and his staff in the Drawing Office of the Department of Geography, University of Durham. Photomechanical reproduction was by Mr D. Hudspeth and his staff of the same department. The doubtful privilege of producing a decent typescript fell on Mrs Bell and her typing colleagues in the Department of Geography. R.H. would also like to thank the University of Durham for one term's sabbatical leave in the Easter term of 1978, which enabled him to make substantial progress with his contribution to the book. Both authors would also like to thank the same institution for granting D.R. sabbatical leave in the Michaelmas term of 1979 – the pressures of his resultant impending departure to the Antipodes served to concentrate our minds wonderfully on the task of completing the text.

D.R.
R.H.
Durham
July 1979

Acknowledgements

The authors and the publishers would like to thank the following for permission to reproduce copyright material:

Tables

US Geological Survey, Reston, Virginia, for 3.1 and 3.5. Dr A. Coleman, Kings College, London, for 3.3 and 3.4. Tyne and Wear County Council Joint Information System for 3.6. Department of the Environment, London, for 4.1 and 6.4. The Council of Europe for 4.2 and 4.3. The Editors of *Remote Sensing of the Electromagnetic Spectrum* for 5.1. Institute of British Geographers, London, for 6.2, 6.3, 6.9 and 7.2. The Editors of *Urban Studies* and Longman Group Ltd for 6.5 and 6.7 Department of Land Economy, Cambridge University, for 6.8. Chief Planning Officer, Cleveland County Council, for 6.10. Harper & Row, Publishers, Inc., New York, for 7.1. Hutchinson & Co. (Publishers) Ltd, London, for 7.3. Association of American Geographers, Washington, D.C., for 7.4. Edward Arnold (Publishers) Ltd, London, for 7.5.

Figures

Ordnance Survey, Southampton, for 3.4, 4.3, 4.15, 5.4, 5.5 and 5.6. Tyne and Wear County Council Joint Information System for 3.5. Institute of British Geographers, London, for 4.1, 4.9 and 8.20–8.22. IPC Magazines Ltd for 4.2. Open University Publications Ltd, Milton Keynes, for 4.4. The Controller of Her Majesty's Stationery Office and Department of the Environment, London (Crown Copyright reserved) for 4.5 and 4.17. US Geological Survey, Reston, Virginia, for 4.6. LARS, Purdue University, Indiana, for 4.8. The Council of Europe for 4.11. The Editors of *Progress in Physical Geography* for 4.13. The Remote Sensing Society for 4.14. Hamilton Publishing Co., Inc., Santa Barbara, California, for 4.20. UNESCO, Paris, for 5.3. Department of Natural Resources, Ohio, and the American Planning Association, Washington, D.C., for 5.14. Harper & Row, Publishers, Inc., New York, for 7.1. Hutchinson & Co. (Publishers) Ltd, London, for 7.2–7.4 and 7.13. The Editors of *Geographical Review* for 7.5–7.9. Mrs Marianne Van Valkenburg Carey for 7.10. The Editors of the *American Economic Review* for 7.11. The

ix

Editors of *Human Geography* for 7.12. Edward Arnold (Publishers) Ltd, London, for 7.14, 8.2, 8.12 and 8.14. American Academy of Political and Social Science, Philadelphia, Pennsylvania, for 8.8. Clark University, Worcester, Massachusetts, for 8.9. University of Iowa, Iowa City, for 8.10. Cambridge University Press for 8.11. University of Washington Press, Seattle, for 8.13 and 8.19. B. J. L. Berry for 8.15 and 8.17. Northwestern University Press, Evanston, Illinois, for 8.18. Prentice-Hall, Inc., Englewood Cliffs, New Jersey, for 9.1–9.5. Association of American Geographers, Washington, D.C., for 9.6 and 9.7. University of Illinois Press, Urbana, Illinois, for 9.8. Pergamon Press Ltd, Oxford, for 9.9.

Figures

Glossary of abbreviations

AERE	Atomic Energy Research Establishment (UK)
AGRG	Applied Geochemical Research Group (USA)
CSIRO	Commonwealth Scientific and Industrial Research Organisation (Australia)
CSO	Central Statistical Office (GB)
DoE	Department of the Environment (England and Wales)
DLUS/NLUS	Durham/Northumberland Land Use Surveys
ECU	Experimental Cartography Unit of the Natural Environment Research Council (UK)
EROS	Earth Resources Observation Systems Program, Department of the Interior (USA)
GB	Great Britain (England, Scotland, Wales)
GSS	Government Statistical Service (GB)
IGU	International Geographical Union
JIS	See NGPS
LUNR	Land Use and Natural Resources Inventory of New York State
MAFF	Ministry of Agriculture, Fisheries and Foods (UK)
NASA	National Aeronautics and Space Administration (USA)
NGPS	National Gazetteer Pilot Study (joint study financed by the Department of the Environment and Tyne and Wear County Council; when taken over entirely by the latter, it became known as the Joint Information System)
NLUC	National Land Use Classification
OECD	Organisation for Economic Cooperation and Development
OPCS	Office of Population Censuses and Surveys (England and Wales)
OS	Ordnance Survey (GB)
SDD	Scottish Development Department
SLUS	Second Land Utilisation Survey (GB)
UK	United Kingdom (England, Scotland, Wales and Northern Ireland)
USDA	United States Department of Agriculture
USGS	United States Geological Survey
WLUS	World Land Use Survey

Part 1

1 Introduction: issues and themes

> Buy land – they ain't making no more of it.
>
> *Mark Twain*

Land nationalisation is a vital necessity.

Labour Party Manifesto (1918)

The practical and political importance of land use

There can be no doubt of the significance of land use. On the one hand, we all require land on which to live; on the other, the use of any given parcel of land affects not only those who reside there or have use of that land – for whatever purpose – but also those who live on or have use of adjacent and surrounding areas. Moreover, as Mark Twain pointed out, there is only a finite amount of land. A consequence of this finite supply is that, for certain locations perceived as particularly desirable, the purchase price of land can reach extremely high levels in Western Society: in two large redevelopment schemes in central Paris, La Défense and Front-de-Seine, land changed hands at $2.5 million and $4.0 million per hectare respectively (Rubinstein 1978). Since the financial ability to purchase land and the consequent right to influence or control land use may bring considerable power to those who possess it, control of land and land use has been and remains a politically contentious issue. In Britain, for example, there have been repeated calls over a period of some 200 years to take into public ownership either land itself or the increment in value deriving from development. In the 1780s both Thomas Spence and William Ogilvy called for national ownership of the land and in the early years of the present century considerable support was given to the slogan 'God made the land for the people' (Ambrose 1977, p. 72). Not surprisingly, then, the growing Labour Party latched onto the issue; its 1918 manifesto proclaimed land nationalization to be a vital necessity. Land nationalization, control of land use change and the taxation of 'windfall gains' arising from such change are issues which have since emerged periodically as major political controversies in Britain and which have, to some extent, been tackled by legislation (see chapter 9).

Elsewhere, it is patently obvious that land has also frequently been at the centre of struggles over its use and control – some of these involving physical aggression and war, others more subtle means. Bombing of dykes in the Vietnam war (Lacoste 1973) was, for example, a strategic attempt to disrupt land use for military ends. Less violently, land reform programmes have been seen in many countries as vital to economic and social progress and have often been fiercely resisted by those with vested interests in land; such reform programmes have often affected not only land ownership but also land use (see King 1973) as, for example, in the collectivization of agriculture in the USSR and China.

At a more mundane level, interaction occurs between everyday behaviour and future land use patterns: existing land use arrangements in part determine where people live, where they work and how and when they travel there, where they shop, where they play, etc., while such behaviour in turn helps to shape future land use patterns. It was recognition of this mutual inter-relationship between land use and travel behaviour that underpinned the development of land use/transportation planning in the 1950s and 1960s (see, for example, Bruton 1975; Starkie 1976). Indeed, the central position of land in economic and social life – quite apart from the political heat generated by the issue of land – has generally led to considerable State intervention, both direct and indirect, in land use control and the land market. In Britain, the perceived importance of the inter-relationship between the supply of development land and 'proper' patterns of urban and regional development has led to much legislation intended to produce effective state control of land for the development process. The most recent significant – if short-lived – addition to this legislation was the Community Land Act, intended both to skim-off development values for public benefit and to give local authorities the statutory powers, though not the finances, compulsorily to purchase land needed for development (see Gazzard 1978). As a consequence of this State involvement, regulation of land use is, for some people, their job and their ambition: at least some influential British planners such as Ash (1978) see their primary role as ensuring 'the proper use of land', Coppock and Gebbett (1978, p. 119) expressing this as 'Although . . . town and country planning is now extremely wide-ranging, the control of land use remains its essential basic function . . .'.

One particular recent manifestation of this concern for land to be allocated to its 'proper' use is the concern with derelict land which developed as part of the more general environmental movement in the 1960s (see Barr 1969). More recently, there has developed a specific concern with the identification of urban wasteland and derelict land and the subsequent creation and implementation of plans to return this land to more productive use. The Civic Trust have estimated that no less than 56,000 hectares of derelict land existed in England and Wales in 1977, as well as uncounted hectares of 'dormant land'. This may be compared with the estimate of 51,000 hectares in 1954 (Willatts 1961). Such concern for wasteland and the 'proper' allocation of land is certainly not new. Rather the context of concern has changed. As Darby (1951) pointed out, there were periodic outcries from the 18th century onwards against the wastelands of Britain that could not be or were not devoted to agricultural use. 'Proper use' may be variously interpreted: in the USA, information on land use is a statutory requirement for various purposes under the National Environmental Policy Act, the Coastal Zone Management Act, the Forest and Rangeland Renewable Resource Protection Act and section 208 of the Federal Water Pollution Control Act Amendments of 1972 (Gallagher *et al.* 1977).

The intellectual tradition of land use studies

In addition to, and also because of, such practical considerations, the past, present and future arrangements and juxtapositions of land use have occupied academics – drawn from a number of disciplines and including agriculturalists, economists, geographers, planners and sociologists – for many years. It is no exaggeration to identify a well-established intellectual tradition of studying land use, both in rural and urban contexts. Initially, agricultural land use was the main focus of attention; for example, both Ricardo and von Thünen were concerned mainly with questions of rent and location in the context of agricultural land use, a reflection of the fact that the economic and social basis of the early 19th-century societies in which they lived were primarily agricultural. While agricultural land use remains a vital issue in a large part of the contemporary world, the increased importance of urbanization and the growth of urban areas from the 19th century to the present day (in Britain, for example, about 80% of the total population currently live in urban areas) have led to an increased study of patterns and extent of urban land use, the conversion of rural to urban land and the conservation and preservation of rural areas. The growing crises in many Western cities in the later 1960s and early 1970s, which were expressed partly in mass protests against living conditions, provide further compelling reasons for focusing upon the determinants of urban land use pattern and land use change.

These are the more obvious and important relationships and areas of intellectual concern in land use studies; beyond them, though, the use of land can have vital, though less immediately apparent, impacts which are reflected in the work of a variety of academics in other disciplines. Such impacts can arise in one of two ways: spatial variation in land use acts either as a back-cloth to work in these disciplines or, alternatively, is an integral part of multi-disciplinary research. For example, to the geochemist carrying out regional reconnaissance studies (see AGRG 1978), knowledge of present and past land use is crucial if anomalous geochemical concentrations are to be regarded as indicators of areas requiring further, more detailed investigation – as opposed to samples contaminated by previous industrial processes. Land use can also be seen as a back-cloth to studies of climate: nocturnal 'heat islands' generated by urban areas are well substantiated (Pease *et al.* 1977). On the other hand, the incorporation of the same land use data in multi-disciplinary studies may have practical importance: this was emphasized recently by some of the results of a major geochemical survey of England and Wales, which revealed that cadmium levels in the Somerset village of Shipham were one hundred times the national average. These contemporary levels reflected the mining of zinc in the area from Roman times until its cessation some 200 years ago. Despite the health risks which such cadmium levels pose, leading to possible respiratory troubles and even kidney failure, at least some residents were reported to be less concerned with this than the possible harmful effects on property values in the village as a result of its newly acquired 'doomwatch image' (_Sunday Telegraph_ 21 January, 1979). Another related example concerns those studying the causes of mortality, for whom data on land use – both at work-place and home – could provide ideal information on which to build or test hypotheses. From many points of view, then, a knowledge of the use of land is of crucial importance.

Why is land use as it is?

While knowledge of what currently exists is often a necessary condition for answering questions related to the use of land, it is rarely a sufficient one. To know _how_ a particular parcel of land came to have its present use – for example, turning from forest to enclosed farmland to huge, hedgeless fields or from green field to urban sprawl to decaying inner city slum – demands at a minimum a longitudinal profile of changes in use through time. Some such data exist for particular time periods and places. For example, the US Department of Agriculture have reported that, during the decade from 1960 onwards, an average of 296,000 hectares of land within the USA were urbanized each year while transportation land uses expanded by 53,000 hectares and recreational land uses by 400,000 hectares per annum. In France, the current demand for additional urban land use is of the order of 15,000 hectares per annum (Rubinstein 1978, p. 91).

But even this sort of information – generally available only on an incomplete and fragmentary basis – may be insufficient for some explanatory purposes. In order to understand 'why' land use changes as well as 'how' the changes occur, it may be necessary to have information on who currently owns and who has owned the land in question: Ambrose (1977) and Denman (1970) for example, have argued that this is essential. In an agricultural context, Munton (1978, p. 60) has argued in a similar vein by saying: 'Government legislation . . . in particular with regard to capital taxation, has made the question of ownership critical, for as owners seek legal means to reduce Capital Transfer, Capital Gains and Development Tax liabilities, their decisions may well have important management implications for those who are actually farming the land.' In general terms, these contentions are indisputable for both understanding past and present land use patterns and in any attempt to predict the future role and use of land: thus, to account for the majority of apparent transgressions of building regulations in the London Green Belt requires the knowledge that these largely involved Government-owned research laboratories and the like which did not have to go through the same planning procedures as other potential builders. About 5% of the agricultural land in the UK is owned by or leased to government and the Crown (CSO 1979).

Yet information on land ownership may be – indeed, usually is – potentially sensitive and, as a consequence, is not always easy to obtain accurately and in detail. A recent case in point is the inventory of ownership of land in Scotland compiled by McEwen (1977) which, despite certain short-comings in accuracy, pointed out the undoubted domination of land-ownership in Scotland by non-nationals – again a subject of considerable political significance in view of the resurgence of nationalist sentiment in Scotland. Such an interest in land-ownership is by no means confined to Scotland and is, of course, scarcely new, as Pattison (1957) has shown in relation to the USA rectangular survey system in the 1780s.

The data problem

It is evident that, for both academic and practical purposes, information concerning a variety of aspects about land other than its use is needed in order to understand why past, present and future land use patterns are as they are. The multi-faceted character of interest in land is illustrated by Rowley (1978) who listed ten items of information required by those concerned with land – such as current use or activity, intensity of use, restrictions on use, value and ownership. While such data may be *desirable* – indeed even essential – it is altogether another issue as to whether they are *available* in practice. Data sources vary widely from country to country, within countries and between rural and urban areas. The existence of a comprehensive and computerized ownership register for part of Sweden (Rystedt 1977) represents one extreme of the data availability spectrum, although, as we point out in chapters 4 and 5, satellite imagery and air photography may well result in a complete picture of land cover in the USA in the near future. At the other end of the spectrum are some parts of, for example, Africa where next to nothing is known about the detailed distribution of land use even though, for other parts of the same continent, there are numerous empirical studies of land use (Floyd 1972).

In Britain, detailed land use data are available down to the resolution of individual buildings, even parts of buildings, for certain areas; other data are available to cover the rest of the country but at widely different resolutions and for different moments in time. Even in this comparatively happy situation, however, it is possible for well-known research workers to claim that: 'At present we are taking land unnecessarily, wastefully, blindly and much faster than we realize ' (Coleman 1978) and that '. . . there is no real land problem in Britain at the moment. Most of the problem is simply in the mind; it is not out there on the ground' (Best 1978). The contemporary existence of such widely divergent views is salutary and arises primarily because the available data upon which they are based are unsatisfactory for the task at hand, being wholly or partially out-of-date, of dubious accuracy, or, perhaps most commonly, are inappropriately classified. Not surprisingly, both the academic and the practical consequences of inadequate land use data are serious and this may be readily demonstrated. In the course of a lecture given to the Royal Geographical Society in London on 11 February 1974, summarizing the results of a major study of post-war British planning systems, Professor Peter Hall (1974) commented that the attempt to carry out regional-scale analysis of parts of the English Metropolis: 'was among the most frustrating and least reliable pieces of our entire research. The difficulties . . . arose from the necessity to compare land use surveys developed by different agencies for different purposes, with slightly different classifications of land use.'

These points were elaborated in the discussion of the paper. Diamond (1974) commented: 'Objectively a rather extraordinary situation exists. We have legislation, the impact of which is directly on and concerned with land use change and we have a national system of local planning authorities who can collect, collate and publish such information. *Yet no really reliable or adequate data exists*' (emphasis added). Coppock (1974) added: 'I . . . should like to reinforce Derek Diamond's point about information. This is a very important topic but there is a great complacency about the lack of suitable information, *without which we cannot adequately plan*' (emphasis added). To this, Hall replied: 'As to the points about data limitations. . . I can only reinforce them. Having struggled for many long months with the researchers who were trying to analyse the land use variations and finally discovering that the incompatibilities in classification made the results of many, many thousand man-hours and woman-hours to some extent invalid, then I can only emphasise that we desperately need some national Domesday book for land use, preferably updated every ten years at the time of the population census.'

If this was the position in the mid-1970s in Britain, with reputedly the most sophisticated planning systems in the Western world, what is the situation in other countries? Furthermore, when multi-national land use variations are considered, the complications and problems multiply – not merely because of the generally uneven level of detail of available data. Discrepancies arise for rather more fundamental reasons, particularly the fact that the pressing problems in one country may be largely irrelevant in another and these are reflected in what classes of data are collected. This point was made by the OECD (1976): 'The demand for land for non-agricultural purposes has been increasing as a result of rapid economic growth . . . . What is acceptable in the United States, a vast country where agricultural production greatly exceeds its domestic requirements, may raise serious problems in countries like Japan or the Netherlands with high population densities or the United Kingdom or Norway which import agricultural products.' Thus, the incompatibility of international statistics on land use, except at the most aggregate levels, is no more than one would expect: such data may well be collected in relation to quite different perceived needs in markedly different environments. It should be noted, however, that the domination of relevant satellite imagery by the USA may well permit, at a particular level of aggregation, a standardization of data collection and so make possible the comparison of land use in different countries – with the possible consequence that such data may fail to meet the needs of some and perhaps all of them.

Our objectives

The rest of the book is not, then, primarily oriented to a detailed analysis of land use in a single country or to national comparisons of land use patterns. Such studies would be of great value but, in the present state of the art, would be difficult to carry out and likely to be error-prone in the absence of data collected specifically to facilitate comparisons. Nor do we discuss issues to do with land reform programmes and their use, the relationship between land and national and regional economic development and so on. Rather our approach reflects the parallel existence of three paradigms within con- temporary human geography – locational or spatial analysis, behavioural approaches and structural approaches (see Johnston 1977). We first examine the philosophical and definitional aspects of the nature of land use and the variety of ways in which land use data can be and have been collected, together with the effects that different methods of data collection may have upon interpretations of land use patterns. Following on from this examination of the data base, we briefly examine what can be said about the frequency of different land uses encountered in one country. This is almost entirely non- geographical or aspatial; it is based largely upon national statistics and, while of considerable practical importance, is a rather abstract description, devoid of any idea about how the different uses have come into being. In the third section of the book we go a stage further and examine how order may be extracted from chaos – the modelling of land use patterns so as to explain these and to enable comparisons to be drawn between land use patterns in different parts of the world, other than on the basis of aspatial summaries. Consideration is given both to 'traditional' approaches, and to newer perspectives on land use patterns.

We stress repeatedly the crucial inter-relationship between the sections; between methods of defining and collecting land use and attempts to compare, understand and explain land use patterns. Essentially these represent different facets of the one process of attempting to order and make sense of the world. Currently available data and theoretical interpretations of those data reciprocally transform one another and lead to the measurement or analysis of additional data and fresh interpretations.

Part 2

2 Land use data and the user

Who needs which land use data?

The case for needing land use data is frequently ignored in the published literature, either because the answer is believed trivially obvious or because the users are so numerous and diffuse that to list them is banal. One exception to this is Horton (1974); another is Rowley (1978).

Although both of these attitudes may be legitimate, it is helpful for what follows to enumerate some of the users and the type of data that they require. Manifestly, a planner concerned with national affairs or even regional ones rarely needs to know what exists at 42 South Street, Durham. Equally, regional summaries are of little interest to the Fire Officer intent on planning fire prevention measures in fire-prone industrial premises. We can systematize description of requirements by use of the scale defined on pp. 31 and 32, ranging from level IC (coarse resolution in space and time) to VA (extremely fine resolution in space and up-dated whenever any changes take place); we should remember that, if required, data can always be degraded to a coarser spatial and temporal resolution but that improving the data on either count requires the input of additional information, often from a new survey (see chapter 3).

The types of known user and their data requirements are summarized in table 2.1. Although this can only be a very crude approximation to the real picture, several points of some importance arise from it. The first is that there are many inter-relationships between the users listed: the most obvious one is the one-way flow between local planners who collect, or at least compile, much of the data in Britain and the central government which collates the individual contributions into a national picture. Other links, especially the informal and *ad hoc* ones between academics and local planners, are also important and occasionally the situation is inverted, where work by academics is used directly by local government (Coleman 1978) and central government (Champion 1975). The multi-national comparisons made of land use by academics, some of which (e.g. Stamp 1965) have been fostered by the World Land Use Survey, have proved of value to professional users.

But these inter-relationships do not end at the stage of data collection and supply. Consider, as an example, the case where land is changed in use from

Table 2.1 An outline of the uses and users of land use data.

Type of use/user	Examples	Data type*	Frequency of use	Areal extent for one user
'House-keeping' or administrative chores	District planner checking planning applications, sending out zonal detail (UK)	VA (mostly urban)	Moderate and spasmodic	District
	Central planner involved in planning appeals	VA	Low, but critically important	Sub-district
	Equalization of tax assessments in many states of the USA	VA		County
	District planner making statutory returns on land use change to central government	IVA	Annually (in theory)	District
'Positive' planning initiatives				
inventorying	Agriculturalists, foresters; Police, Fire, Health officers	IVB–IC		Area of administrative responsibility All levels
monitoring	Local, regional and national planners monitoring change, possibly as statutory requirement	VA – IB (UK) VA – IC (US)	Highly variable but often frequent and of critical importance	All levels
prediction	Local, regional, national and international planners carrying out suitability (e.g. Environmental Impact Assessment studies)	VA – IC	Enormous range, but a statutory obligation in US and under discussion or an obligation in many parts of Europe	
'Academic' or non-policy orientated research	Comparing different areas and modelling land use patterns in cities and rural areas (see chapters 7 and 8) by geographers, economists, sociologists	Whatever available		Selected urban areas (e.g. Niedercorn and Hearle 1964)
	Collection of data (e.g. Coleman 1961) and analysis of classification effects	VA – IVC		Usually local but cf. Second Land Utilisation Survey

* The meaning of these terms is defined in chapter 3.

14

agriculture or forestry to urban use: surface water run-off increases in magnitude, flood peaks become sharper, surface and ground water quality may well deteriorate and the volume of water used increases dramatically. Without some close collaboration between those involved in initiating and steering this land use transition, effective flood control, water supply and waste water treatment is unlikely.

The second important point is that some of these applications of land use data are statutory requirements – notably those for Environmental Impact Assessment studies, such as those necessitated by the US National Environmental Policy Act of 1970 (Stoel and Scherr 1978) or in certain European countries (Lee and Wood 1978): most of these require detailed land use information over comparatively small areas around a proposed new development. At the other end of the scale is the UK Department of the Environment's circular 71/74 to all Local Authorities, requesting annual land use change information (DoE 1974a): this was intended to provide information for each of the 403 districts in England and Wales but, in its first year of operation (1974/75), nothing of any value could be derived from the responses. In 1976/77, the second year in which responses were mandatory, nearly half of the districts responded to the circular (Rice 1978). The existence of the statutory requirements does not, then, necessarily guarantee the availability of data or the quality of those which are available.

The third point is one which is fundamental to all management – the higher level the function, the less predictable is the type, volume and quality of the data required to meet user demands. Thus, within a given planning system which is not subject to revolutionary change, it is much easier to anticipate the needs of those involved in 'house-keeping' functions than it is to prepare for the next high-level crisis facing the Chief Executive.

A final point is also important – that of temporal continuity. There is clearly little point in obtaining land use data for two moments in time if the data are not comparable, either by virtue of the way that they have been collected or because of the way that they have been stored. The options here are reviewed later (pp. 18–35).

What are the data used for?

In considering land use – or indeed any other – data and their uses, it is useful to consider the functional ends to which these are put. In other words, individuals as diverse as epidemiologists and foresters may use the data for the same types of task and, as a result, be happy with the same sort of data in the same sort of form.

Jeffers (1970) postulated that the usual aims of conventional land use surveys were merely two-fold:

(i) to produce estimates of the proportions of land used for various defined purposes and hence of the actual area of land devoted to these purposes;

(ii) to produce maps of the area surveyed, showing the spatial distribution of the various land use classes.

Although conceptually distinct, recent technological developments in the handling of spatial data by computer have ensured that both of these are now feasible from one source – the land use data file (see chapter 5; also DoE 1978; ECU 1978). We may also note in passing that Jeffers' concern and experience was largely with ecological data: he thus emphasized the 'areal extent' or land cover, rather than the 'number of functional units' or land use *sensu stricto* approach to land use (see p. 20).

Coppock (1970) has, in counter-distinction, seen the role of land use data in a more policy-orientated sense – to guide the formation of new policies and to assist the implementation of those policies that have been chosen. It is both possible and desirable, however, to examine the technical uses of these data in more detail. Amplifying Dueker and Talcott's (1973) list, we can state these as follows:

 (i) to provide area and/or volume descriptions of the land uses within defined regions, usually on a statistical basis, or to define the land use at a particular point in space;

 (ii) to 'overlay' data for an area at different moments in time and thus produce rates-of-change in land use;

 (iii) to overlay different data sets for the same area – land use with soil, geology, geochemical distributions and so on – to determine coincidence of physical features and, hence, possibly get hints as to factors responsible for the observed land use;

 (iv) to overlay different data sets for the same area to observe relationships between physical features and socio-economic or medical attributes, or transport and other network configurations – for the same reason as (iii);

 (v) to carry out statistical analysis to explore relationships within an area – either aspatially (such as 'is there an inverse correlation between the extent of land use A and that of land use B?') or spatially ('is land use A next to land use D more frequently than one would expect from a random scatter of uses in space?; is there clear evidence of radial or sectoral structures in the city's land use pattern?'; see p. 101);

 (vi) to produce comparisons between areas at the same moment in time; such comparisons may be carried out at many different levels, such as the comparison of towns or of countries;

 (vii) to produce graphic representations of the data, either as maps or graphs.

Conventionally, in the past, most of these uses have been manually based. Important developments in geographical information systems since the mid-1960s have, however, led to a variety of facilities for carrying out these functions by means of computers. Given the continuing diminution in the costs of information storage, retrieval and processing – by about an order of magnitude every five years at present – these are becoming increasingly widely used and are discussed in chapter 5.

The ideal land use data

Clearly, there is a wide variety of users of land use data, many of whom have different requirements by the way of resolution, timeliness and reliability, as well as different analytical capabilities and needs. By way of conclusion to this chapter, it is interesting to conjecture on the feasibility and form of land use data which could meet all these varying needs. The only alternative to this ideal is multiple survey of the same area, carried out for individual, specific purposes.

Such ideal data would have to describe both functional and formal differentiation of space: in the American sense it would have to describe both land use and land cover (p. 20). It would have to describe 'atomic' areas, i.e. areas which were homogeneous both in form and in function and which could be aggregated to whatever larger areas were required. It would have to be classified in such a way that it not only permitted re-aggregation to whatever level of detail and whatever grouping a user might require (p. 102), but in which it also permitted comparison with the results of previous surveys: in other words, it would have to be stored in a very detailed form indeed. Complete surveys of the areas of interest would have to be carried out at or about the same moment in time. Finally, it would have to relate to all the time periods which users might require and meet the most demanding of their accuracy specifications. In other words, it would have everywhere and all the time to meet the most stringent demands. Given this, it is not surprising that special purpose surveys exist and that the same area may be surveyed several times!

3 Conceptual and technical aspects of land use

The danger is clear: national land use statistics are, potentially, a meaningless amalgam of figures based on different classifications applied to dissimilar areal units with varying degrees of precision.

Dickinson and Shaw (1978)

Thus far, we have dealt with the needs for land use data as seen by various groups in society. It is now essential to consider in rather more detail the great variations, both conceptual and technical, which it is possible to produce in the characteristics of such data. Without this understanding, it is quite impossible to compare different surveys or even to evaluate any one survey in any meaningful way. We shall proceed by considering each of the relevant data characteristics in turn.

Activity or form?

A fundamental underpinning of any survey of land use is whether the information recorded relates to some activity carried on at different places, or whether it relates to inherent physical characteristics of those places. In urban areas, such a distinction is usually straightforward. Thus a distinction can be made between use of two buildings on the grounds that one was an office while the other was a residential property; alternatively, a formal distinction might be made on the basis that one was multi-storey and the other was single storey. Analogous situations do occur in a rural context, although here a duality of viewpoint is clearer – a stream or the growth of a crop may be regarded both as an activity going on at a place and also as a physical entity there. In general, the same land can be classified as being used for agricultural, recreation, transport or residential purposes or, alternatively, on the basis of woodland cover, the existence of water bodies and so on. Whether the classification is functional or formal will, in these circumstances, depend partly on the objective of the study. Fig. 3.1 illustrates the results of classifying the same area on activity and on formal bases.

In the rural case, a further difficulty may exist since the criteria on which detailed land use assignations are made often reflect short-term management considerations. Indeed, many users of agricultural land use data require not so much 'present coverage of the land' as 'present capability' data. The result is a further confusion of functional and formal characteristics in the land use description – leading to what is, in effect, a multi-dimensional classification. Generally speaking, only the physical characteristics of the land or soil have

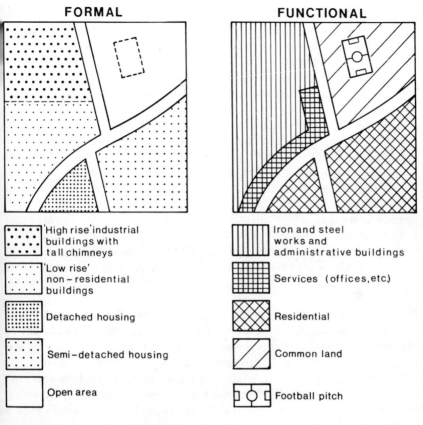

FORMAL

FUNCTIONAL

⬚	'High rise'industrial buildings with tall chimneys
⬚	'Low rise' non – residential buildings
⬚	Detached housing
⬚	Semi–detached housing
⬚	Open area

⬚	Iron and steel works and administrative buildings
⬚	Services (offices,etc.)
⬚	Residential
⬚	Common land
⬚	Football pitch

Figure 3.1 Land use in the same area classified on formal and functional bases.

been considered in such 'capability' maps and the area is divided into capability classes on the basis of physical restraints to development, such as depth of soil, stoniness and slope. Rarely is any allowance made for chemical, as opposed to physical, limitations to development, and distance to market, types of road, farm structure and managerial efficiency are not generally incorporated; good examples of such surveys are Klingebiel and Montgomery (1961) and the British Ministry of Agriculture, Fisheries and Food's Agricultural Land Classification map of England and Wales (MAFF 1968, 1974). It is interesting to note that economic criteria were included in the latter's proposed classification at an earlier stage (MAFF 1965) but were dropped for the publication of the mapped results.

There is common agreement (Coppock and Gebbett 1978; Dickinson and Shaw 1978) that 'activity' or, more specifically, 'principal activity carried on at a site' is the main concern of many people in collecting land use data; Clawson and Stewart (1965) defined land use as 'man's activities on land which are directly related to the land'. Yet there is also considerable interest, especially in rural areas, in what may be termed 'land cover'. This has been defined by Burley (1961) as 'the vegetation and artificial constructions covering the land surface'. Indeed, in many recent American studies (e.g. Anderson, 1977), the two are invariably used in association; this partly reflects the collection of data by satellite imagery (from which it is difficult to distinguish many activities) but also reflects the occasionally inter-dependent nature of activity and form and the conceptually fuzzy distinction between them. We shall see later that such inter-dependence is a critical assumption in some land use surveys but, at this stage, it is as well to note the results of Hofstee's (1976) study in the Netherlands – considerable field work was necessary to convert 'formally' classified land use data taken from air photographs into functional or 'activity-based' data. In some circumstances, such distinctions are un-necessary. We shall henceforth use 'land use' as a general term covering either or both activity and formally-based data in these circumstances. 'Land cover' will be used in the sense defined by Burley (1961) and 'land use *sensu stricto*' or land use *ss* will be used when activity-based data alone is under discussion.

Spatial units

We normally think of land use *ss* or land cover as spread over an area of land. In practice, however, there are several different ways in which the data may be collected over space and stored and presented. Choice of the 'geographical individual' – the section of ground which is considered as a unit for subsequent purposes – has considerable implications for analysis and even more for the level of effort needed for any ground survey. Frequently, however, choice of spatial unit is outside the scope of the end-user of the data and, if particular technology is used, of even the data collector – as we shall see.

The most obvious way of considering geographical individuals as spatial units is on a dimensional basis: use of the dimensions 0 to 2 gives point, line and area representations although, for some purposes, extension to the third dimension (producing a volume) is of some importance.

POINT REPRESENTATION

Clearly, a point representation may result either from a sample from an unknown population (Coleman 1978; Dickinson and Shaw 1978; Frolov with Maling 1969; Nunnally and Witmer 1970) or simply as a convenient, if abstract, means of describing each of a number of features, such as houses, in an area. In the first case, a sample drawn in a random or suitably stratified random fashion (Berry and Baker 1968; Wood 1955) permits the calculation of a figure summarizing land use over the area sampled and also some measure of the likely extent of error in this estimate. It is particularly appropriate where information about the nature and degree of change, rather than its location, is required. It also offers an effective method for deciding whether up-dating of a previous survey is needed. Robertson and Stoner (1970) discuss the cost and accuracy aspects of land-based surveys of this type. Such a procedure is eminently suited for macro-studies of rural or urban – residential type of land cover, except in so far that the transport involved in any field-based study may be expensive or simply impossible (see chapter 4). It also depends upon the existence of adequate topographic base maps.

The point sampling procedure, as normally carried out, gives land cover information and not land use *ss*. In addition, it gives only 'crop' information as opposed to 'fields', i.e. since there is no knowledge whatever once the samples have been collected of where the boundaries of the real geographical units lie, the only summary statistics which can be given are of the area of land use type A (either as a percentage of the wider area of interest or in terms of absolute units like hectares). Fig. 3.2 illustrates this: from the point samples, it

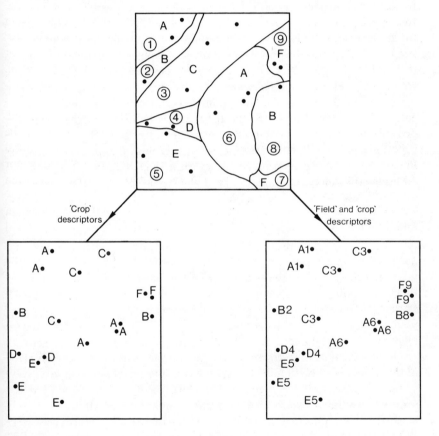

① 'Field' number

A 'Crop' or land cover type

• Sample point

Figure 3.2 Point sampling of land use: the distinction between 'fields' and 'crops' of land use.

is impossible to determine the percentage of the total area covered by 6 as opposed to the total area covered by all the As unless two descriptions are stored for each sample point – the 'field number' (e.g. 6) and the 'crop' (i.e. land cover type A). Such a procedure is possible, if tiresome, when working from maps but is often unrealistic when working in the field (see chapter 4).

Where points are stored so as to represent, say, each and every house or property or each and every field, this generally indicates that no over-riding need was seen for the areal extent of each such geographical individual when the survey was planned or, alternatively, that the level of available technology and human resources suggested this was a suitable approach (DoE 1973; Rhind and Hudson 1980; Rystedt 1977). In these circumstances, the feature described may either be land use *sensu stricto* or land cover since the decision to allocate a particular point is taken *after* the survey is carried out. Clearly, then, the use of points as geographical individuals may either be adopted as a rapid means of sample survey or, alternatively as a compact way of storing geographical information about all of the geographical individuals in an area (see p. 96). In the latter case, it may be possible to construct a more traditional-looking, if imprecise, map of land use areas by employing one of various assumptions: fig. 5.4, for example, is a map of modal land use *ss* for each of the 100 m squares in the town of Darlington. Alternatively, it is possible to recombine the points into zones using a Thiessen polygon procedure, as done by Rhind (1973a) for drift geology mapping: this assumes that all areas in the map are of a type found at the nearest data point. Although the same procedure may be applied to sample data, this is generally unwise unless the sample is very large.

TRAVERSE LINES

Another form of spatial unit is the traverse line, along which different land uses are recorded, the cumulative 'length' of each land use type representing its relative occurrence over the sampled area. This has been much used in earlier times (see Colby 1933; Proudfoot 1942) in ground-based land use survey, especially in poorly mapped areas with air-photo coverage. Unlike the use of points as spatial units, it has found virtually no major use as a data storage method. Robertson and Stoner (1970) describe one such survey. In general, randomly orientated traverses are essential if some measure of the likely error in the results is to be obtained – essential for any legitimate sample survey. Thus, inferences as to the land use characteristics of an area based upon the results of a single traverse by aircraft are of unknown reliability.

Much soil sampling and mapping has been based upon the use of traverses; since it is generally held that in Britain the greatest rate of change in the soil characteristics is down the hillslopes, many traverses are deliberately orientated down-slope to maximize the variation studied, interpretation and interpolation being used in between the traverses, together with topographic information, to complete areal coverage. Some *a priori* postulates of this kind can also be used for observing the maximum rates of land use change with the minimum effort (radial traverses out of a city centre form one such sampling scheme), but all suffer from the disadvantage that the non-random sampling may create the illusion of the form of land use originally suspected (in this example a set of radial land use zones).

ZONES

Much the most common way of treating land use, in terms of survey and of storage in map form, has been as zones-polygons within which the land use is homogeneous or as near this as makes no difference for the use to which the data were originally collected. Zonal data collected by ground survey are zonal in type largely because it is relatively straightforward to collect it thus, usually by walking streets in urban areas or because fields are convenient units in cultivated rural areas. We shall see in chapter 4, however, that land cover data collected by remote sensing is already zonal in part. The polygons completely cover or exhaust space within the area of interest and their boundaries are often taken as physical features in the landscape. This concept of homogeneity is an important one since only at the survey stage or by repeating the survey stage can any user of the data find out just how varied is the land use within any one zone. As an example, fig. 3.3b illustrates a

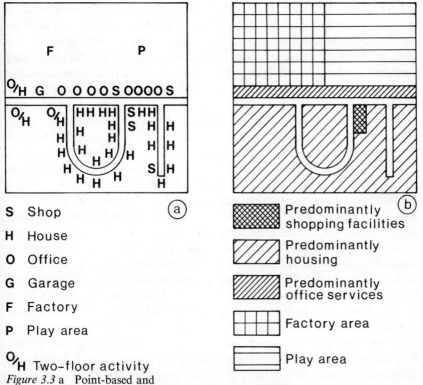

S   Shop   (a)

H   House

O   Office

G   Garage

F   Factory

P   Play area

$^O/_H$ Two–floor activity

     Predominantly shopping facilities

     Predominantly housing

     Predominantly office services

     Factory area

     Play area

Figure 3.3 a   Point-based and
        b   zone-based representations of the same urban land use data; zonal representation 'submerges' some land uses.

hypothetical land use zone-type map while fig. 3.3a shows a detailed plot of the same information, showing individual properties. It is also clear that the degree of homogeneity is linked with data resolution and with the type of classification recorded. If mixed categories are permitted (such as 'mixed residential and commercial'), then some indication is given of the land use 'mix' – but this is often unsatisfactory since such qualitative classes give no indication of whether 0.1% or 70% of the land use is commercial. In statistical terms, it is usually held that such regionalization (for such it is) should ensure that the between-areas variance is much greater than that within areas. Grigg (1965, 1967) gives a good account of classification and regionalization of areas in space. Considerable work in the 1960s and the early 1970s (see Hodgart 1979) was devoted to the definition of optimal zoning systems: the resulting procedures could be employed to get the best possible zonal representation of very detailed land use data. In one sense, though, such considerations are now largely irrelevant – computer facilities exist such that extremely detailed data, if available, can be held as such and aggregated individually as any user requires. Where such mechanical aids are available, data should never be immutably transformed to a coarser form than that in which they were collected.

Like all classifications, this dimensional consideration of the spatial units used for recording land use data is imperfect. One hybrid form must be mentioned – the point sample whose value is not 'instantaneous' but is averaged over a certain area. Thus points on a regular grid, each point being identified as what is found for, say, 40 m around it, are a special but important combination of point and zone recording: such an approach is not limited to remote-sensed data. Floyd (1978) describes its use in Puerto Rico, and Duffield and Coppock (1975) have long used it for many different data types in Scotland.

What we have considered thus far is the form of geometric abstraction which we may use to record our observations of land use. There are, however, at least three other important aspects of the spatial units chosen. All of these apply almost entirely to zonal representations. The first of these is to distinguish between what Harvey (1969, p. 351) has termed *natural* areal units and *artificial* ones. Here the former term encompasses such discrete entities as farms, lakes, fields, street blocks, states and so on. These are generally only 'natural' in so far as they have physically observable extremities and, often, in so far as they relate to functionally-orientated organization. We may also note that some 'natural' areas, such as the street block, may be regarded as a functional (i.e. activity-based) entity for some purposes and not for others. Further, a 'natural' unit is not natural for all purposes: there are often many alternative 'natural' units which one may detect in the landscape – a farm or field unit may not match to an area of similar soils. Even so, it is generally the case that rural land use is built up from the observable molecular elements of the rural landscape such as fields and the street pattern often gives the same degree of 'naturalness' to urban surveys.

Contrasted with this are the artificial areal units, often defined as being constant in size and shape and employed for ease of survey or because of the survey technology, as in remote sensing. It can validly be argued, however, that such regular spatial series are more than just a convenience of survey – they are to geography what collecting information by years (rather than say, by king's reigns) are to history (Evans 1979). In other words, they give a simple means of point sampling the area on an exhaustive and consistent basis and certainly facilitate comparison through time – the contents of each cell at time p is simply compared with the contents at time q; none of the extremely nasty problems of comparing areas of different shapes and sizes occur. If we must use natural units, the extent of such difficulties of comparison suggests that it may be sensible to use pre-existing 'natural' or 'semi-natural' areas as land use zones: a particular concern in Britain, for instance, is the linking together of land use and population census data (Dickinson and Shaw 1978; DoE 1978). Since the basic census data collection units (the Enumeration Districts or EDs) are chosen on a multiplicity of criteria but are only changed where necessary before each decennial census, any data comparisons are greatly facilitated by mapping land use with EDs or, if there is too much variation within these, in smaller units whose boundaries are coincident with those of the ED, as shown in fig. 3.4. The additional provision of Census data for 1971 by artificial units (1 km grid squares) simplified certain land use and population matching operations (see chapter 5). The disadvantages of artificial units are, however, immense: except fortuitously, one unit does not describe either a formal or an activity unit. It may sometimes, with suitable human experience, be possible to amalgamate such artificial units into formal units but almost never is it possible to create activity units of any reliability in such a fashion. In passing, we should note that, just occasionally, what appear to be artificial areal units to the observer may turn out to be closely related to some natural ones. An example of this is the selection of 40 acre rectangular areas for the 'atomic spatial units' in the Minnesota Land Management Information System (Hsu *et al.* 1975) because these parcels are the smallest consistent unit in the US land survey system and most blocks of land, whether in public or private ownership, have as their edges the boundaries of these 40 acre parcels – to the extent that they are reflected in the field boundaries, in forested areas and within cities as major streets. The landscape of Minnesota is thus partitioned into what elsewhere would be widely regarded as artificial units.

The penultimate aspects of spatial units to which we should refer are also discussed in some detail by Harvey (1969, pp. 351–4). This concerns the singularity or collectiveness of the areal units. A land use *ss* zone in which one manufacturing enterprise exists is an example of a singular zone, a farm in one land use *ss* zone is another. Alternatively, a set of semi-detached houses might form one land cover zone and a set of farms or fields another. Occasionally, though, the same unit (such as a farm) may be thought of as either singular or collective. Even if it is singular in nature when collected, subsequent use may

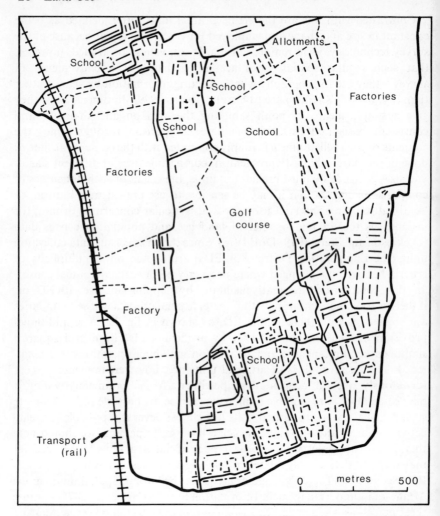

Figure 3.4 Selected land uses (derived from a large scale Ordnance Survey map) superimposed on the outline of the 1971 Census Enumeration Districts in Birtley, Tyne and Wear County; note that the land use character of the EDs is markedly different and also that the ED boundaries occasionally subdivide entities such as streets.

produce collective units: if we wish to know the land use breakdown by district and county (England) or by county and state (US), we will wish progressively to aggregate the initial data (though problems may occur where the boundaries of the land use zones do not coincide with those of the administrative units). Such considerations are important largely because of how we subsequently analyse and interpret the data. At the very least, we must compare like with like: to say that 20% of the plants in given area A are industrial while 40% of the extent of area B is industrial compares different kinds of areal individuals and is patently absurd. Yet this is the common result of comparing activity-based natural unit land use schemes with formally-based ones. The situation is liable to be even worse when artificial units are utilized.

In addition to the need to compare like with like, the use of collective data units in sophisticated analyses can lead to what has been termed the ecological fallacy (Johnston 1976). Consider an areal unit which, in England at least, will always be a collective one – the county – and suppose we wish to measure the relationship between the percentage of land devoted to urban areas and the density of population over all the counties in the country. Even if a high positive or, more likely, negative correlation were found to exist, this does not necessarily imply any causal connection between these two variables; many other factors could be conspiring to suggest such an association.

The final important aspect in relation to spatial units returns us to the concern expressed on p. 18 and anticipates in part that of succeeding pages: how, in practice, do we decide where to stop sub-dividing space and creating more and more detailed land use parcels? As we shall show, there are practical limitations to what can be achieved given any data collection – or, more evocatively, data capture technology. But there is more to it than that – at least where we are dealing with singular functional units, such as steel works, which are surveyed by human means. Even where we are dealing with land cover, as compared with land use *ss*, difficulties often exist. To distinguish land from water would seem, at first sight, of trivial difficulty – but what of seasonally wet areas, tidal flats or marshes with various kinds of plant cover? Dickinson and Shaw (1977, 1978) have discussed the 'sub-divisions of space' problems in some detail in relation to the British urban situation. They point out that a factory complex may be treated *en bloc* as a 'curtilage' used for manufacturing, where that term denotes 'a cohesive area of land to which some or all users normally have access by virtue of their participation in its use'. We may note, in passing, that this democratic definition is scarcely clear-cut; it is one which attempts to disguise the different views and hence sub-division of land use taken for different purposes. Alternatively, they suggest, the manufacturing complex can be broken up into its constituent 'activity spaces' such as manufacturing, offices, storage and transport. Fig. 3.5 illustrates how the latter principle was applied within the National Gazetteer Pilot Study (see also pp. 42–8). Some of these activity spaces need not be spatially contiguous: playing fields used primarily by one or more schools, and hence basically educational in function, may be separated from the school(s).

Such 'atomic units' of activity space were discussed in the 1972 report 'General Information System for Planning' (HMSO 1972) and termed Basic Spatial Units or BSUs. BSUs may consist of only one floor or part of a floor in a high-rise block, providing no other inter-dependent activities go on within the block. They were generally defined as heriditaments (rating or local tax units), the equivalent of heriditaments for non-rated premises or sub-divisions of heriditaments in urban areas: outside the built-up areas, they conform to

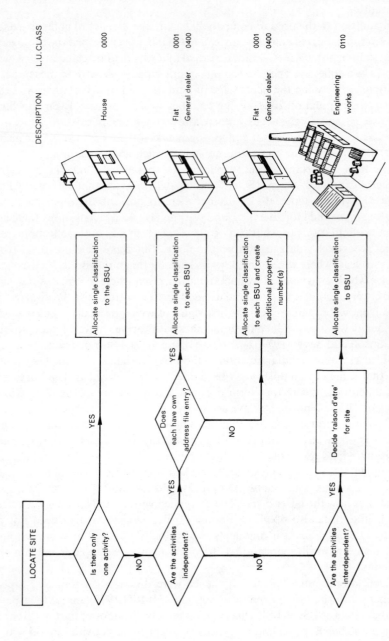

Figure 3.5 The definition of geographical individuals, as done by NGPS (after NGPS 1974).

28

the parcels of land shown on Ordnance Survey plans and large scale maps (and thus are often arbitrary rather than natural units). Both the GISP report and the National Land Use Classification report (HMSO 1975) stress the need to define such units by natural or by man-made physical boundaries, such as fences. Both stress the advantages of compiling data on as small an areal basis as possible, thereby permitting aggregation whatever larger units are required.

Dickinson and Shaw are fierce critics of the BSUs, arguing that the boundaries of curtilages are usually unambiguous and main users are easily agreed; in contrast, detailed activity spaces may be differently defined by different analysts and, in any case, necessitate much more surveying effort. They are undoubtedly correct in saying that gross confusion of statistics will occur if some surveys are based upon curtilages and some upon detailed activity spaces: in summarizing their comments on the shortcomings of British land use statistics, they make the statement heading this chapter. They are, however, misleading in implying that the use of the curtilage principle will solve all land use *ss* definition problems. Consider the situation where a major chemical plant is separated from another by an intervening road but supplies the latter with 50% of its output for further processing, the other half being sold elsewhere. What then is the curtilage? In addition, as demonstrated above with the educational example, functional organization may well not be contiguous in space – the larger the organization, the less likely is this to be the case. In the Dickinson and Shaw view, contiguity is vital and inter-area relationships are expendable, if only because of the difficulty of obtaining such information.

The moral is clear: there is no magical set of 'natural' areal units which will meet all purposes and which are easy to survey. In practice this may or may not have serious implications and, by and large, we do not know in what situations the implications are serious: comparatively little empirical work seems to have been done by way of multiple surveys of the same areas on different bases. It is patently obvious, however, that the Dickinson and Shaw (1978) call for standardization makes sense: without attempts to do this *and* explicit statements of the spatial units used in the survey, comparison with other surveys is liable to be misleading and possibly absurd. In the short term at least, the only sub-national land use figures likely to be of real value are those compiled on the basis of one survey by one person or group.

The measurement scale

Land use is looked upon as a nominal-scale variable. By 'nominal-scale variable' we mean one in which the possible states are discrete and not on any regular measurement scale: they are different in kind. In other words, a residential area is to a manufacturing one as are apples to elephants. If such, it is now comparatively unusual since geographers and others have increasingly turned to the collection over space of quantitatively scaled data during the last twenty years (Unwin 1979). Little can be done in any statistical analysis of such data apart from counting the frequency of each class, unless the observations are grouped into larger units in which a number of geographical individuals exist, e.g. larger 'semi-natural' areas can be compared on the basis of their component land uses (see chapter 5). The other available measurement scales – ordinal, interval and ratio – provide increasing possibilities for sophisticated analysis.

Yet we may reasonably ask whether land use is really a nominal-scale variable. Certainly, fairly simple transformations applied to the data can sometimes convert it to a higher level of sophistication: calculating the income from each area of agricultural land by multiplying the area of each field by a unit for what is being produced therein is a case in point. Even without such transformations, which generally require 'external' information such as unit value, any zone of land use which is collective is necessarily based upon a frequency distribution of the component parts and is not totally homogeneous. But it is also clear that the functional or formal attributes of a place, upon which the land use is allocated, are frequently themselves on an ordinal, interval or ratio scale: surveying the age of houses and producing a map which shows the extent of residential development at different periods is one common example of these procedures. In addition, obvious relationships exist between land use classes, such as the juxtaposition of industry and Victorian housing for the factory workers. Given this symbiotic or ecological view of land use, the concept of nominal scaling is not always appropriate.

In summary, then, while we may often have to regard land use (particularly where few categories exist in the classification) as a nominal-scale variable, we can often escape the limitations that this places upon our analysis either by aggregating to larger spatial units or by transforming the data onto a higher level measurement scale. Sometimes we are fortunate enough to find that the land use of interest is already measured on such a scale.

Resolution of the data

SPATIAL RESOLUTION

It is self-evident to anyone ever involved in field survey that there are practical limits to the details which may or should be collected on variations in land use – or on anything else! This may be due either to the limited human resources available, to the technology being used or, most sensibly, to the objectives of the survey and the intended use of the data. While botanical surveys may very well cover small areas down to the resolution of individual plants, almost all land use studies are much coarser in resolution. The national survey of 1969 Developed Areas in England and Wales, for example, excluded any discrete areas of built-up land less than 5 ha in extent, while the minimum size of mapping unit in the new land use *ss* and land cover maps of the USA is 4 ha for urban areas and bodies of surface water, and 16 ha for most of the other land uses (see pp. 65–8). Naturally, coarser resolutions may always be created from finer ones: a generalized, smaller scale map of land use in which the smallest zones shown are, say 50 ha in extent, could be produced from the more detailed data if required. Such generalization is well, if largely intuitively, understood by map-makers (Rhind 1973b).

Any feature which is smaller than the basic spatial resolution of the survey does not exist so far as that survey is concerned. In fieldwork-based surveys, the human being frequently adjusts the lower limits of his resolution in response to what seem to be important in terms of function: even if the basic resolution of survey is 1 ha, the surveyor finding a missile silo may be tempted to include it! Indeed, in survey in urban areas, the basic resolution may be not specified in terms of a fixed spatial size – it may be specified as functional units such as heriditaments, or as detached blocks of property, both of which will vary considerably in physical size. In machine-based sensing systems this flexibility is rarely possible and a constant spatial resolution is provided. Ideally, the technology must here be chosen to detect the smallest object likely to be of interest; in practical terms, what happens at present is that the resolution of available imagery from civilian satellites is such that some feature may be detected while others, however desirable, may not.

Clearly, then, different types of data capture methods will provide data of different spatial resolution and thus data suitable for different tasks. It is useful, therefore, to be able to categorize such information from different surveys. Table 3.1 is such a categorization and is based upon that used by the United States Geological Survey (Anderson *et al.* 1976) but modified in one important respect: it contains an extra level (V) to cope with the more detailed surveys recently carried out in Britain. It also incorporates other ground surveys. To give some idea of the publishable resolution from such data, a list of the corresponding map output scales is attached, even though it is technically feasible to make both larger and smaller scale output from the same input data: maps ranging in scale from 1/24,000 to 1/250,000 have, for example, been produced from level II data.

Table 3.1 Data resolution and their sources (*after* Anderson *et al.* 1976). Note: certain terms in this table are defined in chapter 4.

Classification level	Data source	Map output scale
I	Landsat or similar (see pp. 80–8)	1/250,000 to 1/1 million
II	High altitude (12,500 m +) photography; reconnaissance survey	1/80,000 and smaller
III	Medium altitude (3–12,500 m) photography; field survey	1/20,000 to 1/800,000
IV	Low altitude (below 3,000 m) photography; ground survey	1/2,500 to 1/20,000
V	Individual building or sub-building	1/100 to 1/10,000

TEMPORAL RESOLUTION

There is little point in carrying out detailed local planning with data which are twenty years out of date. Similarly any land use survey which is not approximately synchronous, i.e. carried out at the same time, is liable to be highly misleading. Thus up-to-dateness and temporal consistency are both important elements in the usefulness of such data. As in the previous section, we may with benefit categorize the data on such criteria (see table 3.2).

Certain observations may be made in regard to table 3.2. Level A data, by their very nature, are both up-to-date and synchronous since they are the current picture. Level D data are largely historical and minor variations in synchronicity are usually of little consequence: they may still be a useful and relatively accurate description of the land use picture in some rural areas, although it is well known that substantial changes occurred in these areas in Britain during and after the 1914–18 and 1939–45 World Wars. Some interaction occurs between spatial and temporal resolution: for many house-keeping purposes, for example, it is essential to have both level IV or V data and that residing in level A or, at worst, level B.

For convenience, we may describe data sets in future by amalgamating the two classifications. Thus the numerous land use maps produced in formulating Development Plans for many British towns following the Town and Country Planning Act of 1947 would now be level IID. Satellite imagery from the Landsat satellite (see chapter 4) would be IA and the land use data enshrined within the topography on Ordnance Survey large scale plans obtained via the SUSI (Supply of Unpublished Survey Information; OS 1976) systems would be VA or VB in level.

In all data pertaining to phenomena which are subject to change more rapidly than they are sampled, i.e. most land use data of levels B to D (certainly levels C and D) the problems of aliasing are likely to be severe. We can demonstrate such generation of spurious results by considering fig. 3.6; on the basis of three surveys, an apparent trend for a steady increase in the percentage of land use type A would be seen, even though the more detailed picture indicates considerable variation about a diminishing trend. A further illustration may be taken from Best's (1978) graph of the rate of conversion of land to urban use. Taking the period from 1945 to 1975, a ten yearly survey

Table 3.2.

Classification level	Temporal characteristics of the data
A	Up-dated when change occurs or within a few days
B	Collected within last two years or up to two years between surveys
C	Collected between two and fifteen years ago or between two and fifteen years between surveys
D	Collected more than fifteen years ago

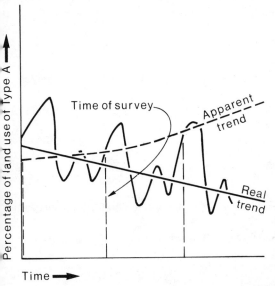

Figure 3.6 Aliasing: spurious trends can be obtained by taking samples of land use at different time intervals and in different years.

recording the change in the previous year would give a quite different trend from a set of similar surveys starting in 1950. Thus 'one-off' surveys give us 'one-off' results; even where combined into a time series, the results may be extremely misleading.

The classification of land use

For most purposes, we need to arrange our detailed observations into groups, using some classification process. That many land use classifications exist should not surprise us, especially when we consider the succinct summary by Anderson *et al.* (1976, p. 4):

> There is no one ideal classification of land use (*ss*) and land cover, and it is unlikely that one could ever be developed. There are different perspectives in the classification process, and the process itself tends to be subjective, even when an objective numerical approach is used. There is, in fact, no logical reason to expect that one detailed inventory should be adequate for more than a short time, since land use and land cover patterns change in keeping with demands for natural resources. Each classification is made to suit the needs of the user, and few users will be satisfied with an inventory that does not meet most of their needs. (our emphasis)

The fundamental question remains, however: how do we compare surveys if they use different terms and different categories to describe their data? If we cannot do this, then each survey becomes an island, separate in space and time from all other surveys.

In practice, much land use survey leads not to classification in a statistical sense but to a discriminant analysis – rather than grouping the geographical individuals (BSUs, heriditaments, picture elements, etc.) on the basis of similarity to provide groups of like individuals for which names are then sought, each individual is compared with an *a priori* scheme; the individuals are then slotted into pigeon holes ('residential', 'manufacturing', etc.) one at a time. This distinction, however, says more about the differences in terminology between laymen and statisticians than anything of practical importance. We shall proceed on two fronts: first by considering the functions which a 'classification' should meet, and secondly, by comparing some existing and widely used schemes.

DESIDERATA OF A CLASSIFICATION SYSTEM

These are as follows:

(i) the classes must be mutually exclusive, i.e. any geographical individual can only fall into one class;

(ii) it has to meet the detailed needs of the primary user, who may have paid for the survey;

(iii) it has to meet as many of the needs of secondary users of the data as is possible, concomitant with (ii);

(iv) it has to be easily understood and applied;

(v) it has to produce repeatable results with use by different surveyors using the same survey technology. Both this and (iv) imply the need for the classification to be explicit, i.e. well-documented;

(vi) it has to be exhaustive in that all 'geographical individuals' under consideration must be classifiable – even if only in an 'other uses' dustbin;

(vii) it has to be hierarchical, to cope with surveys at differing levels of resolution in differing areas;

(viii) it has to be structured in such a fashion that, if different survey technologies are ever used, the results from both can be compared (this overlaps with (v), but is not identical to it);

(ix) it has to be sufficiently stable for surveys carried out at different moments in time to be compared;

(x) it has to be sufficiently flexible for new interests and tasks to be met from a modified, rather than a completely new, classification;

(xi) it must incorporate some recognition of seasonal or other cyclic changes so that aliasing is not embalmed in the results;

(xii) wherever possible, it must be based upon quantitative criteria (thus contributing to (v)).

Clearly this is a tall, even impossible, order. Item (vi), for example, may lead to a need to deal with both rural and urban areas in great detail (see pp. 49–50). The longer a classification remains unchanged (ix), the easier it is to monitor changes through time yet the less likely it is to be suitable for contemporary purposes (x).

An interesting characteristic of classifications concerns the number of classes used. It is often found that, with small or very large numbers of different classes of land use, little difficulty is found in allocating geographical individuals to classes, though much information is obviously lost in the first circumstance. With medium numbers of classes, particularly in urban surveys, the difficulty is at a maximum: yet it is in precisely this level of classification accuracy or representativeness (say 50 to 100 classes) that many surveys such as the Second Land Utilisation Survey and that of the Greater London Council have worked.

In other words, any classification is a compromise between conflicting anticipated needs. This is amply borne out by our detailed examples.

SOME CASE STUDIES OF CLASSIFICATIONS

The World Land Use Survey (WLUS) and the Second Land Utilisation Survey (SLUS)

Both of these surveys and the classifications they have used stem largely from the work of Sir L. Dudley Stamp and others such as E. C. Willatts in the early 1930s (Stamp 1931; Stamp and Willatts 1934). The World Land Use Survey was a Commission of the International Geographical Union with Stamp as its first chairman, succeeded by Hans Boesch; the second was directly encouraged by Stamp as a second look at the same area – Britain – as was covered in his first survey in the early 1930s. The World Land Use Survey classification, adopted in 1949 and orientated towards agricultural interests, was always intended to be further sub-divided in local circumstances; it is set out in table 3.3. Drawn from Kostrowicki (1970, p. 82), this is compared with

Table 3.3 A comparison between first order categories in the World Land Use Survey and Second Land Utilisation Survey classifications.

WLUS	SLUS
1 Settlements and associated non-agricultural lands	1 Settlement (residential and commercial)
2 Horticulture	2 Industry
3 Tree and other perennial crops	3 Transport
4 Cropland	4 Derelict land
5 Improved permanent pasture	5 Open spaces
6 Unimproved grazing land	6 Grass land
7 Woodlands	7 Arable
8 Swamps and marshes	8 Market gardening
9 Unproductive land	9 Orchards
	10 Woodland
	11 Heath and rough land
	12 Water and marsh
	13 Unvegetated land

Note: the numbering sequences are those given in the source documents.

the most general level of the Second Land Utilisation Survey classification (Coleman 1961; Coleman and Maggs 1962). It is worth noting that in examples of Stamp's preliminary classification for the WLUS, the whole of London was painted red and thus considered as 'wasteland', given the agricultural bias of the scheme!

Ignoring, for the time being, the sub-divisions in both classifications, leading to 16 divisions in the WLUS and 64 published divisions in the SLUS, we can 'map' one classification into the other roughly as follows:

WLUS

SLUS

Although this is a very crude simplification of a correspondence which would always be carried out at the greatest level of detail possible, it illustrates a general problem. To convert the results from one classification, A, into the terms of another, B, may not only require the fusion of classes (thereby wasting detail present in classification A) but also the splitting of some classes. If no further sub-divisions are available in A, then the only logical thing to do is to group some of the classes in B. In the example above, this would seem to necessitate grouping classes 2 and 3 of the WLUS together, plus 5 and 6 together. The consequence, particularly in very incompatible and coarsely sub-divided classifications, is a gross reduction in the number of classes available. On occasions it may be necessary to group together classes which are intuitively unlike and the utility of the classification and of the data (and hence of any subsequent analysis) will suffer accordingly. It goes without saying that all matching of differently classified data is dependent on a clear and correct understanding of the scope of each class in each classification.

The above example is partly hypothetical, not because the classifications are imaginary (they are not) but because they grew apart from a common stock to suit different purposes. The WLUS classification in its basic form was designed (Kostrowicki 1970) to suit the production of maps at *circa* 1/1 million scale, and to be sub-divided for more detailed work. The great majority of the mapping for the Second Land Utilisation Survey, begun in 1960 and completed some ten years later (though 60% of the survey was done in 1960–64 in England and Wales and post-1965 in Scotland), was carried out at 1/10,560 scale and published at 1/25,000 scale. Even so, it is noticeable that simple, further sub-division of the WLUS would not necessarily make the classifications compatible and aggregation of the SLUS classes to produce a map to fit with the WLUS series is not a strictly objective procedure.

The sub-divisions of the first and second SLUS classes are of particular interest in so far as they correspond to classifications used by planners and administrators with a direct interest in settlement and industry. The sub-

Table 3.4

1	*Settlement* (residential and commercial)	Continuous, mixed commercial and residential Houses with gardens Newly built areas Public buildings Caravan sites
2	*Industry* (based upon the industrial classifications in the 1951 Census; this is therefore incompatible in certain respects with the later Standard Industrial Classification and hence with the NLUC (HMSO 1975, p. 10))	Treatment of non-metalliferous mining products other than coal (glass, ceramics, cements, etc.) Chemical and allied trades Metal manufacture Engineering, shipbuilding and electrical goods Vehicles Metal goods, not otherwise specified Precision instruments, jewellery Textiles Leather, leather goods and fur Clothing Food, drink and tobacco Wood and cork manufacture Paper and printing Other manufacturing industries

divisions in the published maps were as in table 3.4. It will be readily appreciated that these categories need significant modification for many contemporary uses: electronics and the computer industry, for example, would be submerged with shipbuilding. The sub-divisions of industry, however, are largely on a functional or activity basis; those of settlement are a hotch-potch and also contravene the first tenet of a good classification as set out on p. 34: i.e. they are not mutually exclusive. Overall, it is clear that much of the classification is orientated towards rural areas – only about 22 of the 64 published categories are primarily urban. Finally, it is clear from Coleman and Maggs (1962, p. 3) that at least part of the restriction on the numbers of categories is due to the survey procedures utilized – surveying, often by school children, was carried out largely on 1/10,560 scale maps – and the scale of maps (1/25,000) used to publish the results. These comments on classification should not be taken to detract from what has been a truly staggering achievement – as will be made clear in later sections.

The United States Geological Survey (USGS) and the Department of the Environment (DoE) Developed Areas classifications

Both of these classifications have been designed for the collection of data from remote-sensed imagery, in particular that of spatial resolution levels I to III (see p. 31). Anderson (1978) has defined criteria, in addition to those earlier specified, which classifications for remote-sensed data should meet. In brief, the important additions are:

(i) the minimum level of interpretation accuracy in the identification of land use (*ss*) and land cover categories should be at least 85%;

(ii) the accuracy of interpretation for the different categories should be about equal;

(iii) repeatable results should be obtainable from one interpreter to another and from one time of sensing to another;

(iv) the classification system should be such as to permit vegetation and other types of land cover to be used as surrogates for activity;

(v) it should also be suitable for use with remote sensor data obtained at different times of the year.

An important difference between the two classifications is that one (that of the USGS) is designed to be extensive, covering both rural and urban areas, whereas the DoE one is primarily for urban or, as they prefer to state, Developed Areas (there are wide variations in understanding of the meaning of 'urban'). In addition, the American classification differs in being produced by an inter-agency committee which included representatives of the Association of American Geographers and the International Geographical Union. From its inception in 1971, this produced several possible classification systems which were reviewed at a conference of Federal, State and local government representatives and many others. On the basis of this and an avowed requirement to fit in with other, more detailed field-based land use surveys (such as those based on the Standard Land Use Coding Manual published by the US Urban Renewal Administration and Bureau of Public Roads, 1965, or the inventory of Major Uses of Land made every five years by the Economic Research Service of the US Department of Agriculture) a prototype classification was evolved and 'field tested', particularly for levels I and II data, and published as USGS Circular 671. This was followed by widespread further discussions and concluded by the publication of the seminal work, USGS Professional Paper 964 (Anderson *et al.* 1976).

In contrast, the DoE classification was created largely for internal purposes in order to produce a speedy, country-wide set of consistent land use figures. Smith *et al.* (1977, p. 158) state that 'the broad land use groups were defined in terms of information obtainable from the photography, rather than in terms of any ideal classification suitable for planning purposes'. The same authors describe the rationale for needing such figures in the British context and also point out that the Developed Areas survey, and hence its classification, should be seen as only one of a number of initiatives put in hand by the Department concerned with the recording or analysing of land use information, including satellite-based studies (see chapter 4). The immediate and limited aims of the survey, for which the DoE classification was concocted, were to establish a 'base line' of *area* of land within Developed

Areas, as compared with that outside and to examine how this varied throughout England and Wales. In so far as this was possible, the classification had to be 'mappable' (relatable) to the National Land Use Classification (see below). The definition of Developed Areas is given in DoE (1978) as ' . . . all areas of continuous development, development being taken to include all areas covered by bricks and mortar or structures of other materials. This includes transportation features as well as buildings. Also included are land uses associated with these features and open spaces as existed primarily for "urban" uses.' Table 3.5 compares the two classifications and includes the first level of the US Standard Land Use Code for good measure.

The US Standard Land Use Code is highly orientated towards human activities – the first seven of the nine major categories occur on less than 5% of the US land area. As was intended by its designers, the scheme put forward by Anderson *et al.* (1976) is a national one, designed to cover, with considerable equity, all of the features in or on the landscape of the USA. Even so, it is possible roughly to 'map' the first six major categories of the Standard Code into the sub-divisions of the first category in the USGS classification though (as is predictable) with much aggregation of classes. The DoE classification is much more conservatively described – the use of the adjective 'predominantly' to describe categories A to C indicates some considerable subjectivity in the allocation-to-classes procedure. It is, however, substantially an activity-based classification and, particularly for the educational category, required supplementary information from medium scale topographic maps to permit the categorization of the areas defined on the air photographs. Like all classifications, it constrains the scope of future developments: any more sophisticated future system for monitoring land use changes will, to produce results comparable with the existing study, have to be based upon a like, even if expanded, classification. As Cline (1963) perceptively noted, 'A classification can prejudice the future'.

Comparing the USGS and DoE classifications, it is clear that they treat indeterminancy in different ways. Classes 16, 17 and 24 of the former are, in effect, dustbin categories for those geographical individuals whose nature cannot be recognized or which are irrelevant to the purposes of any anticipated task. No such 'dustbins' exist in the DoE classification – the classification is exhaustive in that all developed areas are either residential, industrial, educational, for transport uses or are open space. The explicit omission of urban open space – football pitches, parks and so on (plus cemetaries in the DoE scheme) – from the USGS classification is an interesting one. Presumably such areas are lumped together with classes 12, 14, 16 or 17. It may be that this difference between the two schemes reflects the American primary concern with data from levels I and II, as compared with the DoE main, initial concern with levels II and III. Some interesting allocations have been made in the DoE scheme: local government offices, for example, are included in class B although law courts and

Table 3.5.

US Standard Land Use Code	USGS classification	DoE Developed Areas classification
1 Residential	1 Urban or build-up land	1 Developed Areas
2 Manufacturing (9 second-level categories)	11 Residential	A Predominantly residential use
3 Manufacturing (6 second-level categories)	12 Commercial and services	B Predominantly industrial and/or commercial use
4 Transportation, communications and utilities	13 Industrial	C Predominantly educational/community/health/indoor recreational use
5 Trade	14 Transport, communications, utilities	D Transport use
6 Services	15 Industrial and commercial complexes	E 'Urban' open space
7 Cultural, entertainment and recreation	16 Mixed urban or built-up land	2 Non-developed areas
8 Resource production and extraction	17 Other urban or built-up land	
	2 Agricultural land	
	21 Cropland and pasture	
	22 Orchards, groves, vineyards, nurseries	
	23 Confined feeding operations	
	24 Other agricultural land	
	3 Rangeland	
	31 Herbaceous rangeland	
	32 Shrub and brush rangeland	
	33 Mixed rangeland	

9 Undeveloped land and water areas

4 Forest land
41 Deciduous forest
42 Coniferous forest
43 Mixed forest

5 Water areas
51 Streams and canals
52 Lakes
53 Reservoirs
54 Bays and estuaries

6 Wetland
61 Forested wetland
62 Non-forested wetland

7 Barren land
71 Dry salt flats
72 Beaches
73 Sandy areas other than beaches
74 Bare, exposed rock
75 Stripmines, quarries and gravel pits
76 Transitional areas
77 Mixed barren land

8 Tundra
81 Shrub and brush tundra
82 Herbaceous tundra
83 Bare ground tundra
84 Wet tundra
85 Mixed tundra

9 Perennial snow or ice
91 Perennial snowfields
92 Glaciers

recreation centres run by local authorities are in class C. The breadth of the classes is very considerable; C includes:

> schools, universities, colleges and research establishments; places of worship, social meeting places, law courts, prisons, borstals and fire stations; hospitals, clinics, medical auxiliary service centres such as ambulance stations, convalescent homes and non-medical care homes; indoor centres of recreation and leisure, such as sports halls, libraries, museums and galleries, together with amusement and show places, including film and TV studies.
>
> Grounds in which these buildings stood are included....However, playing fields associated with schools, etc. are included under 'urban' open space. (DoE 1978, p. 2)

In essence, then, both classifications are broad-brush and essentially reconnaisance tools intended, at best, for regional planning ends. The American classification is comprehensive and tested; the British one is highly selective and pragmatic, was pressed quickly into service but must form the basis of any future expanded classifications if change in land uses is to be detected. Both classifications attempt to work with activity, rather than formal, units. It is interesting to note that the American scheme, with minor modifications, seems capable of producing the level of published detail in the Second Land Use Survey. Subject to the availability of adequate remote sensing imagery (chapter 4) and supplementary information, therefore, it may soon be unnecessary ever to mount again the sort of field-based survey organized by Coleman (1961), unless much higher resolutions and individual crop designations are required.

The National Land Use Classification (NLUC) and the National Gazetteer Pilot Study (NGPS)

Both of these classifications are very much more detailed than any of the others considered thus far: both are designed to be capable of application down to the Basic Spatial Unit level of spatial sub-division, although they can be used at a much more aggregate level. As we have already seen and is expanded in chapter 4, such detailed survey presently demands ground-based methods. No understanding of these classifications is possible without knowing something of their chequered histories.

The NLUC grew out of the early concern with Development Planning after the landmark 1947 Town and Country Planning Act. In 1949 and 1951, the then Ministry of Town and Country Planning issued Circulars 63 and 92 to all local authorities in England and Wales which recommended standard land use notations for survey and development plans – in effect, a standard classification. Unfortunately, the definitions of land uses which were given proved insufficiently precise to avoid being interpreted in different ways. After the equally momentous Town and Country Planning Act of 1968 (and subsequent amendments), which required a new style of development plan, two study teams were set up by the responsible Ministry to study the general information needs for planning (the GISP report, HMSO 1972) and 'to develop a land use classification which would serve the various purposes of planning throughout the country and would also have regard to the needs of other users of land use data' (HMSO 1975). This ambitious aim – to provide a vehicle of utility for all planners in local and central government, plus other interested parties – was begun in 1969. The team was drawn from local and central government and from the Local Authorities Management Services and Computer Committee. It published a final scheme, after several drafts, six years later (HMSO 1975). From the point of view of its intentions, the effort devoted to it, the detail it encompasses and the adoption of it by a number of local authorities plus other data collectors (see chapters 4 and 5), it is therefore of prime importance – whatever Dickinson and Shaw (1978) might feel. In addition, the DoE Circular 71/74 to all local authorities (DoE 1974a) requests annual returns on land use change classified into the fifteen major orders of the NLUC – so that it now has some legislative substance. Finally, the decision to try to relate the NLUC to the headings of the Standard Industrial Classification (which is already widely used in the collation and publication of information concerning manufacturing) meant that some limited connection was forged between economic and land use information (CSO 1968).

The National Gazetteer Pilot Study was also an initiative of central government: it was set up by the Department of the Environment in conjunction with what later became the Metropolitan County of Tyne and Wear. Its aims were to devise, implement and test procedures for providing a gazetteer of Britain. The gazetteer was to contain a record for each and every BSU and in this record was to be included a postal address, a National Grid co-ordinate reference, a unique property code *and* a land use code. The gazetteer was to give a complete land use description of an area and one which was up-dated monthly. It is important to note that the land use code, while critical for many of the uses of the gazetteer, was not its main function – to provide a form of common referencing for data obtained from different sources, so that these could be inter-related. This function will be elaborated in chapter 5 but it is clear that the data on land use in the gazetteer are of level VA (see p. 31).

Since it was initiated by the same department as fostered the NLUC, it would have been logical had NLUC been utilized for the gazetteer. Unfortunately (NGPS 1974), substantial changes to draft forms of the NLUC – it was not originally hierarchical – ensured that it was not in final form before the NGPS began work. As a consequence, the Study team adopted the land use classification of the old Newcastle upon Tyne County Borough. Subsequently, the NGPS has been taken over by the County of Tyne and Wear and now functions as the Joint Information System of that County (Spicer *et al.* 1979).

The NLUC is a hierachical system which is ostensibly based on activity considerations (HMSO 1975, p. 8): we shall soon see that it is, in fact, a hybrid classification encompassing both activity and form. The four-level structure of the NLUC is as in fig. 3.7. The code MAØ1BC denotes an iron and steel plant. Although there are just over 600 lowest level classes in the NLUC, the index in HMSO (1975) lists over 2,500 items – most of these are other common land use terms which have been subsumed in this classification or are synonyms for the NLUC descriptions of land use. The fifteen Orders are: Agriculture and fisheries; Community and health services; Defence; Education; Manufacturing; Mineral extraction; Offices; Recreation and leisure; Residences; Retail distribution and servicing; Storage; Transport tracks and places; Utility services; Wholesale distribution; and Unused land, water and buildings.

At the most detailed level – the Class – some surprising omissions occur. For example, while there is a category for 'photographic service shop', there is no specific category for 'chemists'. Some of the categories can be interpreted as being non-mutually exclusive – the presence of both 'fried fish' and 'hot food' shops are a source of some confusion in survey, especially in so far as they relate to traditional eating habits in the North of England! Most of these problems relate to the finest level detail, however, and can be cured by adding a few extra codes at this level. Some 'dustbin' categories, e.g. 'other non-food retail distribution' establishments, exist. More serious is the mixture of activity and formally-based classes; the Group 'Self-contained residences' (RSØ2) exemplifies this. The list of dwellings (RSØ2A) distinguished is as follows:

	RSØ2A
Building converted to more than one dwelling	A
Bungalow	B
Detached house	C
Maisonette	D
Non-residential plus single dwelling	E
Purpose-built block of flats	F
Semi-detached house	G
Terraced house	H
Other dwelling	I

In addition to this duality of definition, category RSØ2AF illustrates the complexities introduced by the need to cope with different spatial units. The NLUC is (HMSO 1975) applicable at the level of the BSU, the heriditament or at some more amorphously defined zonal level: 'Purpose-built block of flats' is an agglomerative term required for zonal-level mapping. Fortunately, the detail available in the classification is such that it is usually possible (with careful planning) to pick terms which either reflect an activity basis or a formal one.

The NGPS classification is broadly similar in that it is a four-level hierarchy, although – confusingly – the levels are termed Order, Group, Class and Sub-class. The authors (NGPS 1974, p. 12) state categorically that land use is taken

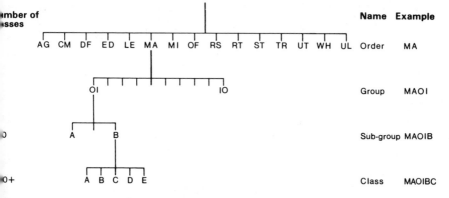

Figure 3.7 The hierarchical organization of the National Land Use Classification.

as an activity and that such differentiation as between terraced and detached houses is irrelevant to their purposes. However, such determination is tempered by circumstance: their classification *does* distinguish between 'houses' and 'flats' since changes between these are considered as development under the Town and Country Planning Act of 1971 (s. 22(3) (a)). Thus the purpose of the gazetteer and its method of up-dating through statutory monitoring of development by the local authority is reflected in the classification: since it costs no more to accumulate that type of distinction – the data are provided by the development control system (see chapter 4) – the classification may as well recognize it.

For a variety of reasons, not least the need to make annual returns on land use change to central government, it is important to be able to cross-relate the NGPS classification to that of NLUC. In principle, some matching is simple, especially the aggregation of the NGPS sub-classes to the 15 NLUC Orders needed for statutory purposes. Table 3.6 illustrates more detailed matching and indicates how the structural content of the two classifications differs: some of the detailed 'storage' categories in NGPS are spread over the Storage, Transport and Agriculture Orders of NLUC. This in itself is not of major importance – provided there are equivalent classes in each classification, their location in different parts of the hierarchy is not usually crucial. What is striking about this comparison is that only eight of the sixteen or so NLUC storage categories (counting TRØ2CA to F as one) are used to map to the sixteen of the NGPS. And of these sixteen, no less than ten are matched by 'dustbin' (i.e. 'Other') categories. The implication is inescapable – it is impossible to compare NGPS and NLUC at the same level of detail; only by converting NGPS sub-classes to NLUC sub-groups is comparison possible. In more general terms, when class splitting is needed because a class in classification A covers two or more of those in B, then the difficulties become onerous. We have already seen this when comparing the WLUS and SLUS classifications but can summarize the situation as below (p. 48).

Table 3.6 Comparison of the NGPS and NLUC classifications – an example. Source: after NGPS (1974).

Order	Group	Class	Sub-classes		NLUC classes
02 Storage*	020 Covered storage	0200 (Covered storage)	02000	Perishable foods (meat, fruit, vegetables, milk)	ST∅3AC[1]
			02001	Other foodstuffs	ST∅3AD
			02002	Clothing, footware, textiles (fancy goods)	ST∅3AD
			02003	Durable household goods (inc. furniture, glass, electric appliances)	ST∅3AA
			02004	Paper, books, stationery	ST∅3AD
			02005	Builders' materials yard	ST∅2AA
			02006	Timber (under cover)	ST∅2Ac
			02007	Industrial materials (steel, petroleum, paint, machines)	ST∅AC, ST∅1AD
			02008	Depository, transit shed, bonded stores	ST∅3AD
			02009	Other goods	ST∅3AD
	021 Open storage and Stockpiling	0210 Land use for storing goods and materials not under cover	02100	Timber and storage	ST∅2AC[2]
			02101	Scrap and waste metal dump	ST∅3AD
			02102	Coal storage	ST∅2AC
	022 Vehicle storage	0220 Private open air vehicle storage			TR∅2CA-TR∅2CF[3]
		0221 Private covered vehicle storage			

023   Animal storage   0230   Animal storage inc.
                                  stables, kennels and
                                  cattery

---

*This Order is concerned solely with storage; wholesaling functions are treated in 044.

Key to NLUC categories. NGPS Sub-group designation in brackets

STØ1AD	Industrial and office machinery (equipment) store
STØ2AA	Builders yard (bulk materials) store
STØ2AC	Other materials store
STØ3AA	Furniture depository (other stores)
STØ3AC	Refrigerated store
STØ3AD	Other (other stores) store
TRØ2CA-TRØ2CF	(Storage place for vehicles) aircraft hangar – railway siding
AGØ1BA	Animal boarding place (animal welfare places)

Notes

[1] These will not always be equivalent. STØ3AD is the conservative equivalent.
[2] NLUC does not distinguish explicitly between outside and covered storage.
[3] NLUC does not distinguish explicitly between private and public storage.

Classification A (e.g. NGPS)	Classification B (e.g. NLUC)	Operation
Many (e.g. Sub-classes)	Few (e.g. Orders)	Usually easy
Few (e.g. Orders)	Many (e.g. Classes)	Impossible
Many (e.g. Sub-classes)	Many (e.g. Classes)	Difficult; some satisfactory
Few (e.g. Orders)	Few (e.g. Orders)	Difficult; likely to be misleading

The amount of necessary class splitting is related to the level in the hierarchy at which survey occurs, as compared with the level at which the final results or use of the two classifications are needed: if the matching process is always a 'many-to-few' one, insignificant problems may be expected. On the other hand, with certain methods of acquiring land use data (chapter 4), obtaining detail is costly and likely to induce certain sorts of errors. As a general conclusion, we should not expect to be able to compare surveys based on different classifications other than at a level of detail far inferior to that of either survey. In addition, the level of classification and spatial resolution at which the survey takes place may well condition what is found.

Multiple uses of the same land

The same land may be used for more than one purpose on an on-going basis. This is conceptually different from the situation where one land use replaces another on some semi-permanent or permanent basis. It is also quite distinct from the situation where different but closely inter-dependent activities are carried on at the same location and is, finally, also different from those situations where different activities take place at different levels above or below the ground. Both of the latter situations have been discussed earlier (see p. 27). The multiplicity of uses which occur on one site, stemming from the legal concept of land running from the centre of the earth to the skies (Coppock and Gebbett 1978, p. 11), are circumvented by considering each level as a separate piece of land where activities change between levels.

True multiple use exists where two or more activities proceed on the same physical expanse of land but are not so intimately connected that they contribute to one single industrial, commercial, socio-economic or agricultural process. Necessarily, the definition and thus classification of multiple use is therefore rather subjective. Multiple use can occur simultaneously, as in the instance of agricultural land or forest being used for recreational activities – such as hunting or camping, or the growth of vine and root crops on the same ground (as in parts of Northern Portugal). Alternatively, the use may be sequential and cyclic – where a street, a transport thoroughfare during the week, becomes the site of a market at the weekend; a reservoir, whose primary function is flood control in one season and water supply in another, is a second example of sequential but multiple land use.

Certain repetitive types of survey may not detect the latter type of multiple land use (see chapter 4) or may detect a biased picture. Consider the situation where markets are observed on simultaneous satellite imagery of the Middle East: the fact that these are periodic markets and travel to other settlements, with consequent land use implications, will not be detected. Of course, whether multiple uses are worth detecting will depend entirely upon the primary purpose of the survey. Since few surveys seem specifically to take account of multiple uses, it is generally the case that those interested in the topic have to carry out special-purpose surveys and to utilize classifications which explicitly permit multiple uses to be recorded. This is comparatively straightforward in a good computerized system for storing land use records (see chapter 5).

The urban–rural dichotomy

As late as 1968, Best was able to contend that an excessive contribution had been paid to rural, rather than urban matters

> . . . the rural bias in geography has been so pronounced that the actual term 'land use' is frequently misinterpreted as referring primarily or wholly to *agricultural* land use, with the urban sector almost completely excluded. . . . The rural weighting is just as marked in land-use statistics. The supply of urban data has lagged far behind the information for rural areas. In particular, agricultural statistics have been collected since as long ago as 1866. . . . Urban statistics, in great contrast, were practically non-existent in any fairly comprehensive form until analyses were made of the development plans compiled under the 1947 Town and Country Planning Act. (Best 1968, p. 89)

Quite apart from this situation, two quintessential points stand out from our discussions thus far in relation to the urban–rural dichotomy. The first is that a dichotomy also exists in the literature: most authors are still primarily interested in one type of area rather than the other – even those concerned with the extent of the transfer of land into urban uses seem to be driven primarily by a concern for the preservation of agricultural land (see, for example, Rogers 1978). The second point is that land use *ss* seems more commonly to be of interest in urban areas and land cover in rural ones, although both relate to man's activities in many Westernized landscapes.

A consequence of all this is that the scales of interest to professional users often differ – the person working on urban land use data will usually wish to deal with much larger map scales than will his compatriot dealing with rural data other than the archaeologist. This divergence of interests is of course recognized in the provision of topographic maps, particularly in Britain where plans at 1/1,250 or 1/2,500 scale are available from Ordnance Survey (as of

1980) for about 70% of the country (Harley 1975) while the basic scale coverage of the rest of the country is now 1/10,000.

Even more important than this, however, are the effects of different concepts of what constitutes an urban area. As Smith *et al.* (1977) and several other Department of the Environment publications (DoE 1974b, 1975) have clearly indicated for England and Wales, what is defined as urban will differ depending on whether formal or functional characteristics are concerned. Such characteristics as continuity of built-over areas (DoE 1974b, 1978) population density and journey-to-work statistics (Goddard *et al.* 1976; Hal (ed.) 1973) have been used (*de facto* units) as well as administrative definitions (*de jure* units). The general outlines of the pre-1974 administrative units which dated from the late 1880s, distinguished sharply between local authorities responsible for urban areas and those responsible for rural ones however, the build-up in urban areas since their inception had largely vitiated their utility. The post-1974 administrative units are not consistently differentiated on urban and rural status, the exception being the metropolitan counties. This situation thus has implications for the availability and type of land use data, e.g. the Joint Information System (see pp. 43 and 117) is an urban system which is administratively defined in terms of its areal scope. In general, then, different land use surveys concerned exclusively with urban or with rural areas have taken inconsistent criteria for definitions of their study areas. As a consequence, the comparison of their results becomes ever more complex.

Furthermore, a crude distinction of the country into urban and rural ignores the complex transitional areas which exist around many major urban complexes. Coleman (1976) has examined these 'rurban-fringes' and sub-divided the country on the basis of the Second Land Utilisation Survey data. Yet rural–urban transitions are dynamic: thus data pertaining solely, say, to urban areas of the 1930s will not cover the same area of ground as an urban and rurban-based study today and this difference in the types of areas studied may be of real significance in analysis of change over time – even if the definition of what is urban remains unchanged.

Data accuracy

Most analyses of land use data and any policies stemming from them are predicated upon the belief that the data are correct or, at worst, are sufficiently correct for the conclusions drawn still to stand. In rare circumstances, the reality of data capture are recognized and a minimum acceptable accuracy built into the specifications for the survey. It is now well known that accuracy, like (and partly because of) resolution, has to be paid for. The cost of progressing from, say 95% to 98% accuracy is generally very much greater than that of going from 92% to 95%; in other words, the increases in cost rise sharply for any unit increase in accuracy above quite mediocre levels. It is worth noting that accuracy can only be truly determined if you already know the answer: in practice, partial re-survey is usually carried out to check accuracy but this, while helpful, checks only *consistency*. Office checks which can be made upon the data, such as in the Durham Land Use Survey, check only the *feasibility* that the data are correct (see p. 92).

Clearly there are several considerations in regard to accuracy, and timeliness' is one of them. Certain types of land use, once established, are much more stable than others – suburban housing areas are likely to remain suburban housing areas long after the functions of some inner city shops have changed several times. In addition, some land uses are much easier to survey than others. Because of these two considerations, it is possible to suggest that, in general terms, the accuracy of some land use identifications will be much higher than others unless special arrangements have been made – such as the organization of a gazetteer.

However, the concept of accuracy is much more complex still (Hay 1978; Jord and Brooner 1976; Turk 1979; van Genderen and Lock 1977). Let us consider only the accuracy of classification of geographical individuals: it is often suggested, for example (following Anderson 1978), that at least 85% accuracy of identification is required if land use results from remote sensing are to be at all useful. By specifying a percentage accuracy of x, it is intimated that x out of every 100 geographical individuals have been correctly identified and allocated to the appropriate classification 'pigeon-hole'. Three weaknesses of such a crude measure of accuracy – quite apart from how we know what is appropriate – are obvious. The first is that the chances of misclassification increase the more classes are available: thus 75% accuracy in one land use study with 40 classes used may be much more impressive than 90% in another with five classes. The second weakness concerns the homogeneity of the classes: the first three categories in the DoE (1978) Developed Areas classification are preceded by the adjective 'Predominantly'. In such a circumstance only gross errors can be detected. The third obvious weakness is the crude counting of misclassification: some 'errors' are very much worse than others. To identify a building as a school when it is a university building is, for many purposes, manifestly more satisfactory than identifying it as a manufacturing concern.

From these examples and the numerous options that we have already discussed for defining areal units and other aspects of land use, it is clear that statements of data accuracy are fraught with hazards for the unwary. In pointing this out, we do not imply that there is no need for such statements. Quite the reverse: unless some examination of the likely errors has been made and vigorous checking has taken place, the data are worse than useless – the discovery of a single error will then render the rest of the data unreliable except at the most gross and superficial level. Such statements are echoed by van Genderen *et al.* (1978) and by Hay (1978) who attempt to provide improved methods of estimating the accuracy of interpretation of remote-sensed images.

4   Obtaining land use data

... to have suggested that within a decade we would see a thing
called a multi-spectral scanner used in conjunction with a computer
to produce crop production assessments and land use maps of
millions of hectares on cost effective and time effective bases would
have caused raised eyebrows if not outright guffaws in most circles.
I see no reason why 10 years from now we cannot be viewing results
which would be equally incredible to us today.

Landgrebe (1976)

No baseline or benchmark land use and land cover maps and
data have ever been compiled for the entire United States.

US Geological Survey Circular (1978)

Thus far we have discussed what *is* land use; if we do not have a clear
understanding of the nature of the phenomenon it is singularly unlikely that
we can subsequently say much of value about it. Now we turn our attention to
how data pertaining to it may be collected, checked and compiled, up to the
stage where some map or set of land use statistics or computerized data file
have been produced. The process is summarized in fig. 4.1; the interac-
tions between certain types of data collection procedures should be
noted – questionnaire surveys, for example, usually produce data lists.

Perhaps the most important distinctions to draw at the outset are those
between the base line and the *ad hoc* survey and between repeated surveys and
continuous up-dating. The base line survey is designed as a 'snap shot' of land
use at one moment in time, but with an eye to the likely future needs for land
use data and the methods by which it may be up-dated; the *ad hoc* survey,
usually smaller in scale, is often designed to answer some immediate questions
with little regard as to how this might be maintained as accurate and up-to-
date. Repeated surveys and continuous up-dating are two different means of
achieving the same end – a time series of land use, often to monitor the effects
of some decision stemming in part from the results of earlier survey. Without
some flow of 'intelligence' as to where changes are taking place, it is difficult
to run a continuous up-dating system. Repeated surveys run the risk of
producing aliased results (chapter 3) and must be at least compatible with
those preceding in terminology, classification, spatial units and resolution if
comparability is to be possible without jettisoning much of the expensively
collected detail. Willatts (1933) is, though, an example of making the best
of imperfect data. It will become obvious that different methods of data
collection produce surveys which fall in each one of the above categories. With
these considerations in mind, we can now consider the different methods by
which land use data have been captured, beginning with the most indirect

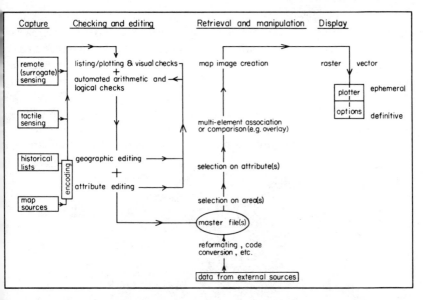

Figure 4.1 Procedures for collecting spatial (especially land use) data (from Rhind 1977).

methods and proceeding towards those which give the ability to collect whatever data are required. Coppock and Gebbett (1978) should be consulted for specific British examples of the data sources mentioned below and on pp. 57 and 69.

Data from lists and texts

The most important characteristic of data extracted from texts is that their extraction is usually time-consuming and often necessitates expert knowledge of the source and, possibly, of the geographical area concerned. Despite this, such lists provide the earliest land use records which exist in Britain and, indeed, in most other countries. Perhaps the most striking of these sources is the two-volume Domesday Book: Darby (1973, p. 38) has called it 'probably the most remarkable statistical document in the history of Europe'. The information is arranged under the heading of each of the then counties; within each county, details of the holdings of the principal land holders is given for each village. Darby, in a number of different publications, has shown that the information available falls into two categories. The first are those items which occur in almost every village: plough lands, population and so on. The second group consists of such items as mills, meadows, pasture, woodland and less common items such as fisheries, marsh, salt pans, vineyards and wasteland. The interpretational difficulties may be exemplified by the response to a question of 'How much wood?' put by the Domesday Commissioners; the more precise of the answers given (Darby 1973, p. 43) were couched in terms of the land being able to support a specified number of swine, in terms of imprecise statistics defining some of the lengths of sides of a field of unknown shape, or in terms of 'acres'. Unhappily, we do not know what area was implied by this 'acre' nor what levels of consistency were adhered to throughout the country. Finally, the remarkable level of detail is present only for the country areas; the detail relating to towns is fragmentary and incomplete. All reference to London is, for example, missing. Despite this considerable reconstruction of land use is possible, as exemplified by fig. 4.2 showing all occurrences of land which had gone out of productive use.

Where necessary, it may also be possible to extract information on land use

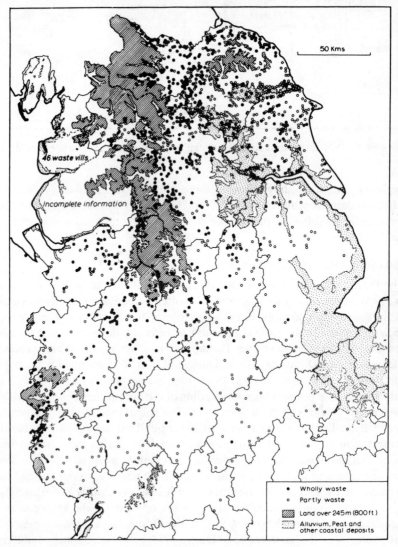

Figure 4.2   Wasteland in England in 1086 (from Darby 1973).

particularly on activities, from the work of regional novelists. Such 'soft data' are usually only valuable as a fill-in between the 'harder' variety or where none of the latter exists, but such works as those of Thomas Hardy, D. H. Lawrence, J. B. Priestley, George Orwell and John Steinbeck often provide and use commentaries, however personalized. Pocock (1979), in discussing the novelist's feel for place, incidently illustrates the way in which novelists writing about Northern England have included land use information.

Not all lists and text sources provide only historical material. The cadastral surveys in some parts of Europe define land ownership and, to some extent, land use boundaries both now and, in some cases, at times in the past. These boudaries are defined by sets of bounding co-ordinates stored, until recently, in manuscript form: in England and Wales, by contrast, the definition of ownership of land held by the Land Registry is based upon generalized boundaries, most of which follow physical features shown on the Ordnance Survey large scale plans (Dale 1977); but the explicit definition of the location of these boundaries is a verbal one. It has been variously estimated that between 70% and 90% of all property boundaries are physical features visible on OS maps. The situation in the United States is, according to McLaughlin and Clapp (1977), rather different: 'In the settlement of North America the land was largely regarded as a free good and neither the quality of the cadastral arrangements nor their subsequent maintenance were deemed of significant public importance.' Other textual sources of land use data include the valuation registers available for inspection by the public in each British Local Authority office: since some property is unrated, such lists are not comprehensive and, worse than this, no indication is available of how much is missing. All too frequently, such lists are still in manuscript form but the progressive change toward holding the data on computers and the proposed changes to the methods of rating ensure that this could be an important secondary source of land use information in Britain in the future (ECU 1978).

We should note that some important sources of land use information are widely used in tabular form, even though they have been derived from field mapping: as such they have incurred several stages of interpretation. Examples of this are the County Series of Reports derived from Stamp's Land Utilisation Survey and the Department of Environment study of Developed Areas (DoE 1978). Both of these are discussed in the succeeding section.

Penultimately, other data lists have been used in Britain to provide answers to a topical and pressing land use problem, essentially connected with land use change rather than with a detailed geographical description of contemporary land use. Best (1968, 1978) has used returns from the Annual Agricultural Census of England and Wales, which includes statistics on losses of land from agricultural use, to suggest that the rate of absorption of agricultural land for urban land use is not significant. Champion (1975) has used other listed information—population change data compiled from decennial censuses—as surrogate, or alternative, ways of measuring land use change. Although the statistics are available for long periods—agricultural statistics were first collected in 1866 – such procedures are not without their difficulties. Best (Best 1978; Best and Coppock 1962) himself has pointed out that official estimates of urban land in 1937, which were based upon what was left after totalling other uses, now appear to have been 50% in error. Comparisons with the first Land Utilisation Survey of Great Britain showed that both massive under- and double-counting of land areas had occurred in some contemporary Government statistics – a deficiency of no less the 500,000 ha existed in the Ministry of Agriculture statistics in 1950. In part, such problems stem from the classification of land use – and change – by the Ministry and in part from the use of self-enumeration by farmers in the Agricultural Census. As Coppock (Best and Coppock 1962) has pointed out: 'the field which the Welsh hill farmer would return as permanent pasture would probably be classified by the Leicestershire grazier as rough pasture.' Coppock (1978) has also pointed out that the geographical individuals for which these data are available are also rather unsatisfactory: owing to confidentiality considerations, they are only available by civil parishes or groups of parishes. In Scotland, only 891 parishes exist and these vary in size from less than 40 to more than 100,000 ha.

Champion's (1975) estimates of the percentage of urban land in Britain are based upon more consistently collected data but are only valid if his assumptions on the relationship between population density and land use are everywhere substantially correct or if the 'errors' cancel out over-all. Even if these assumptions are largely correct, equally reasonable but different estimates may be obtained by use of different surrogates. In passing, we might notice that the inverse of Champion's approach – to estimate population from the extent of urban land – has proved feasible and potentially valuable when based upon satellite imagery for certain areas (Tobler 1969; Wellar 1969). Horton (1974) has obtained limited success in attempting to predict the populations in small areas within cities from urban characteristics detectable on 1/50,000 scale photographs. Such indirect methods of detecting land use may be exploited from a variety of other sources. Coppock and Gebbett (1978) have listed a variety of sources ranging from the Annual Census of Employment, the data from which are available by Employment Exchange Areas, to the decennial Census of Population, statistics from which are available by the 110,000 or so Enumeration Districts in the country.

In practice – and in Britain at least – the abstraction of land use data from a variety of data lists has given some activity- and some form-based data, relating mainly to the micro- or to the national (rather than district or regional) level of resolution and the results have been of highly variable accuracy. The spatial units by which data are available have either been functional ones, such as the individual farm, or administrative units such as a County Borough. Except where on-going agricultural censuses have been involved, the results from such data abstraction from lists constitute only *ad hoc* surveys. Even in on-going censuses, changes in definition and self-enumeration have undoubtedly led to complications of comparison through time or over space. In short, there are comparatively few purposes for which the available data are ideal and the imprecisions resulting from their mis-use are extremely difficult to quantify.

Data from maps

We can think of maps as having several functions – to display spatial patterns and to act as a geographical index to tabulate figures are two examples. So far as land use is concerned, however, maps are extremely common data stores. Like data lists and information on land use culled from text books, data from maps are taken from a secondary source: some other survey has taken place, the results have been collected and translated into map form – subject to the training, skills and inclinations of the cartographer and the space and time available to him (see Robinson *et al.* 1978). Consequently, maps of land use (and particularly small scale ones) should be treated with some care as data sources. As an example, it is difficult to draw and annotate any area smaller than about 2 mm across on a map: this indicates that, on maps of 1/50,000 scale, the minimum-sized area which can be depicted, irrespective of what has been found on the ground, is one hectare.

The longest geographically detailed historical 'time series' is available from topographic maps, in which land use information – both activity- and formally-based – occurs incidently. In Britain, the comparatively high frequency of up-dating of the topographic maps ensures that these may be used for a crude land use 'base-line' and for rolling estimates of change. Fordham (1975) has, for example, utilized Ordnance Survey 1/63,360, 1/10,560 and 1/2,500 scale maps to determine the extent of urban areas at the several points in time. On the basis of about 134,000 point samples, he has calculated that Best's original figure for the area of urban land in 1950–51 is incorrect by no less than 14% (see chapter 6). Although Fordham castigates Best's results, he acknowledges some deficiencies of his own data, in particular the gross generalization on the 1/63,360 scale maps: such generalization is shown in fig. 4.3 in which land uses from different scales of OS maps are compared.

Such a use of topographic maps is not restricted to British maps: fig. 4.4 reproduced from Hansen (1960) via Mills, (1973), illustrates the suburban growth of Copenhagen in the period 1860 to 1960. The over-riding problems of reliance upon general purpose topographic maps as a source of land use data are their lack of synchroneity (different map sheets are revised at different times), their crude, and occasionally inconsistent classification of land uses and the fact that, since the map production is usually outside the control of the persons needing land use data, maps covering the particular area of interest may be very out-of-date when required. The further problem of cartographic generalization has already been observed. Converting such maps to computer means for subsequent analysis, if necessary, is also not a trivial undertaking (Rhind 1977) although much progress is being made towards this end and the computerized processing and analysis of land use data is discussed in chapter 5. The over-riding advantage of maps is that they are extremely

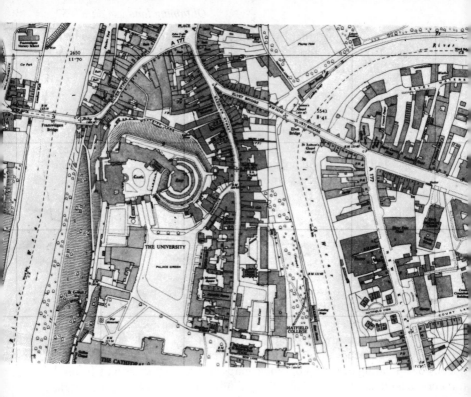

DURHAM (DURHAM AND FRAMWELGATE) MB

a + b + c

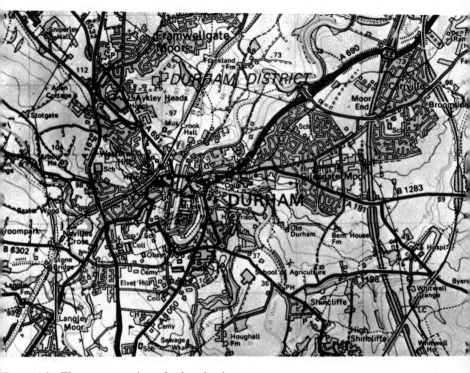

Figure 4.3 The representation of urban land use on
   a 1/1,250
   b 1/10,000 and
   c 1/50,000 scale

OS maps

inexpensive data sources, normally provide both good resolution and good position fixing and are conveniently sampled to obtain general land use statistics.

Maps of land use are now available for most of the areas of both Great Britain and the United States of America. Sources of these maps and other land use information are tabulated in the appendix. The maps are, however, very different in their level of detail, up-to-dateness and in what they show. In Britain, a remarkable variety of evidence is available in map form. The Down Survey, for example, carried out in Ireland between 1654 and 1658 was recorded on maps at 1/7,920 scale. Initiated primarily by the need to define land parcels which were allocated by lottery to soldiers fighting for Cromwell, the survey recorded the existence of arable, pasture, meadow, timber or bog; the value of the land was largely inferred from its then use. The earliest maps which cover large parts of mainland Britain are those of the Tithe surveys, following the Tithe Commutation Act of 1836 (Kain 1977). Some three-quarters of the then rural landscape of England and Wales is depicted exactly in these field-by-field surveys and, in addition to the maps, the accompanying schedules of apportionment give the names of the owners and occupiers of

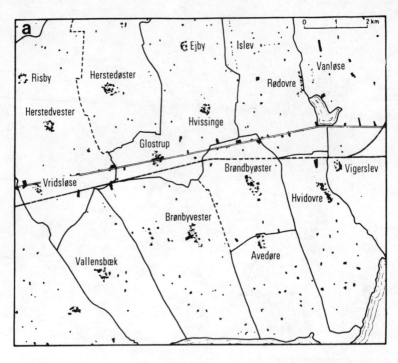

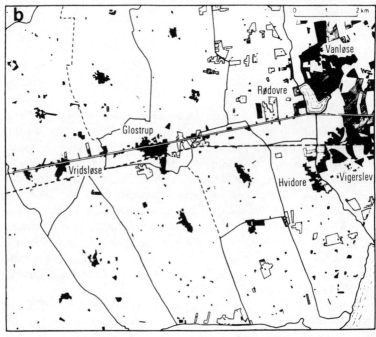

Figure 4.4 The growth of Copenhagen, as shown by topographic maps, a 1860; b 1910; c 1930; d 1960 (Mills 1973, after Hansen 1960).

each field, its state of cultivation and area. For some areas, a series of parish tithe files provide extra information on the nature of farming practices.

Recent work by Harley has elaborated on a little-known source of historical land use data. He has pointed out that:

> ... from 1855 to 1918 the Ordnance Survey carried out what was in effect a simplified form of a national land use survey. Throughout this period, a fairly standard range of land use types – including arable and pasture – were systematically recorded as part of the cadastral mapping and revision at the 25 in. scale. For roughly quarter of a century the information was published in the Books of Reference and by the 1880s, when this series of pamphlets was discontinued, land use information had been published for several thousand parishes in Great Britain. (Harley 1979)

Well over 40,000 maps contained such land use information.

Almost exactly a century after the Tithe maps, another set of maps was published as a result of the Land Utilisation Survey of the early 1930s (Board 1968; Stamp 1948) and upon which the comprehensive series of county reports were based (e.g. Willatts 1937). This was initiated by Sir L. Dudley Stamp and directed by him and Willatts from a base in the London School of Economics. A similar survey of Northern Ireland was carried out by D. A. Hill between 1938 and 1946. Derived from field survey in Britain by 20,000 volunteers on OS Six Inch maps, these multi-colour maps were produced using the 'one inch' (1/63,360) scale Ordnance Survey maps of the day as an underlay and employed a simple classification, largely orientated towards agricultural objectives (see p. 35). The use of a limited number of simply recognized classes in the classification was enforced by the large numbers of indirectly supervised field surveyors – mostly school children. Subsequently, a summary map of land classification in the whole of Britain at 1/625,000 scale was published, having been derived from a generalization of the one inch maps; at the time, this was almost the only consistent basis for the classification of agricultural land in Britain.

This was by no means the only land utilization survey of its time (see, for example, Beard 1941). Wood (1955) has described another contemporary survey as follows:

> The Wisconsin Land Economic Inventory, organised in 1928 and expanded when funds became available in the 1930's, sought to map all of the land cover in the state except that in Milwaukee County. Data for the maps were gathered by field men who made foot traverses one eighth of a mile apart in the southern counties and one quarter of a mile apart in some of the sparsely settled northern counties. These field men used a pace scale to record the distance travelled through each specific type of cover. The plan was to have the traverse data incorporated into maps, but before maps could be made for all counties, the work slowed down

considerably because of lack of funds. Published maps at a scale of one inch to one mile are available for most of the counties in eastern Wisconsin.

Although it was not the only one, the Land Utilisation Survey was, by any standards, a towering achievement. It is proper, however, to note two factors contributing to the feasibility of the project: the first of these is the pioneer British work on land use field mapping by Fairgrieve, Baker (1926) and Field (1930) and other members of the Geographical Association. The second was the availability of semi-skilled labour for the field survey, a consequence of the rapid expansion of geography as an academic discipline in Britain around the turn of the century, after the disasterous situation in schools was revealed by the Keltie report of 1886. The Land Utilisation Survey of Britain was thus a consistent, nearly synchronous and comparatively accurate inventory which has been used for many one-off purposes since the publication of the results.

We may note in passing, however, that several authors – notably Balchin (1976) – have attached an even greater significance to the survey and to Stamp's work on land use. They have traced to it much of the development of formal land use control and other planning in Britain.

Nearly thirty years later, a second survey was set up and carried out (with Stamp's enthusiastic blessing) on an equally impressive scale. The director was Dr Alice Coleman who, with the minimum of resources, initiated the survey in 1960 (Coleman 1961; Coleman and Maggs 1962). Like its predecessor, this was intended to cover the totality of the land area of the country. Areas such as fields, defined as homogeneous on formal or functional characteristics, were shaded appropriately on the maps by the surveyor, being classified into one of about 90 categories (p. 35). Survey was carried out by appealing to senior schools, local geographical societies, colleges and university departments of geography and the like, with consistency checks being applied by a centrally organized group of surveyors. Most survey was carried out on the basis of 1/10,560 scale OS maps and a number of the resulting, final maps were published at the 1/25,000 scale, again utilizing an OS base. It is interesting to note that this procedure made effective use of the national topographic map series – many of the smaller scale maps were, at that time, photographically reduced versions of those at the larger scale and, as such, transference of detail from one map to another was a simple matter. Such compilation of detail is often much more complicated, especially in those areas of the world where maps of highly variable reliability exist and where some map series are on different map projections. The classic example of such difficulties must be in the United States where much large scale survey is carried out on maps based on State co-ordinate systems.

The second survey of England and Wales was largely completed in the 1960s: that of England was completed in 8 years, the 'halfway' year being 1963 while Wales took a decade to complete, the median year being 1966. Some 3,000 volunteer surveyors were involved and the problems of training and

Figure 4.5 The area around London (Heathrow) airport and the Developed Areas (labelled A to E), interpreted from aerial photographs (from Smith 1978; Crown Copyright reserved).

inculcating consistency are obvious. Sample re-surveys were carried out in about 5% of England and Wales in the 1970s. The consequence of all this labour is an accessible archive of land use maps maintained in London, plus derived statistics. The contents of the maps may be deduced from the classification given on pp. 35–7. On the basis of the definitions on pp. 31–2 we would presently classify the data as level IIIC; Stamp's data would be classified as IIID. The importance of the temporal factor was evident in early 1979, when the British government formally announced their rejection of a proposal to publish all the sheets, noting that, while land use information was a critical input to any planning, Dr Coleman's maps were out-of-date and employed an 'unsuitable classification'. Some alternative action was implied to be forthcoming from research then under way in the relevant government body, the Department of the Environment.

The most consistent and up-to-date national coverage of high resolution urban land use data available within England and Wales is almost certainly that produced, in the main, from 1969 air photography between 1977 and 1978 (DoE 1978; Smith *et al.* 1977) i.e. of level IIIB at the time of writing. The methods of survey are discussed under a later heading; the results are transparent overlays to each of the 124 Ordnance Survey 1/50,000 maps covering these two countries. Fig. 4.5 is an example of land use boundaries overlaid on one photograph. It should be noticed that the classification is a coarse one (see p. 38); only five different land use classes are involved and only areas of 5 ha or more in extent were mapped. Set against this, such mapped data have the considerable benefit of synchroneity and consistency of interpretation in different areas. Being based on formal rather than functional considerations, they do not integrate well with the results from many ground based surveys: table 4.1, for example, illustrates how residential land uses occupy some 60% of the land in the town of Darlington, County Durham, while the same individual land uses make up about 90% of all functioning land use units. At the time of writing, this is regarded as a bench-mark survey although active research (e.g. Carter and Jackson 1976; Smith 1978) is being carried out on various means of up-dating it.

A much larger scale operation was initiated in 1975 in the USA. Scheduled for areal completion by 1982 and to be followed by the provision of regular up-dates, the land use maps are also largely compiled from aerial photographs. In this case, however, earlier land use maps, especially for metropolitan areas, are used to supplement aerial photographs and other remote sensed data; the maps are compiled at a scale of about 1/125,000. A minimum homogeneous parcel of 4 ha is used for urban areas and bodies of surface water, quarries, gravel pits and some agricultural features. A minimum mapping unit of 16 ha is used for all other categories of land use: in general, the resolution accords to level IIB of the classification of surveys given in chapter 2. The resulting maps are available for reproduction at the major offices of the USGS, on paper or on film. Where the newly compiled USGS topographic maps at 1/100,000 scale are available, the land use overlays are

Table 4.1 Land cover and land use (ss) in Darlington district, County Durham, using DoE (1978) classification.

	A: predominantly residential use	B: predominantly industrial and/or commercial use	C: predominantly educational/community/health/indoor recreational use	D: transport use	E: 'urban' open space
DoE	60.4	20.1	0.6	9.2	9.9
DLUS	92.7	5.4	1.1	0.5	0.3

Sources: DoE figures from DoE (1978), pertaining to 1969.
DLUS figures aggregated from DLUS survey (Rhind and Hudson 1980) pertaining to 1976. The land use types in the DoE project total only 97.9% of those on the DLUS; the latter have been rescaled to make them directly comparable. The discrepancy is largely due to the omission of much of the 'UL' category (unused land and water) from the DoE study.

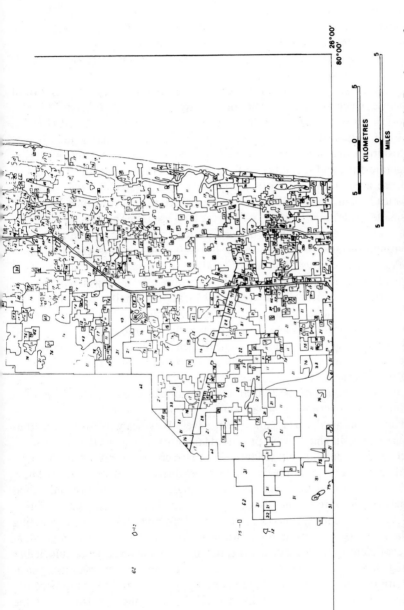

Figure 4.6 A section of the United States Geological Survey land cover and land use map for the Palm Beach area of Florida; the numbers refer to different land use classes (see p. 40).

also available at this scale; in the bulk of the areas, they are available only at 1/250,000 scale. In total, no less than 487 map sheets at 1/250,000 scale are involved to cover the 9.36×10^6 km^2 area of the USA. Fig. 4.6 illustrates a sample of the maps, emphasizing their basic cartographic nature as boundary lines and the identification of land use by parcel numbering. What is particularly distinctive is that these maps are not produced in isolation – identically scaled overlay maps of the boundaries of political units, hydrological areas, census areas and federal land ownership are also available for the user to combine as appropriate.

The relationship of map scale to accuracy is a complex one, but is important to the user when alternative scales of map are available for analysis; it is also important to the person planning the compilation of a map-based land use survey. Comparatively few studies appear to have investigated the relationship in one study area. One of the few studies to do this is that by Fitzgerald-Lins and Chambers (1977); they concluded that, on the basis of land use areas measured both on 1/24,000 and 1/100,000 scale maps, no statistically significant differences between these were discernible. However, the smaller scale maps had only 42% of the land use zones present on the larger scale maps. In essence, then, the errors due to enlarging some areas and obviating others were self-cancelling throughout the map sheet. Two comments follow from this: first, use of smaller scale maps may be acceptable if aggregate, statistical summaries alone are required. If the objective is to store and retrieve accurately land use at *all* locations, smaller scale maps are unsatisfactory. The second comment is that it is difficult to say how general is their conclusion: intuitively, it might be expected to hold in areas where most land parcels were of a similar size. In general, however, the individual cartographer compiling the map will partly control which areas are generalized out of existence.

It is not without interest that all of the examples cited thus far have been produced by government departments, encouraged in many instances by academics, or by the academics themselves. It is scarcely surprising that commercial bodies have rarely produced land use maps, given the main uses to which land use data are put (chapter 2). An exception to this, however, is the Goad maps available for the central business districts of British towns. These are based on use of OS large scale plans and record the use of individual properties; they are frequently up-dated on the basis of field survey.

With very rare exceptions, maps compiled from ground survey and acting as data repositories have been produced on the basis of the individual surveyor identifying homogeneous zones, or assessing one area as sufficiently homogeneous for the purposes of the survey. The shortcomings of using such data are manifest – field checking is often impossible and the map becomes reality, all analysis being totally dependent upon the consistency of the 'homogenization procedure' between different surveyors. We shall see (chapter 5) that maps can store very substantial amounts of information in a compact form; they are easily handled and generally inexpensive. But, although some questions may be answered extremely easily with them – such as 'what land use is at this point?' – others, notably involving statistical summaries, are often difficult, error-prone and time consuming. Finally, and especially true where topographic maps are used as data sources, it is uncommon to find that the maps have been compiled at ideal times for the users' requirements. In addition, different elements of the contents of one map will have last been up-dated at different times. Even in a country as well mapped as Britain, adjacent topographic map sheets in rural areas may have almost half a century between their last substantial revisions.

Data from remote sensing

The term 'remote sensing' dates only from the late 1950s (Estes and Senger 1974). Its scope is, for some, a matter of debate. Here we consider the field to subsume all the sometimes disparate disciplines of air photo interpretation, photogrammetry and the use of imagery from satellites. In essence, we assume remote sensing to embrace the detection and, perhaps, the measurement of objects by some device physically separated from them, often by a considerable distance.

The overwhelming advantages of remote sensing methods over tactile methods based on ground survey are the consistency which can be ensured in at least one stage of data collection, the rapidity of survey and the small number of skilled workers required at the data collection stage: it is possible, in principle at least, to collect photography for all of Great Britain in one field season, even taking into account a statistically average summer, and produce medium scale (say 1/50,000) maps before the succeeding summer. In West Germany, the multiple uses of such air photography have ensured that the country is now over-flown every 2 years. Indeed, imagery for a whole country at scales such as 1/1 million may be obtained in a few hours from satellites. Unlike the preceding data sources, the direct use of air photographs or satellite imagery ensures that a minimum of interpretation has been carried out by others. Provided the imagery has been collected in reasonably similar circumstances, then the user can be confident that his data source is internally consistent and its synchroneity, or lack of it, is explicit. If the imagery is being collected especially for the purposes of the survey, the client will be able to specify time and environment conditions which are best for his purposes, such as mid-day in winter conditions. In considering how accurately land use data may be obtained by remote sensing and how confident we may be about these results, the following considerations are important:

(i) Characteristics of the imagery: scale of the photography
                                      geometric fidelity
                                      contrast, sharpness, resolving
                                          power of film etc.
                                      waveband(s) used
                                      photographic or digital format

(ii) Characteristics of the land use: consistency of the relationship
between form and function
degree of multiple use
the amount of ground control
change since imagery was obtained

(iii) Characteristics of the user and   interpretation skill
of his tools: use of stereoscopic techniques
the classification used
the extent to which accuracy is
checked by the interpreter

For convenience, we shall sub-divide our consideration into two main parts, that of photographic imagery and that of material in digital form. Before that, however, we must examine the physical basis of remote sensing.

THE ELECTROMAGNETIC SPECTRUM EMS AND SENSORS

It is impossible to understand recent developments in remote sensing without understanding something of the radiation – such as light – whose impact creates the image on suitable recording devices – such as photographic film. Equally, it is impossible to choose from available imagery without such understanding because the physical constitution of the ground surface and different types of land use thereon are recorded differently by different methods of remote sensing. Although some forms of remote sensing are done acoustically and others are based on surveys of gravity or magnetism, the vast bulk of surveys are based upon use of electromagnetic energy.

The term 'electromagnetic spectrum' is applied to all energy that moves with constant velocity of light and has a harmonic wave-form: visible light and heat are two physiological manifestations of electromagnetic energy of different wavelengths. Sound, then, is not part of the electromagnetic spectrum. Fig. 4.7 illustrates the meaning of the commonly used terms and sets out the conventional divisions of the wavelengths used in remote sensing. Different objects or surfaces characteristically radiate energy differentially at the various wavelengths. Water, for example, strongly absorbs infrared energy and reflects shorter wave radiation. In this way, we may consider that given objects or surfaces have 'spectral signatures' or, in effect, finger prints and can be recognized on this basis. Fig. 4.8 illustrates the spectral signatures of different land uses in urban areas (after Carter and Jackson 1976). Unfortunately, a number of complicating factors occur. These include scattering and absorption in the atmosphere of the energy being transmitted between the object and the sensor: as a consequence, parts of the spectral signature may be suppressed in transit of radiation. The degree and type of such scattering and absorption vary through time, with geographical location and with the wavelength of the radiation (Estes 1974). Certain types of land use, notably vegetation, also have spectral signatures which vary greatly throughout the year.

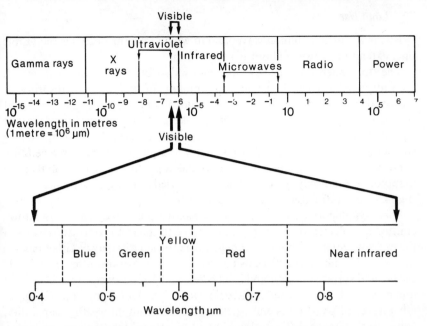

Figure 4.7 The sections of the Electromagnetic Spectrum which are normally used in remote sensing; the enlargement shows those wavebands in or near the visible part of the EMS and the colours associated with them.

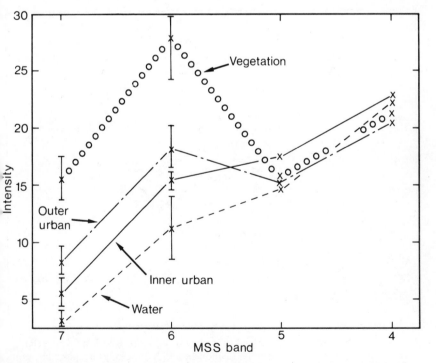

Figure 4.8 Some spectral signatures detected by Carter and Jackson (1976) from Landsat MSS data in the Reading area; the bars at each point on each graph summarize the variation encountered.

By far the most common waveband in which imaging occurs is the visible one, extending between about 0.4 to 0.7 μm.

The atmosphere contains several 'windows' so far as radiation is concerned, i.e. wavelengths at which insignificant amounts of radiation are absorbed or scattered. One of these is between 8 and 14 μm in the thermal infrared wavelengths and, as a consequence, smoke and atmospheric haze do not detract from the imagery obtained. This, and the possibility of measuring smaller temperature variations which reflect variations in crop or vegetation conditions on the ground, has led to the rapid development of thermal mapping. Commonly such mapping is carried out by a scanning device (fig. 4.9), the Infra-Red Line Scan or IRLS.

Photographic and IRLS sensors are passive ones: they collect radiation emitted or reflected from the ground surface to them. In contrast, sensors in the microwave (from about 0.5 mm to 1 m) wavelengths may be either passive or active. The latter generates its own signal which is transmitted until it hits the ground surface or cover and is reflected back to the sensor. It is, of course, much better known as radar (RAdio Detection And Ranging). The great advantages of passive systems are that they have an all-weather capability, being able to image through cloud and at night, and that they can observe a very wide range in the strengths of emitted signals. However, they have a low

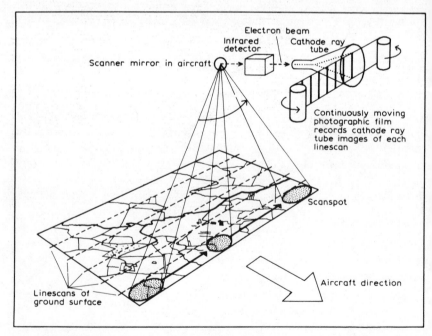

Figure 4.9   Diagrammatic portrayal of survey using Infra-Red Line Scan (IRLS); many other scanners work in a similar fashion although these may be replaced by more reliable solid state devices in the future (from Cooke and Harris 1970).

spatial resolution – few systems can detect features on the ground much smaller than 1 km across. Active systems also have these advantages but, in addition, it is possible to simulate the presence of very large radar aerials by using the movement of the aircraft in conjunction with Doppler techniques. Synthetic Aperture Radar (SAR) thus has the capability for much higher spatial resolution, down to 30 m or less, even though much processing of the data is essential.

Increasingly, the image is being stored in computer-compatible or digital form. Even imaging in the visible wavebands is now often carried out by scanners which store the image directly on a digital tape. Some of the reasons for this will become obvious later (p. 96) but one of these may be noted here: such data can be readily plotted in photographic form on any one of various kinds of film recorders, i.e. the computer can be organized to plot output visible to the naked eye from those wavelengths which are far beyond the eye's sensitivity.

Finally, the role of 'ground truth' is a particularly critical one. By this term, we mean information on what *actually* existed at selected points on the ground at or about the time the remote sensed imagery was taken: the synchroneity is more important for some land uses than others – crops, for instance, change their characteristics more rapidly than houses. This is then used to 'calibrate' those sections of the imagery: all interpretation of imagery proceeds on the basis of analogy – areas which look similar to those constituting the ground truth or to prior experience of the interpreter are identified on the basis of this analogy. All those areas which are not 'similar' within some tolerance have to be left as unclassified.

PHOTOGRAPHIC IMAGERY

The major impetus to studies of land use from photographic imagery arose in war-time. Although the French photographer Tournachon was probably the first to take aerial photographs (he intended to make a topographic map of the environs of Paris from his photographs taken from a captive balloon in 1858) major developments in techniques began from its use by the Union Army in the American Civil War in 1862: photographs were originally taken from captive balloons to gather intelligence on the Confederate defences of Richmond. As early as 1906 the German, Alfred Maul, demonstrated a compressed air-driven rocket which rose to 800 m, took pictures and then parachuted the camera back to earth (Colwell 1960). Aerial photography on an operational basis, however, dates from the First World War and almost immediately it changed the nature of warfare – information on the creation of new transport facilities, troop movements, and the like gave immediate intelligence of the enemy plans. By 1918, American photo interpreters had detected and identified 90% of the military installations on the adjacent enemy side of the front lines.

Although enormous strides were also made in civilian applications of measurement from, and interpretation of, aerial photographs in the inter-war years, the most rapid developments were again to take place in war-time. Both German and British forces made intensive and critical use of air photographs throughout the Second World War, to be followed by Russian and American forces. Observation of unusual patterns of land use on photographs led to such important discoveries as the launching pads for V-1 rockets a full year before they were launched against England. Improvements in the quality of photographic films and the developments of new ones – such as those sensitive to infrared radiation, enabling dead vegetation used as camouflage to be detected – paralleled the development in cameras and in sensing platforms, i.e. the aircraft. Before being disbanded at the end of the war, the extensive photo-reconnaissance facilities of the RAF were employed to make the first complete photo-coverage of Britain. Although highly variable in quality because of the cloud coverage, these photographs are an important bench-mark, essentially synchronous for most practical purposes. Of more general significance was that, in 1946, many military staff familiar with the advantages of aerial photographs returned to civilian life; many military aircraft equipped for photo-reconnaissance were sold to commercial firms. Since then, developments have been extremely rapid and it is now the norm in most countries for topographical mapping to be produced by photo-grammetric means.

Frequently, at least in the past, only one waveband has been used; this band is usually a composite one obtained by using panchromatic film which is sensitive to light throughout the visible part of the spectrum. The most common recording device used in these wavelengths is the camera. Indeed, photographic emulsions have been developed which have a sensitivity extending to 1.1 pm, the photographic infrared region of the EMS. Such cameras are now commonly multi-band in that they record information in different sections of the visible and near-visible wavelengths, either by simultaneously photographing the scene via several lenses and filters onto one wide-tolerance film, or alternatively, via several lenses directly onto separate films of more limited spectral tolerance. Camera designs and sensing platforms are now extremely sophisticated, particularly in military aircraft: moving the film to avoid blur of the image while the photograph is being taken is now necessary, for example, in medium-altitude high-speed aircraft. Films in common use include black and white panchromatic and infrared and (true) colour and false colour (infrared sensitive) film.

Interpretation of the photographic image

Almost all interpretation of air photographs is carried out on vertical aerial photographs, i.e. those in which the camera is pointed vertically downwards. In land use studies in urban areas, of course, there is sometimes much to be said for having a supplementary oblique view since it provides details not obvious from directly overhead. In reality, and unlike a map, no aerial photograph is an orthogonal projection of the world: scale varies across it and buildings apparently lean outward towards the edge of the photograph. These characteristics of air photographs have profound advantages and some disadvantages: by taking successive photographs which overlap and also overlap along flight paths, it is possible to produce stereoscopic images when viewed through a stereoscope (Colwell 1960, p. 30). This use of parallax is the basis of photogrammetry and is useful in urban studies in detecting or measuring heights of buildings and other structures; in rural areas it may be useful in measuring the growth or height of stands of trees.

The disadvantages of air photographs stem from the distortions inherent in them. These are of three main types and are illustrated in fig. 4.10: (i) those due to the camera in the aircraft not being vertical; (ii) those resulting from variations in altitude of the aircraft; and (iii) those due to variations in height of the terrain. Unless compensations are made, the distortions can result in considerable errors in measurements made directly from the photography. Colwell (1960, p. 139) and Dickinson (1979, p. 150) illustrate how these come about and how scale variations can be as much as 50% within one photograph, depending on the relationship between flying height, the focal length of the camera lens and variations in the ground altitude. The first two causes of distortions are comparatively easily negated by a procedure which simulates the attitude and altitude of the aircraft when the picture was taken. A device such as a Multiplex projector is used to recreate the aircraft tilt, etc. Until recently, though, the extraction of the distortion effects due to topography was much more difficult. Now, however, the increasingly common use of orthophoto equipment (Petrie 1977) has ensured that air photographs can be produced without distortions – in practice, to the same standards of geometric accuracy as normal topographic maps. This is still relatively uncommon in Britain although the resulting orthophotos have been used as a base map for a series of planning maps in Sweden and have proved of considerable benefit in mapping urban change in the USA. Recent ingenious developments combine the advantages of stereoscopic viewing of normal air photos with the

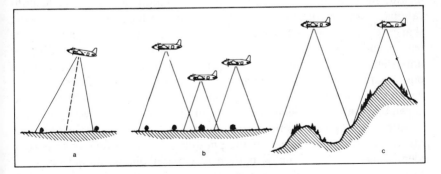

Figure 4.10   Scale variations within aerial photographs
    a   due to tilt of the aircraft
    b   due to variations in flying height
    c   due to variations in ground altitude.

geometric fidelity of the orthophoto by creating an 'orthophotomate' – an image which, when viewed with the orthophoto, gives stereoscopic viewing. The role of computer-based techniques is extremely important here since the processes which are used to create the new products are increasingly changing from optical and mechanical to computerized ones.

The strategy and tactics which an air photo interpreter uses will partially control what he or she finds by way of land use. Most experienced interpreters prefer to begin by scanning the area as a whole or a large part of it, usually by laying down a group of air photographs and studying these visually before proceeding to look at individual prints. Where detailed examination of individual photographs is concerned, one of two tactics is employed (Colwell 1960, p. 109) – either the 'fishing expedition' or the logical search. The first of these involves looking at every object in every photograph and, as a result, yields much redundant information although it is likely to miss little. The second approach is based upon probabilities established in the interpreter's mind by previous experience – certain areas are disregarded after an initial scan as being unlikely to contain relevant material. Here the use of an explicit key for what is being sought (such as features which indicate different kinds of industry, given by Colwell 1960, p. 701) usually restricts the search effort required. In practice, the usual approach is a combination of these with some integration – the interpreter returns to some material he has previously interpreted as he gains more experience in an area. 'Ground truth', supplied either via topographic maps or from visits to part of the area, are usually essential 'control' in the interpretation. Circumstantial evidence is also widely used, e.g. heavy industry often has direct rail communications. Over-all, though, the difference in approach is important – the 'fishing expedition' approach is likely to give information which is useful for a much wider variety of tasks but will cost more to compile and check.

The interpretation of a particular parcel of land may be carried out on the basis of several criteria (Colwell 1960, p. 100). The first of these is size; measurement of this often permits the elimination of alternative identifications. Another criterion is shape and, allied to this, shadow cast by the shape – particularly useful where no great contrast exists between one feature and another. In rural areas, especially, tone and colour are extremely important criteria although the grey tones reproduced on black and white photographs do not always correspond to our perceptions of the objects in nature: a body of water may appear any colour from white to black, depending on the angle of the sun and the form of the water surface. Texture – the tonal repetition of objects too small to be individually identified – varies with scale of the photograph but is often an important identifying criterion. Finally, pattern is a major diagnostic aid – clues to former land uses are often detected from regularities of features seen in photographs of the natural landscape.

Several studies have compared the relative merits of different types of photography for defining different types of land use. Nunnally (1974), summarizing many of these, claims that colour and colour infrared film are generally superior to black and white photography: in general, the additional cost of flying colour is only a small overhead compared with the basic costs of survey. The wavelength of the radiation significantly affects what can be seen (see p. 70): the land and water boundary becomes extremely marked in infrared photographs although crop classifications are usually much easier in the shorter wavelengths.

Many of the examples of photo interpretation quoted thus far, such as Smith *et al.* (1977), relate specifically to urban areas for which, Horton (1974) has suggested, it is more difficult to interpret photographs than in the rural ones. Many successful applications of air photo analysis exist for rural areas, where the possibility of rapid areal coverage is of considerable value (Colwell 1960, p. 561). Thaman (1974) reviewed many of these studies and pointed out, for example, that the agricultural land use potential of some 600,000 square miles of the Australian Northern Territory had been mapped from air photographs in a decade. Thaman also pointed out the wealth of large or medium scale coverage available – often much better than that of topographic maps. In the USA, for example, more than 80% of the conterminous land area and virtually all the cropland is covered by air photography, much of it at 1/20,000 scale, and has often been photographed three or four times since the 1930s. Correspondingly, well over three million air photographs of Canada exist in the National Air Photo Library and similar or better coverage exists for the UK. The move begun in the 1960s towards maintaining comprehensive computer-based inventories (see chapter 5), has led to several major studies using air photos as a data collection method: by their nature, such studies cover both urban and rural areas. A good example is the LUNR scheme carried out for New York State (Tomlinson *et al.* 1976) and based upon interpretation of air photographs at 1/24,000 scale. It should be noted that not all of the use of air photographs has merely been for inventorying purposes – as early as 1957, Green was using them in attempting to define and analyse the social structure of the city.

Problems with use of air photos

Despite the widespread availability of coverage for most developed countries, a number of important problems remain to be faced by all users. One of these is the restraints imposed by the general scale of the photograph: there is, self-evidently, a minimum size of feature which may be consistently interpreted correctly. Gautam (1976), working in an Indian city, and Smith *et al.* (1977), working on urban areas in Britain, both used similar sized areas on the photograph as the minimum size of consistently interpretable unit – 5 and 3.7 mm square areas or their equivalents, respectively. The effects of this greatly constrain the level of detail in the classification hierarchy. Indeed, Smith *et al.* (1977) make the constraints very explicit: ' . . . the definitions of the main land use categories . . . were determined largely by the photography.' De Bruijn (1978) has illustrated the relationship between the photo

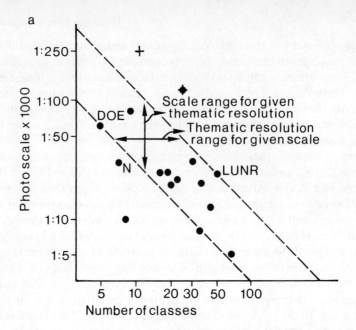

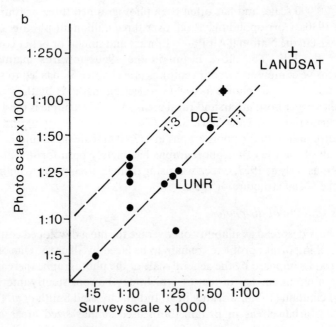

◆ High altitude colour infrared (pilot project)

Figure 4.11

    a Photograph scale and number of classes of land use in different surveys.

    b Photograph scale and scale of land use mapping in different surveys. (Both after De Bruijn 1978)

scale and the number of classes in the classification and between the photo scale and the spatial resolution of the mapping units used on the basis of numerous studies of different areas (fig. 4.11). We might also note that it is often easier to compile a land use map from air photographs from scratch than to identify change between photographs: this is a consequence of human visual characteristics and contrasts sharply with the more automated approaches (see p. 110).

Another problem is one which is at its most severe in urban areas – the assumption of a constant relationship between form and function. Some errors are inevitably generated by this usually vital assumption. Collins and El-Beik (1971), for example, found ground checking to reveal several examples where a building, purpose-built for one function, had changed function without changing form: examples include the frequent conversion of Victorian terraced houses into offices and even the conversion of a church into a computer centre! Changes in the form/function relationship may be very significant where some other variable is being inferred from land use: Horton (1974) gives a relevant example by noting the situation in Des Moines, Iowa where, despite an increase of 150 in the housing stock between 1960 and 1970, the population diminished by over 10,000. It is also obvious that multi-level urban land use data are difficult and frequently impossible to acquire from air photographs.

A final problem is related to the question of form and function and to characteristics of the survey – the accuracy and consistency of the results. There is some controversy over how to measure these parameters (see chapter 3). Claims of 75% to 95% accuracy are common in the literature (e.g. Collins and El-Beik 1971) and most authors agree that certain land uses can be consistently identified to very high accuracies whereas others are much more problematic. An extreme example seems to be the DoE Developed Areas study, where the aims were not ambitious given the quality of imagery but for which Smith (1978, p. 158) has claimed accuracies of identification of between 92% and 99% for the different categories. More worryingly, Nunnally and Witmer (1970) have reported considerable variations in accuracy between different interpreters of the same imagery and stress the need for both formal training in air photo analysis and the need for field experience to marry image and reality together. Over-all, it seems that many studies – provided they do not require over-great detail from their imagery and use trained personnel – may regularly obtain accuracies of between 80% and 90% for those land uses which can be identified from air photographs, i.e. land cover and those land uses *ss* which have unambiguous relationships between form and function.

DIGITAL IMAGERY

Not all remote sensed imagery in digital form comes from satellites and, equally, not all satellite-proved imagery is digital: high quality photographic imagery has come from manned space stations such as Skylab but, until the advent of the Space Shuttle, this has been isolated and often unrepeated. In addition, digital imagery (see chapter 5) can be converted into photographic form and vice versa although some loss of quality is usually involved. Nonetheless, it remains true that the great bulk of remote sensed material is now being collected from satellites and stored in digital form. By digital storage, we mean the storage on magnetic tape or other computerized medium of numbers describing the radiation measured from a particular area of ground (see below). One particular family of satellites – Landsat (formerly the Earth Resources Technology Satellite) – has been of overwhelming importance in land use studies and we will largely restrict our consideration to these.

Landsat

The first Landsat satellite was launched in July 1972 and the second in January 1975. A third was launched in March 1978, just two months after the first was officially retired. The primary objective which led to these launches was to provide repetitive, high resolution, multi-spectral data on a global basis. This objective and others ensured that the result was unmanned space-craft orbiting in a sun-synchronous and near-polar orbit at an altitude of about 915 km and telemetering data back to earth: these satellites always take images at about 10.30 a.m. local time. Fig. 4.12 illustrates the form of Landsats 1 and 2 while fig. 4.13 illustrates the general principles involved in collecting data by these means. The data are collected at various ground stations; by late 1977, over half a million scenes were available, giving useable coverage of most of the terrestrial areas of the world in either digital or paper print form. Various distribution agencies have been set up, such as the EROS Data Centre in the USA and the Earthnet facility in Europe.

Landsats 1, 2 and 3 contain both a multi-spectral scanner (MSS) and two or

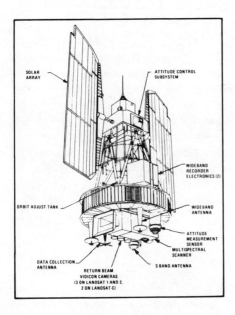

Figure 4.12 Landsat 1 and 2 satellites (from NASA 1976).

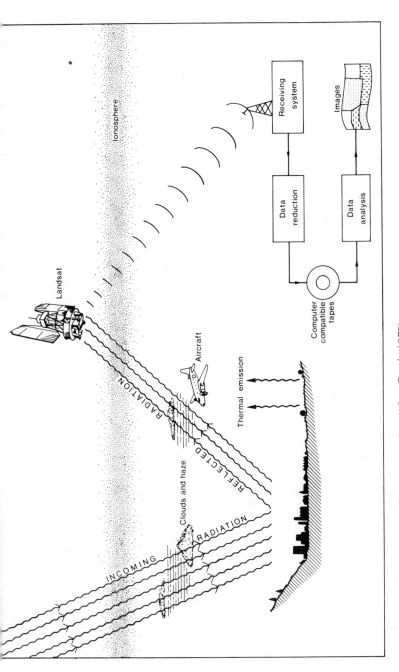

Figure 4.13   The principles of remote sensing (after Curtis 1978).

three return beam vidicon (RBV) cameras – the latter, in effect, very high
resolution TV cameras. The multi-spectral scanner is similar in basic concep
to that illustrated in fig. 4.9 (IRLS scanner): a scene is scanned from side to
side and radiation is measured in each small square area of the ground. Mos
of the data are recorded on a scale from 0 to 127, giving far greater
discrimination than the human eye can perceive in grey tones. Forward
motion of the satellite (fig. 4.14) provides successive coverage of the ground

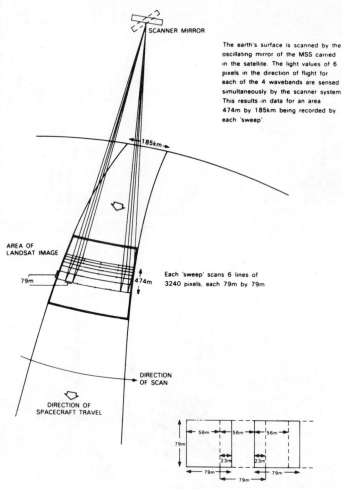

SCANNER MIRROR

The earth's surface is scanned by the
oscillating mirror of the MSS carried
in the satellite. The light values of 6
pixels in the direction of flight for
each of the 4 wavebands are sensed
simultaneously by the scanner system.
This results in data for an area
474m by 185km being recorded by
each 'sweep'.

185km

AREA OF
LANDSAT IMAGE

79m

474m

Each 'sweep' scans 6 lines of
3240 pixels, each 79m by 79m

DIRECTION
OF SCAN

DIRECTION OF
SPACECRAFT TRAVEL

56m   56m   56m
79m
23m   23m
79m   79m
79m

Pixel Distribution along Scan Lines
The multispectral scanner continuously records the light values
from a field of view 79m by 79m along each scan line. The
signals are sampled at 56m intervals so that there is an
overlap of 23m in the ground area viewed.

Figure 4.14 The survey by Landsat MSS of one swath around the
world; the scanner sweeps across a strip 185 km long at right angles to
the satellite (after Carter *et al.* 1976).

Figure 4.15 Landsat pixels superimposed on urban topography (based on an OS map; Crown Copyright reserved); the shaded area is the overlap between adjacent pixels along each scan line. The likelihood of obtaining mixed land use categories is obvious.

Since more use has been made of the MSS than of the RBV, we shal concentrate upon it.

Each MSS image covers an area of 181 km by 185 km. Because of the rotation of the earth under the satellite, the picture is actually a rhomboic rather than a square. Within these pictures, individual sample measurements of radiation are made at 3,240 discrete points along each scan line and there are 2,340 scan lines per picture. The 'field of view' of the scanner i 79 m × 79 m but sampling is done at 56 m intervals along each scan. Hence the result is that the spatial resolution of the basic picture element (or pixels) i 56 m by 79 m, with an overlap of 23 m between adjacent pixels on a scan Fig. 4.15 illustrates how this relates to a British urban area. Carter *et al.* (1976 p. 63) have summarized the ramifications of the resolution of the MSS ir Landsat 1, 2 and 3 thus:

> The detail and spatial resolution of aerial photographs is not at presen available in Landsat images and a comparison of the two shows the relative importance of a change of spatial resolution by a factor of abou 80. Thus [1/60,000 scale] aerial photographs, with a ground resolution o about 1 metre, provide about 100 pixels for a dwelling of size 10 × 10 metres, whereas Landsat imagery . . . necessarily contains many dwell ings per pixel.

Even this basic resolution of 79 m can often be degraded by atmospheri conditions although, on occasions, linear features such as roads which are smaller than the pixel size can be seen because of their contrast. Quite apar from this coarse resolution, we should note that the spatial units are artificia ones (chapter 3, p. 25) and will normally, therefore, be of mixed land use except within large fields, say, in the American Mid-West. Each Landsa satellite orbits the world completely every 18 days. The nearer to the Poles, the more day-to-day overlaps of the nearly square scenes exist (fig. 4.16): at 50° o latitude, for example, 44% overlap exists between adjacent orbits and this rise to 57% at 60° of latitude. On those occasions where two satellites have ru concurrently, they have been placed in orbit so as to provide total coverage o the globe every 9 days, weather conditions permitting. Given these character istics and their spatial resolution, Landsats 1, 2 and 3 have provided level I/ data (chapter 3, p. 31).

For each area, the MSS of Landsats 1 and 2 imaged in four wavebands That in Landsat 3 imaged in five, as below:

Band	Wavelength (µm)	Name	Landsat 1 and 2	Landsat 3
4	0.5– 0.6	Green	√	√
5	0.6– 0.7	Red	√	√
6	0.7– 0.8	Near infrared	√	√
7	0.8– 1.1	Near infrared	√	√
8	10.4–12.6	Infrared		√ (240 n resolution

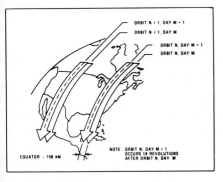

Figure 4.16 The arrangement of images taken on successive Landsat passes (from NASA 1976).

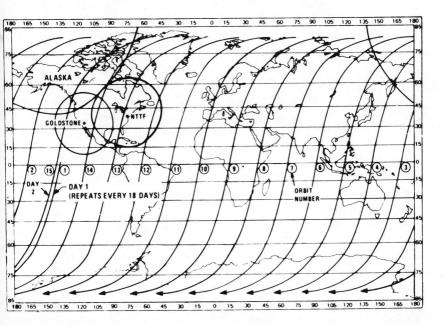

We should note that, even with a spatial resolution as coarse as 79 m, some thirty million numbers are required to store a four waveband Landsat image for one area about 185 km square: to cover all of the UK requires about 900 million numbers. Such volumes of data cause complications even when handled by the largest computers extant. Moreover, this is an image which can be displayed (albeit much more coarsely than the computer can handle) as one photo map. Such mapping is often useful; because of the altitude at which Landsat images are taken, the images are almost distortion-free and, plotted at about 1/1 million scale, are often more accurate than the best topographic maps in some parts of the world. The trend towards higher resolution is presaged by the RBV cameras on Landsat 3 which have a resolution of about 40 m, i.e. similar to some high altitude photography.

Interpreting Landsat imagery

In the first 5 years after the launch of Landsat, the great bulk of successful studies using its imagery were based upon manual interpretation. There is much to be said for such procedures since they use simple technology and treat the Landsat image as a small scale but familiar air photograph (van Genderen *et al*. 1976). Set against this is the need for rapid processing, the vast bulk of the data, the fact that it is originally stored in computer form and that more detail exists within it than is readily apparent to the eye, plus the difficulty of guaranteed change detection by eye. For these reasons, very considerable research has been invested in methods of automated classification of the data by computer.

In essence, there are two different ways of classifying digital remotely sensed data – in supervised or in unsupervised classifications. In the first, a computer program carries out some type of cluster analysis in which the individual pixels are grouped on the basis of the similarity of the amount of radiation measured in each waveband. The results tend to be labelled as groups A, B, etc. i.e., at the analysis stage there is no knowledge of what, if any, land use classes these constitute. The alternative approach is to utilize *a priori* knowledge, derived from 'ground truth'. Using known values from a set of different areas, e.g. say some from woodland, some from urban areas and so on, all pixels are classified on the basis of the maximum likelihood of being in one of these training sets by a procedure such as discriminant analysis. In other words, the first approach groups the artificial recording units on the basis of their common spectral signatures (chapter 4, p. 70), the second groups them on the basis of their similarity to known spectral signatures. Such approaches, according to Nunnally (1974), 'work fine for identification of crops but fail utterly for most urban uses'. It is also relevant to point out that while spectrally based procedures work well for American agricultural land use, they are likely to work less well in the smaller fields of Europe.

If we compare this automated classification procedure with that of the air photo interpreter, its essential crudity becomes obvious. Whereas manual interpretation takes place on the basis of size and shape of feature and of the tone, texture and pattern in the image, only tone is being used extensively in the automated classification (albeit on the basis of four wavebands). Neither size nor shape is easily used by the computer since the spatial unit is an arbitrary one – the pixel – rather than a natural unit, and frequently contains mixed land uses. Despite this, accuracies of between 80% and 85% have been recorded by Jackson *et al*. (1980) for simple division of pixels on spectral grounds into urban or rural areas. Use of more detailed classifications results in a drop in the success rate to between 60% and 80%.

Jaakkola (1978), working in Finland on a one-time, five waveband digital data set collected by aircraft and classifying solely on the basis of spectral signature, has obtained accuracy results in crop classification of as low as 52% (table 4.2).

Table 4.2 Percentage of crops classified as other crops (the diagonal values indicate the correct classification) (Jaakkola 1978).

Crop	1	2	3	4	5	6	7
Pasture	75	0	4	0	2	15	4
Grass	0	95	0	5	0	0	0
Rye	11	2	64	2	0	6	15
Oats	0	0	2	52	0	2	44
Harvested hay	5	5	1	3	78	8	0
Growing hay	10	1	13	1	1	53	21
Barley	0	0	10	4	0	9	77

Three obvious approaches exist to improve this level of success. These are, first, to take into account not only the spectral signature but also the texture in each picture and also imagery taken at different seasons. Among the many studies which demonstrate the utility of such an approach are those by Hsu (1978), in which accuracies of between 85% and 90% were obtained in a seven class classification, and by Bauer *et al.* (1978) who obtained classification performances of crops of 85% or better and were able to predict wheat yields in Kansas to a quite high level of reliability, based on area and proportion of wheat. It is interesting to note that Hsu (1978) stresses the need to program the computer in such a way that the machine replicates the human's vision and decision-making characteristics.

Most automated classifications are 'one-shot' – all classes are regarded as being distinct. The second improved approach being utilized is to use layered classifications, i.e. to make decisions within a hierachical classification framework, since most land use classifications are hierarchical. Thus Jensen (1978) has produced methods which first allocate each pixel to land or water areas, then all land pixels to organic, inorganic or mixed pixel sets, and so on. The obvious complication of all this is the need for the input of thematic information in deciding the layers to be used and how this is to be linked to the remotely sensed data : the advantage is that errors may be restricted to much less significant (i.e. within major class) ones.

The third improvement is not within the control of the analyst – it is the improvement in the spatial resolution of the sensor and hence the reduction in the mixing of different land uses within each pixel. At the time of writing, much technical argument is in progress on whether subsequent Landsat satellites would become an operational (as opposed to experimental) facility, what sensors they would contain and what their resolution, orbit, etc. would be (Calvocoresses 1979; Doyle 1978). What seems likely is a resolution of about 30 m by the early 1980s and, possibly, of resolutions of about 10 m by the mid–late 1980s. Such changes stem not only from user needs but also from changing technology : Thompson (1979) has shown how new sensors will not only have higher resolution but also be more reliable. The implications of such changes are very considerable, even for rapidly improving computer technology – a 10 m resolution would multiply the volumes of data transmitted from the satellite and stored by a factor of 64 over that from Landsat 1 and 2. The implications for the user are even more significant – the data become useful in almost all areas.

The cost of remote sensing

One of the great advantages claimed for remote sensing is its low unit cost for data collection, even though hiring aircraft or launching satellites are intrinsically expensive operations. In practice, it is remarkably difficult to assess how cost effective satellite remote sensing has been in comparison with that from aircraft or, indeed, from ground survey. This is because the Landsat facilities were originally sponsored as experimental and, in addition, it is difficult to assess the benefits of operational procedures from the research studies which have been carried out up till now. Despite this, a number of interesting comparisons of land use studies have been published. These include Rowley (1978, p. 106) who published table 4.3 based on comparisons of costs – not of cost and benefits – of windshield (car traverse) surveys and of interpretation of aerial photographs plus of Landsat imagery in a seven-county area of Illinois. In this case, the photography was out of date, resulting in an overall accuracy of 80% and, in addition, was borrowed at no cost from a federal agency. The car survey was a sample, of unknown precision, which only led to 10% of the land being mapped. Rowley claimed that 85% accuracy was achieved using the Landsat data.

If we consider benefits, the picture is more confused. Although Kalter and Tyne (cited in Allan 1978) informed the US Congress that Landsat-type systems had no useful role in crop yield predictions, Watkins (1978) has

Table 4.3   Relative costs ($) of different surveys in one case study.

Task	'Windshield Survey' 3 counties	Aerial photos 6 drainage basins	Landsat 7 counties
Maps, photos or tapes	119	19	240
Travel	520	minimal	600
Classification (equipment and manpower)	50,000	12,500	2,929
Measure land use and tabulate	30,000	8,200	4,625
Ground checking	Not applicable	minimal	625
Prepare maps	20,000	4,000	5,615
Miscellaneous	500	75	750
	101,139	24,794	15,384

Source: Rowley (1978).

reviewed some of the actual and potential economics of remote sensing and noted, for example, that McQuillan claims a reduction in the margin of error of forecasts of Canadian wheat production from the present 5% to 4% could increase Canadian exports by $7 million dollars – the implication being that this is possible from remote sensing. In more urban situations, the benefits are often even more difficult to assess – counting losses which might not have occurred had a survey been carried out is tricky in the extreme.

Conclusions on remote sensing for land use

Landsats 1, 2 and 3 and similar resolution systems are far from ideal for urban studies in the developed world. They are extremely useful in many rural land use studies: in essence, then, they are ideal for collecting land cover rather than land use *ss* data (see chapter 2). The advantages of satellites as sensing platforms is the frequency and repetitiveness of imagery provided, the consistency of recording and (if automated procedures are used) of interpretation, the low unit cost per scene which may accrue from many users, and the lack of any problems from other air traffic. Conversely, the use of aircraft as sensing platforms gives more flexibility in the time of survey, of photo scale and resolution and of the form of the imagery (colour, waveband used, etc.). If we consider the detection of change rather than the provision of a base-line survey, the relative utility of Landsat imagery and air photography are, as ever, entirely dependent on the detailed needs of the user. Milazzo *et al.* (1977) have discussed some of the advantages of different methods. In principle, however, automated interpretation of Landsat-type data pixel by pixel is comparatively simple and quite reliable by computer, provided that the two scenes can be registered together so that the same areas of ground are covered in corresponding pixels; comparison of photographs by manual means is time-consuming and error-prone. Fig. 4.17, provided by the Image Analysis Group at Harwell, shows change in urban land use in and around Northampton between 1969 and 1976, registered to an Ordnance Survey map. Finally, all forms of remote sensing are liable to lead to errors where land use based on function is being sought.

Data from ground surveys

Some aspects of the collection of data by ground surveys have already been covered (see p. 62); all of the data locked into Stamp's Land Utilisation Survey and Coleman's Second Land Utilisation Survey were collected thus. In practice, it is almost impossible to produce accurate areal summaries of land use without a good topographic base map. Traverses may give samples of land use but, in urban areas in particular, may give biased overall impressions. In urban areas where no appropriate topographic map exists (Winch 1978), it is possible to carry out survey over limited areas by noting adjacency of buildings as well as their use; a crude map may be compiled from such observations. In principle, approximate maps of rural areas can also be reconstructed from recording which fields are adjacent to each other; Kendall

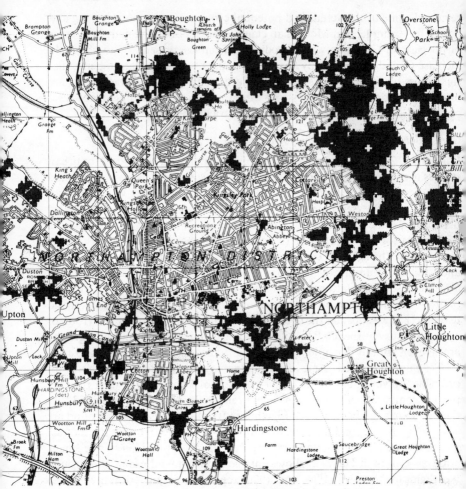

Figure 4.17 Urban development, 1969–76, detected by multispectral scanners carried by Landsat 2; the information was obtained from digital data using automated computer techniques developed by AERE Harwell for the Department of the Environment; Crown Copyright reserved.

(1971) has demonstrated this at a macro-scale for France but the same principle holds true at micro-scales, provided most of the fields are of similar sizes. If metric as well as topological observations are made, the maps may be usable for a number of purposes other than land use. Fig. 4.18 illustrates an example of such a land use map compiled by students on field trips in Tunisia.

Most land cover surveys are spatially exhaustive, although we have already noted (in chapter 3) the possibility of sample surveys. A major disadvantage of sample surveys is that the results are either unrepresentative, through use of roads or other transport links as the sampling framework or, alternatively, that – where a high certainty that the answer is the correct one is

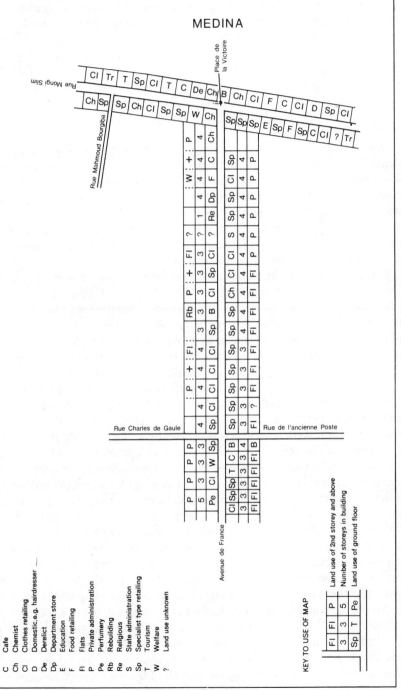

Figure 4.18 A map of land use in Tunis, based upon recording of the land use in adjacent shops and little accurate topographic data.

necessary – more appropriate sampling strategies may require only a little less field work than exhaustive survey. In activity-based land use studies, by contrast, estimates of ground area covered may not be so important and survey then concentrates on detecting what is present, rather than its area extent; consequently, the provision of good topographic base maps, while still extremely useful, is not a necessary condition to be met before survey is carried out. Good examples of this approach are the Durham and Northumberland Land Use Surveys and the Tyne and Wear Joint Information System (see below and chapter 5).

The planning of major ground-based survey is, if anything, even more demanding than that of aerial survey. It is essential that all surveyors allot identical properties or uses to the same category, that they all work with consistent concepts of spatial resolution, and that all work is checked for accuracy. It is desirable that as little as possible overlap of areas surveyed by individuals should take place and any which does should be known so as to avoid double counting: it is essential that all unsurveyed areas be known to give clues to the degree of undercounting.

One example where such considerations have been put into practice is the Durham Land Use Survey (Rhind and Hudson 1980); near-identical procedures were followed in later surveys of Northumberland and Cleveland Counties. Land use (or rather, property use) was surveyed in the field by numerous pairs of school leavers, all of whom had undergone training and testing before the real survey began. Each team was equipped with defined areas to survey on a daily basis and as depicted on Ordnance Survey 1/1,250, 1/2,500 or 1/10,000 scale maps; they recorded the use of each distinct, functional entity on the left-hand side of special coding forms by observation and, where necessary, discussion with those working or living therein. Each spatial unit (a BSU in this case) was defined by a single easting and northing co-ordinate of some central point. In practice, this procedure was found easier and more reliable than designation of quasi-homogeneous areas in the field, as well as providing much greater flexibility. Later, the same group compiled this information into computer-compatible data on the right-hand side of the same coding form (fig. 4.19). Special short-hand facilities were provided, e.g. for use in grid referencing where streets were straight, where all the properties in a street were in the same post-code area and so on. The results were manually checked and sent for conversion to punch cards, then entry to the computer. Thereafter, a number of checks were made on the data by computer program: the national grid reference was checked as lying within the area surveyed, the land use code was checked as existing within the 830 categories of the National Land Use Classification, the house and street codes were checked as being feasible and so on. It must be stressed that these checks do not check accuracy – they check only feasibility. Accuracy can only be checked indirectly, by repeating some or all of the field survey and this was also done periodically: even so, stringent re-survey only tests for consistency, rather than accuracy in a strict sense. 'Errors' detected by re-survey varied by

Left hand form

(HYPOTHETICAL EXAMPLE)

NORTHUMBERLAND LAND USE PROJECT
BASIC DATA CODING FORM

District Name: (NEWBIGGIN) WANSBECK   Encoder: C. Harrison   Date: 7.11.77

Number/Name	Floor Part	Street Name	Land Use	
Sea Shell Cafe		High Street	Restaurant (take away meals)	
	+1	High Street	Residential flat	
1A		Waverley Place	Terraced House	end terrace
1B				
2				
3		Waverley Place	Terraced House	end terrace
Antique Parlour	-1	High Street	Antiques and Furniture (buyers and exporters)	end terrace

Right hand form

(HYPOTHETICAL EXAMPLE)

NORTHUMBERLAND LAND USE PROJECT
BASIC DATA CODING FORM

District Name: (NEWBIGGIN) WANSBECK   Encoder: C. Harrison   Date: 7.11.77

District NZ/NY	East	North	House	Suf	N	Floor	Street	Post Code	Land Use Code
5 NZ	3146	8813	9001		N		3	NE64 6AT	RT03BA
1 2	3146	8813	9002			+1	20	NE64 6AT	RS03AE
	3149	8816	1	A			13	NE64 6AX	RS02AM
			1	B					RS02AH
			2						RS02AH
	3147	8816	3				13	NE64 6AX	RS02AM
	3148	8813	9003		N	-1	3	NE64 6AT	RT01BN

Figure 4.19 The coding form used in the field by surveyors in the Northumberland Land Use Survey: the left-hand section was compiled in the field, the corresponding right-hand section immediately afterwards in the office. Vertical lines denote identical figures for each property; missing grid references are filled in by the computer which assumes straight streets. The land use code is that from the National Land Use Classification.

land use class, from fewer than 1/1,000 occurrences for detached and semi-detached houses to about 1/50 where complex, multi-floor use of space was carried out. In certain land use categories, errors appeared to cancel out and have a mean value of zero; in others, notably separate living accomodation above retail establishments, an under-count occurred.

The Durham and Northumberland surveys were base-line ones; in a space of 2 years all but the smallest groups of dwellings, industry, etc., in two counties of Britain were enumerated at a crude net cost to the community of about £50,000. About 350,000 properties were thus surveyed and recorded. The data were distributed both to County and District level planners and were used in a variety of research projects. In addition, the design of the data structure permitted the land use data to act as an index: thus data collected by one agency on the basis of post codes could be related to that collected by another on the basis of, say, census areas. Apart from use in individual districts, however, no concerted effort was made to ensure that these became on-going, continuously up-to-date land use bases. In this respect, they differ from the Joint Information System in Tyne and Wear County (Spicer *et al.* 1979), the CLUSTER system of various London Boroughs (Irvine 1974) and the various implementations of the LAMIS scheme (Harrison 1978) which have been carried out by local authorities and make, in the main, use of administrative data to up-date records. In the JIS, for example, change data are collected every month by tapping the regular, administrative flows within a range of departments such as architects (starts and completions of council property, site plans); engineers (demolitions, starts and completions of roads, car parks, playgrounds); planning (planning permissions); building inspectors (starts and completions of non-council property) and education (starts, completion and change of use for local education authority properties). It is clear that such a scheme is, again, essentially suited to collection of urban data and, of course, to the monitoring of urban conditions. Even though many of the up-dates are derived from ground survey, problems arise because some are collected at much greater detail than others; considerable detail will be known of structures initiated by the engineers but only those changes of land use necessitating statutory planning permission will be 'caught' by the development control system. Inevitably, perhaps, quality control is diffused throughout the data collecting agencies and can only be monitored either by periodic field checks or by comparing supposedly redundant and independent data: one well known, if crude, method of the latter involves using rating information and comparing changes in this with those in planning permissions granted. It is also clear that up-dating the file is easy if all the property or area changes from one use to another; some complications ensue if sites are split or lumped together. Finally, there may be much to be said for integrating ground-based and remote sensed data collection procedures: fig. 4.20 is one scheme of how this might be applied to detect urban change. It will become obvious in chapter 5 that this poses considerable technical problems.

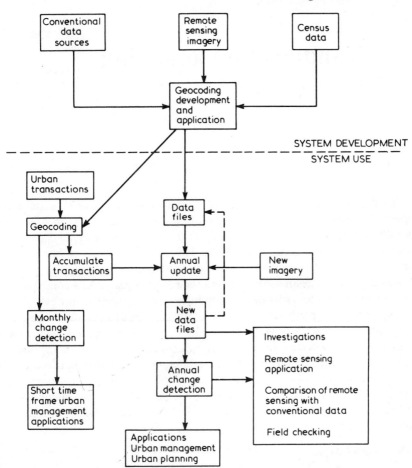

Figure 4.20   A proposed operational system for the detection of change within urban areas, utilizing a variety of data sources (from Horton 1974).

Ground survey is essentially a flexible method of survey, even if it is often expensive and difficult to standardize. It has the paramount advantage of collecting activity-based data in urban areas as a matter of routine. Because of historical factors and the scale of operation involved, it has been more common in Britain than in the United States. The most recent manifestations of it are in local authority information systems (chapter 5). The level of spatial resolution, timeliness and accuracy of survey can be fine-tuned to meet the project objectives, subject to good management and adequate control of resources: results from ground-based survey without in-built accuracy checks merit considerable scepticism.

5 Handling and analysing land use data

It is self-evident that collecting land use data without analysing them has little merit. Equally, it is obvious that handling the very large volumes of data which result from some of the data collection methods in the preceding chapter necessitates using a computer. This method is likely to become still more common: at present, the cost of computing power is decreasing in real terms by as much as an order of magnitude every 5 years. As a consequence, this chapter will concentrate on computer-based methods; however, since many computer methods merely attempt to replicate manual ones, the contents of this section will not be unfamiliar to most readers. Some data which eventually pertain to land cover *are* collected in a computer (or digital) form, notably those from unmanned satellites, but much other data require to be converted from lists, maps, aerial photographs or from ground survey. As a result, we shall discuss the topic under three headings – input, manipulation and output of the data – and will assume the technical uses of land use data are those defined on page 6.

The input of data

For data to be intelligible to the digital computer, they must be stored explicitly as numbers; in all cases what is required are the geography and the land use character of the geographical individual (see p. 20 and Rhind 1974). We have already discussed the possible forms of the geographical individual; here we merely observe that land use is normally stored in the computer either as a point value – requiring only one co-ordinate pair and one attribute – or as a zone which is represented as a series of co-ordinates and one attribute (fig. 5.1). If the units are artificial ones and, say, square, then land use in the whole area under consideration may be represented by a series of land use codes for the geographical individuals or pixels, provided the dimensions of one of these and the orientation and size of the image are known (fig. 5.1). It is important to realize, however, that the units in which the data are stored need not remain sacrosanct at all stages. It is entirely possible to aggregate the data together into different forms after collection, either for the purposes of manipulation or display. Figure 5.2 illustrates this. Examples where such transformations have been carried out are given later (p. 102).

(i) By points

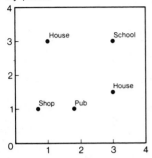

Land use	Co-ordinates
House	1,3
House	3,1·5
School	3,3
Shop	0·7,1
Pub	1·8,1

(ii) By polygons

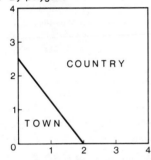

Land use	Co-ordinates
Town	0,2·5; 2,0; 0,0; 0,2·5
Country	0,2·5; 0,4; 4,4; 4,0; 2,0; 0,2·5

(iii) By square areas

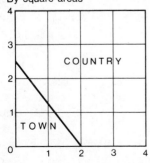

Land use (T – Town, C – Country)

C	C	C	C
C	C	C	C
T	C	C	C
T	T	C	C

Figure 5.1 Representation of points, line and areas on a map and as approximated within a computer.

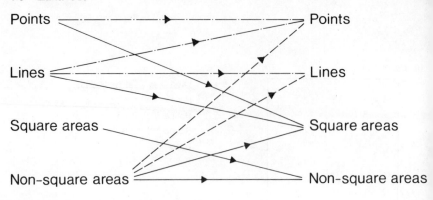

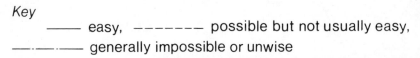

Key
———— easy,   – – – – – – – possible but not usually easy,
—·—·—— generally impossible or unwise

Figure 5.2   Conversion of data from one set of spatial data collection units to another.

Note: Where area-to-area transformations are involved, it is assumed that the 'from' areas are much smaller than the 'to' ones; if this is not correct, assumptions such as uniform spread of land use within each area are necessary and some errors are inevitable.

The exact method utilized to convert data into computer form will depend on the method of survey: historical data locked up in lists will usually be tiresome to convert since hand-written documents are frequently unsuited for computer-controlled optical character recognition. In such cases, the boundaries of the areas may not be known with precision and some approximate centroid will have to serve as the geography.

Where the data are to be encoded from a map or from a photograph, two rather different methods of digitizing have been in use since at least the mid-1960s. The first involves tracing the boundaries of zones – often as segments between intersection points of lines with some label (fig. 5.1). The methods used to capture these data have sometimes been manual, using a romer and measuring successive grid references around a boundary. This is extremely time-consuming but numerous devices now exist (e.g. Rogers and Dawson 1979) partially to automate the procedure: an operator traces around the periphery of the area and co-ordinates are automatically transfered to a storage medium such as magnetic tape; the boundaries of all the Developed Area land use zones in Britain were encoded in such a fashion (Smith *et al.* 1977). The most sophisticated approach to line following is the lock-on follower; with one such machine (the Laserscan Fastrak), an operator steers a cursor to the start of a line projected on a screen. The machine then tracks down the line at high speed, encoding the line as it proceeds and blanking out the line so that it cannot be digitized again. Fegeas and Kewer (1977) have discussed some of the problems inherent in such a line-following approach to encoding land use data, such as the need for understanding of the topology of the map by the digitizer operator, the need to edit and clean up the data and so on. Rhind (1974) gives a general introduction to the principles and practice of line-following digitizing which may also, of course, be used to follow tonal boundaries on an aerial photograph, encode point values, and so on. In essence, the amount of information stored depends upon how closely digitized are points along each line and how much line work exists on each map. Table 5.1 shows the volume of data stored (after redundant co-ordinates had been extracted) from a sample of 24 US Land Use and Land Cover maps at 1/250,000 scale (Anderson *et al.* 1977). The average number of co-ordinates per polygon is 55 while the average distance between digitized points on the map is under 0.5 mm. Anderson *et al.* (1977) estimated that, even with substantial compression of the data, some 37 million co-ordinates would be needed to store the US-wide land use data collected up to 1982. Such figures are not unique. Based upon an analysis of Ordnance Survey large scale topographic data carried out by Adams (1979), the total length on the map of boundaries of buildings in Britain is likely to be over 1,000 km, with perhaps 300 million co-ordinates. On the other hand, crude encoding of property boundaries from large scale urban plans has required far fewer co-ordinates – about six per polygon in the LAMIS project in Leeds.

Table 5.1 Values of data resulting from the digitizing of USGS land use maps.

	Average	*Maximum*	*Minimum*
Number of co-ordinates	131,136	305,916	15,594
Number of polygons	2,402	9,856	392
Total line length (mm)	56,337	102,743	7,290

A quite different approach is to scan the map or photograph, breaking it down into tiny cells which are considered as black or white. Typically, these cells may be as small as 0.1 mm in size: a 50 cm × 50 cm map would then be represented by 25 million on/off values, irrespective of the length of the land use boundaries therein. In such systems, there is no knowledge of what the black cell represents – whether it is part of a residential area or is the boundary between residential and commercial, for example, is not recorded (fig. 5.3). These were the means used to encode more than 1,000 maps by the Canada Geographic Information System: the 'meaning' of the cells was provided at a later stage (Tomlinson *et al.* 1976). In more sophisticated systems (Sci-Tex 1979), different colour codings may be given to different types of land use and a code will be stored to represent this, rather than black/white only.

Photographs may similarly be converted into a numerical representation by converting the 'greyness' of an area of arbitrary size (a 'pixel') onto an arbitrarily numbered scale from white to black. Clearly the results are then very similar to, though of lower quality than, a Landsat digital image.

Both of these methods of data collection have their advantages: line following (or vector notation) usually gives the minimum amount of data for a

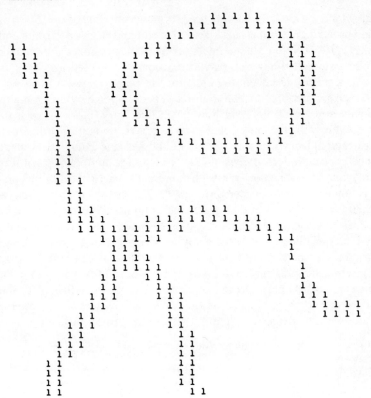

Figure 5.3 The representation of lines after raster scanning; the value '1' represents black in that cell. Alternatively, different areas may be stored as a code number (e.g. '5') in each cell comprising that area (from Tomlinson *et al.* 1976).

given accuracy of representation and the land use is represented directly, tagging the boundaries with a suitable code. The second type of encoding – often termed raster scanning – is comparatively easy to automate and produces a high and consistent throughput of data from maps or other graphic documents, even though the results usually require some processing to make them useful for most purposes (Tomlinson *et al.* 1976, pp. 49–55). It has often been found convenient to convert one method of storage to another; this is comparatively easy in moving from vector to raster but is costly and difficult going through the reverse process.

Whatever the method of initial encoding of the land use data, provision must always be made for two other operations – editing and up-dating the resulting data base. In the first of these, a primary task is the detection of errors (Rhind 1974). The most frequent types of error differ between vector and raster encoding: the more the human element is involved, the more idiosyncratic the errors are likely to be! A variety of methods (Rhind 1974) exist for obviating the errors once detected, from the simple (e.g. Gardiner-

Hill 1972) to sophisticated inter-active procedures (Margerison 1977; Sci-Tex 1979), in which data are plotted on cathode ray tubes and adjusted by an operator until correct (p. 12). Up-dating is a rather different process: here the aim is to detect all change and hence up-date the current land use inventory and, usually, to keep a record of the changes between two time periods. By virtue of the survey being carried out within a defined geographical area, change is easily detected wherever complete re-surveys (chapter 4) have been carried out and, especially, if a raster format for the data has been utilized: the two surveys are simply superimposed (p. 116) and differences detected and stored.

Those ground-based surveys, such as the JIS (Spicer *et al.* 1979) or the Durham and Northumberland ones (Rhind and Hudson 1979), which collect data for individual BSUs are usually encoded as point values and are easily punched on standard cards or other computer media, usually via the intermediate step. Quality checking such data is not trivial and requires a battery of techniques – plotting the raw data for visual inspection when overlaid on topographic maps is one common method. Up-dating is usually achieved by finding the old record with the same postal address or within the same, small geographical area. Encoding both these and those surveys providing zone-based information may be expected to become very much easier in the future – at least so far as Britain, continental Europe and the USA are concerned as more and more topographic data become available in digital form. On many occasions the 'anatomy' provided by the topographic can be re-arranged to provide the geography of land use (see below).

Manipulating land use data

We itemized the detailed, technical end-products which are needed from land use data on p. 16. This section discusses how these may be met, together with the preceding stages necessary to achieve them. In essence, we discuss the procedures for producing statistical summaries of the data, for detecting patterns within the data, for comparing two or more land use distributions and for displaying the results in map or other graphical form. Before these can be carried out, however, it is common to carry out two other stages, often referred to as pre-processing and these are discussed first.

TRANSFORMATION AND RECTIFICATION OF THE GEOGRAPHY

Suppose a comparison of the land use and the soil data over several of the states of the USA is desired and, further, that each state has assembled its data independently. A pre-requisite for computing comparable figures for the different states and, especially, for producing maps is to have them in one common co-ordinate system. This is directly analogous to converting land use maps on different projections to a common projection.

A very common second example of this is where data are being digitized from maps or air photographs – the units in which the digitizer works are usually millimetres (or smaller) on the image; these need to be converted into some more commonly used, global co-ordinate system such as the British

National Grid. In addition, distortion has usually occurred in the image – either in drawing the map or because of differential shrinkage in the paper – and it must be converted to its correct size and shape before, in effect, joining adjacent images together; an identical requirement occurs when up-dates are to be fed into an existing data base – clearly they must fit the pre-existing detail. The procedures to carry out such transformations – or stretching – of the geography are well known and various different mathematical procedures are available. Baxter (1976) and GAG (1977) give simple descriptions and computer programs for carrying them out. It is essential, of course, that, for stretching to take place, the correct, real-world co-ordinates of a number of control points must be available, together with relative co-ordinates in the distorted image or in the local co-ordinate system. Thus some form of ground survey, often provided by the topographic mapping agency, is essential. In some ways, the transformation of raster data is rather more complex than that of vectors since, to ensure no gaps appear between pixels, the size and shape of the pixels may have to vary throughout the image after transformation.

AGGREGATION AND RE-ORGANIZATION OF THE GEOGRAPHICAL INDIVIDUALS

It is often convenient, as we shall see later (pp. 110 and 121), to convert the form of the geographical individual into another, usually one covering more space. Thus fig. 5.4 illustrates the conversion of all the point land use records in part of Darlington into a zonal land use by selecting the most frequent land use type in each 100 m square and suppressing the boundary between like squares. Equally it may be useful to aggregate not by defined areas of space but upon internal characteristics of the data: the DLUS and NLUS data may, for instance, be aggregated by streets, by post codes, and by various other methods for the purposes of reporting.

We should note that, while many such aggregations are easy and desirable for different purposes, two important caveats must be lodged. The first of these is that, in aggregating land use data recorded as points, lines or (smaller) areas to zones, the results are partially controlled by the size, shape and detailed location of the latter zones. This characteristic is not restricted to land use; indeed, Openshaw (1977) and others have demonstrated that in analysing census-type data, the degree of aggregation of the data and the particular aggregation of the geographical individuals can have very substantial effects upon the statistical inter-relationships between the different variables. On a much simpler level, fig. 5.5 also illustrates the point: the use of a 150 m mesh gives slightly different results for the land use pattern from that of 100 m. In addition to this 'scale effect', there are usually also many different principles of aggregating and thus generalizing land use data. Grigg (1965, 1967) has discussed some of these regionalization procedures. It is obvious that, as a result, data for two different areas aggregated on different criteria may well give spurious comparisons.

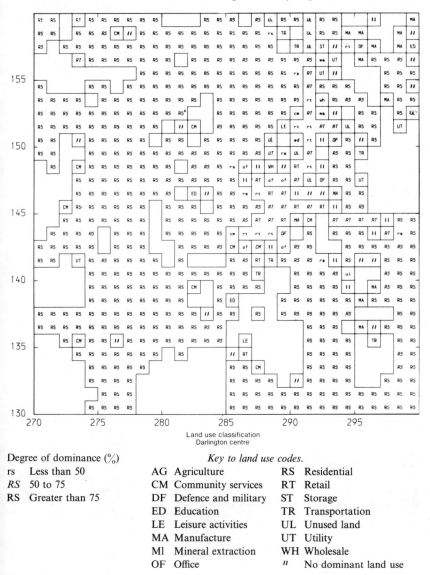

Figure 5.4 The modal (most frequent) land use in each 100 m square covering the town of Darlington, County Durham: based upon about 14,000 individual land use records.

The second caveat is concerned not with the aggregation of geographical individuals but with its converse – disaggregation or the breaking down of these units into smaller ones. This applies mainly to zones, some such procedure often being essential in comparing different data for the same area through the 'overlay' procedure (see p. 116). Strictly speaking, this is totally illogical unless extra information is available on the within-area variations in

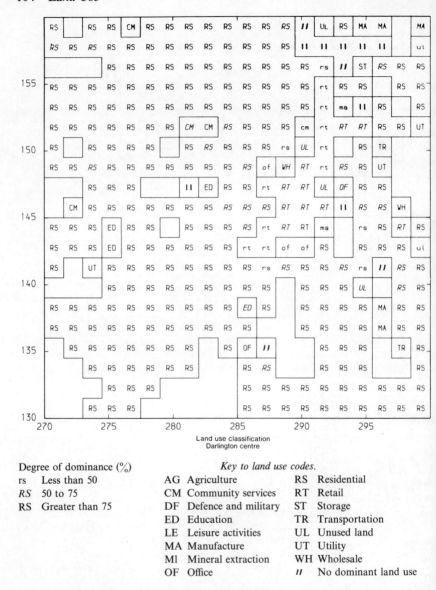

Figure 5.5 The modal land use in each 150 m square covering Darlington, County Durham: based upon the same data as figure 5.4; the differences, both in some of the final classes and in the degree of dominance, are obvious.

land use. Alternatively, assumptions may be made on the basis of an even spread of land use within the zone, a radial increase in density of buildings towards the centre of the zone, or on some other 'guess'. It is also obvious that these assumptions are likely to be in error by unknown amounts and, again, may lead to spurious comparisons.

There are also two clear morals to be drawn from these caveats: it is wise to hold the land use data in computer form to provide flexibility, at least whenever two or more uses of the same data are anticipated and, also, that it is prudent to retain data in as disaggregated a form as possible. By applying this principle not only for the geographical individual but also in the classification utilized and for the time to which the survey pertains, the maximum flexibility in subsequent use and the maximum level of accuracy in any comparisons are retained. Such a *modus operandus* does have its disadvantages; these are that the resources available may not be physically capable of such detailed, disaggregated storage or that the costs of comparison based on these data are too great for the immediate or anticipated benefits. Such decisions must be made in the light of the needs of the primary user but made with the awareness of the possible pitfalls – and of the rapid diminution in the costs of computer processing and storage of data.

Finally, so far as data aggregation and reorganization are concerned, we may reasonably expect that, in the future, more and more of the anatomy of land use will be available to us from topographic mapping agencies. The plans of Ordnance Survey, of the United States Geological Survey (Southard 1978) and many other agencies is to move towards the situation where more and more topographic data are collected and stored in digital form. In 1979 after a 5 year period of pilot production, OS had a total of 7,000 of their 1/1,250 and 1/2,500 scale map sheets stored in digital form; they had also created computer programs for reorganizing these data, originally collected solely for mapping purposes, into units of interest to many other organizations. Thompson (1978) has described how the boundaries of individual properties, i.e. detailed land use parcels or 'natural' units, can be extracted from the cartographic data and this process is illustrated in fig. 5.6. In principle, it is possible to extend this to the stage where each such parcel is labelled with its street address and, to some extent, where the land use can be inferred from the mapped form. Thompson, however, observes that not all land use boundaries are recorded as physical features on topographic maps and, because of this, a complete formulation of a land use inventory will not be possible in Britain by these means alone.

THE STATISTICAL SUMMARY OF LAND USE

It is a common requirement that the relative and absolute proportions of land use are required within a defined area, whether this is an administrative entity, a proposed General Improvement Area, a river basin, within 50 m of a proposed motorway or whatever unit is of immediate interest. In recent years, the identification of land covers and the measurement of their areal extents at different periods of the growing season has become increasingly important in predicting crop yields: major developments have been made by the Laboratory for Applications of Remote Sensing at Purdue University and elsewhere (see, for example, Swain and Davis 1978). This reporting on the *status quo* is much the most simple requirement from a land use data base.

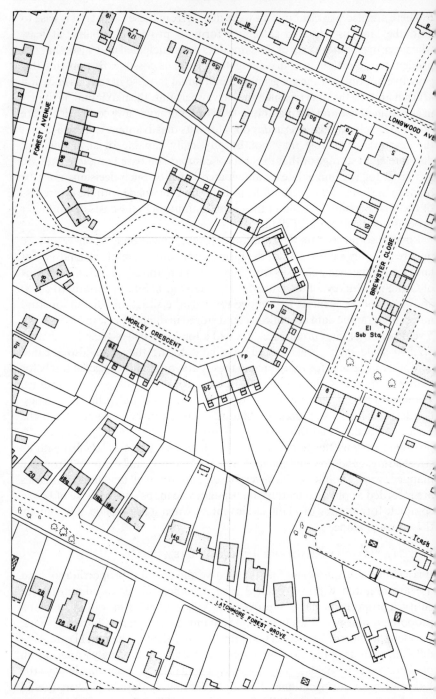

Figure 5.6 The re-organization of Ordnance Survey digital cartographic data to form
property parcels:
   a (above) the original data
   b (on facing page) all line intersections detected
   c (on page 108) the lines reorganized into closed polygons – property parcels.

c

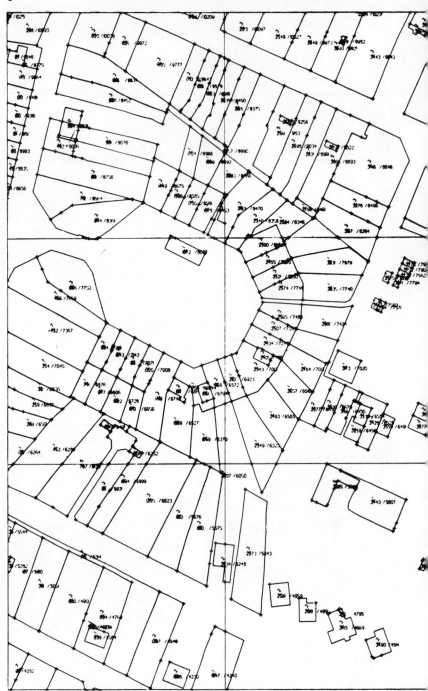

Figure 5.7
  a All 35,000 properties in Darlington district and
  b after filtering through a Point-in-Polygon program to select only those properties in Darlington town.
  This process was followed prior to statistical analysis of land use data for various different towns (see table 5.2 and figure 5.8).

How it is carried out within the computer depends upon how the data are stored: if they are in a raster format (see p. 99) or if the data are stored as point values, the calculation merely involves counting how many units lie in each land use class. Before counting of these begins, a procedure known as Point-in-Polygon (Baxter 1976) eliminates all those geographical individuals which are not inside the area of interest (fig. 5.7). The situation with land use stored as zones is slightly more complex in that the area must be measured using a procedure such as Simpson's Rule and a form of overlay (see p. 117) applied to the data to 'clip out' all zones and parts of zones within the area of interest.

Table 5.2 is an example of the results of applying PIP to a land use file then point counting; the results pertain to various discrete towns within Northumberland, Durham and Tyne and Wear counties and are based on a selection of 212,276 properties from a data base of 837,319. The Tyne and Wear data have been amalgamated into NLUC orders (chapter 3). Obvious characteristics include the ubiquitous preponderance of residential properties especially within new towns such as Killingworth, Cramlington and Peterlee.

Such area summaries are time-consuming and error-prone if carried out by hand: indeed, if the data are in list form, their use may even necessitate conversion into maps as a prior stage before the selection of those land uses within the area of interest. On all grounds, computer processing is here a simple and sensible way to proceed. Such a situation is not, however, invariably true: the answer to a question 'what is the land use at grid reference x, y,' or '. . . immediately east of the specified town centre', is simple to obtain from a map but necessitates a rather sophisticated organization of data within the computer if the answers are not to require much longer than those from the human. Computer systems of this degree of sophistication are becoming increasingly common and some examples are discussed later (pp. 124–5).

THE DETECTION OF PATTERN

Statistical summaries of extent, as described, are almost aspatial. If we wish to add the complication of how the land uses are arranged within a defined area, we move into the much more complex field of pattern analysis. That this, intuitively at least, has formed the basis of most academic preoccupations with land use will become obvious in chapters 7 to 10.

Pattern analysis carried out by eye on maps, air photographs or some other graphical image is, then, the way most land use models have been underpinned in the past. Swain (1978) advocated the value of a computer-based approach to pattern recognition because of its speed, objectivity (in reality, the ability to repeat the same process with the same procedures and data and get the same answer), flexibility and because it produces quantitative results. He subsumed in pattern recognition not only the descriptive pattern in space but also the classification of geographical individuals into groups. We have already discussed aspects of classification from the viewpoint of the schema (p. 34) and from the viewpoint of the two different approaches to

Table 5.2 Percentage table: land use within towns, based upon individual property counts.

TOWN	AG	CM	DF	ED	LE	MA	MI	OF	RS	RT	ST	TR	UL	UT	WH	Key to town codes (fig. 5.8)	
DRLN	0.1	0.7	0.0	0.2	0.1	0.5	0.0	0.8	90.8	3.3	0.3	0.4	2.4	0.2	0.1	DRLN	Darlington
SEAH	0.1	0.9	0.0	0.2	0.2	0.4	0.0	0.3	93.7	2.7	0.1	0.2	0.8	0.2	0.0	SEAH	Seaham
BLYT	0.0	0.7	0.0	0.1	0.2	0.3	0.0	0.6	92.7	2.4	0.2	0.1	2.3	0.2	0.0	BLYT	Blyth
MORP	0.1	1.0	0.0	0.2	0.1	0.4	0.0	1.2	90.8	4.1	0.2	0.1	1.4	0.3	0.1	MORP	Morpeth
DURH	0.2	1.0	0.0	0.9	0.3	0.4	0.0	1.2	90.6	3.2	0.4	0.4	1.1	0.3	0.1	DURH	Durham
CHES	0.1	0.6	0.0	0.2	0.1	0.2	0.0	0.9	91.9	2.5	0.2	0.8	2.2	0.3	0.0	CHES	Chester-le-Street
ALNW	0.5	1.4	0.0	0.4	0.5	0.5	0.0	1.7	85.3	6.3	0.6	0.3	1.8	0.4	0.3	ALNW	Alnwick
ASHN	0.0	1.1	0.0	0.2	0.2	0.3	0.0	0.5	92.3	3.1	0.2	0.3	1.8	0.1	0.0	ASHN	Ashington
BAUK	0.1	1.0	0.0	0.3	0.2	1.0	0.0	1.1	88.4	4.6	0.6	0.3	2.1	0.2	0.2	BAUK	Bishop Aukland
BCAS	0.5	1.3	0.0	0.3	0.4	0.6	0.0	1.4	84.6	6.5	0.8	0.9	2.2	0.2	0.3	BCAS	Barnard Castle
BERW	0.2	1.0	0.0	0.2	0.3	0.6	0.0	1.8	87.2	5.1	1.0	0.1	1.7	0.2	0.4	BERW	Berwick
BEDL	0.1	0.7	0.0	0.1	0.3	0.2	0.0	0.4	93.9	3.0	0.1	0.1	0.8	0.2	0.0	BEDL	Bedlington
CRAM	0.0	0.4	0.0	0.2	0.0	0.3	0.0	0.7	94.4	0.7	0.1	0.0	2.9	0.2	0.0	CRAM	Cramlington
CONS	0.1	1.1	0.0	0.2	0.2	0.3	0.0	0.6	89.5	3.5	0.5	1.1	2.6	0.3	0.0	CONS	Consett
NAYC	0.0	0.5	0.0	0.2	0.0	0.9	0.0	0.3	93.8	1.2	0.3	1.8	0.4	0.5	0.0	NAYC	Newton Aycliffe
STAN	0.1	0.8	0.0	0.2	0.2	0.2	0.0	0.5	91.4	2.6	0.2	1.2	2.2	0.3	0.0	STAN	Stanley
SPEN	0.1	0.8	0.0	0.2	0.3	0.5	0.0	0.6	89.7	3.2	0.3	0.6	3.2	0.4	0.1	SPEN	Spennymoor
PETL	0.0	0.4	0.0	0.3	0.1	0.3	0.0	0.3	94.8	1.5	0.1	0.1	1.3	0.3	0.0	PETL	Peterlee
HEXH	0.3	1.2	0.0	0.4	0.3	1.0	0.0	2.8	83.2	5.7	1.3	0.8	2.1	0.5	0.3	HEXH	Hexham
KILL	0.0	0.4	0.0	0.3	0.3	0.6	0.0	0.3	95.5	0.6	0.1	1.3	0.4	0.3	0.0	KILL	Killingworth
RYTN	0.4	0.8	0.0	0.2	0.8	0.1	0.0	0.4	93.8	1.5	0.3	0.7	0.5	0.5	0.0	RYTN	Ryton
HL.S	0.3	0.7	0.0	0.2	0.7	0.2	0.1	0.5	92.7	2.7	0.3	0.7	0.6	0.4	0.0	HL.S	Houghton-le-Spring
HL.H	0.6	0.6	0.0	0.2	1.3	0.6	0.1	0.3	89.1	2.8	0.7	1.3	1.9	0.3	0.1	HL.H	Hetton-le-Hole
BIRT	0.2	0.6	0.0	0.3	1.3	0.2	0.0	0.5	91.2	2.5	0.3	1.3	1.0	0.6	0.0	BIRT	Birtley
WHIK	0.2	0.6	0.0	0.2	0.9	0.2	0.0	0.5	93.1	1.8	0.2	1.1	0.7	0.5	0.0	WHIK	Whickham
WASH	0.1	0.4	0.0	0.2	0.9	3.9	0.0	0.5	90.0	1.4	0.1	0.9	1.0	0.5	0.0	WASH	Washington

Source: Durham and Northumberland Land Use Surveys and Tyne and Wear Joint Information System data.
Note: The meaning of the acronyms for the 15 NLUC land use orders is given on p. 44.

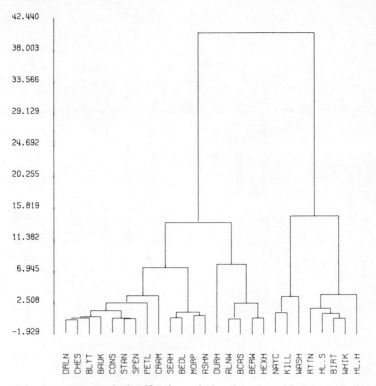

Figure 5.8 An automated classification of the data in table 5.2, excluding the residential, offices and mineral extraction land uses. Produced on the basis of the first four principal components of the data, using Ward's method and the CLUSTAN program. The most similar towns fuse together lower in the dendrogram, the least similar towns at the highest level.

classification – the supervised and the unsupervised (p. 86). Fig. 5.8 illustrates the results of an unsupervised classification of the towns whose land use characteristics are listed in table 5.2; those with similar characteristics cluster together early in the process (near the base of the dendrogram). The results of any such classification may be readily mapped. Fig. 5.9 illustrates an unusual mapping – instead of shading a geographically correct representation of the ground area to show which districts have been classified as similar, we have

Opposite

Figure 5.9 A cartogram to illustrate the classification of districts in Northumberland Tyne and Wear and Durham. Using a procedure and data similar to that in figure 5.8 and table 5.2, each district (rather than town) was grouped with similar ones and the groups are shown by distinctive shading. It would have been easy to produce a standard 'map' but this is probably misleading–the largest areas have few properties. Here each district is scaled in relation to the number of properties within it yet each retains an approximately correct geographical position. The similarity of adjacent districts is obvious, particularly in the inner urban areas.

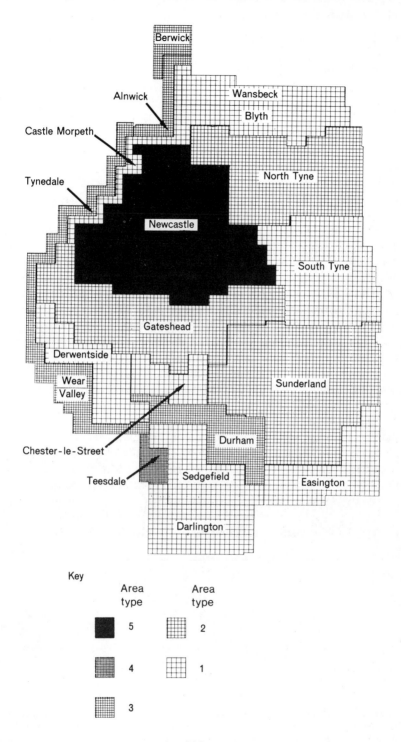

Key

Area type

■	5
	4
	3

Area type

	2
	1

shaded polygons whose size is proportional to the number of properties (and, approximately, to the number of people) in each district. At the price of producing an unfamiliar picture this obviates visual distortion caused by shading large, comparatively 'empty' areas. Such grouping procedures have been mostly developed by numerical taxonomists (e.g. Sneath and Sokal 1973) but are now in widespread use; Alexander (1972), for example, used them in analysing land use in Perth, Australia while Johnston (1968) used land use data from Melbourne city centre as test material to illustrate the properties of different classifying procedures (or algorithms).

Almost all such applications have, however, done one of two things. They have either classified a given area of ground on the basis of various measurements made over all of it (such as on spectral signatures, described in chapter 4) or on the basis of different land uses within the area of ground, such as in characterizing a city block by its component land uses. As such, they are 'data reduction' devices – they condense the wide variability in the natural world into a small set of different possibilities. They are also usually aspatial, in that no direct account is taken of whether parcel 105 is next in space to parcel 342 in the classification process. The most obvious exception to this are texture-based classifiers (chapter 4). On the whole, however, comparatively little appears to have been done in the way of describing *spatial* pattern: the most relevant work seems to be that of Pielou (1965), who produced measures of whether landscape patches of different types (e.g. of land use) were clustered together. Cliff and Ord (1975) have carried out much valuable work devising statistical measures of proximity between like features or auto-correlation. One of the few measures designed to give some direct inkling of pattern, however, is that of near neighbours (see, for example, Haggett *et al.* 1977; Hammond and MacCullagh 1978). In this test, the distance apart of like features is compared with what would be expected from clustered, random and hexagonal distributions (fig. 5.10): it will be appreciated that repeating this analysis several times radially outward from a city centre and obtaining both changing numbers or percentage areas of certain land uses and changing pattern would suggest a particular type of model. In reality, the method has

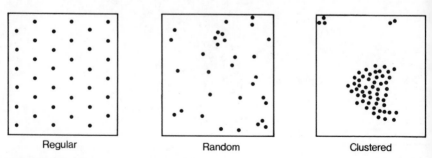

Regular   Random   Clustered

Figure 5.10 Three different forms of spatial distribution characterized by near(est) neighbour statistic; the values of the nearest neighbour statistic for the distribution shown would be approximately 2.14, 1.0 and 0.5 respectively.

many disadvantages, e.g. in its basic form, linear patterns are confounded with the others, and its use necessitates that zones are reduced to point representations. More sophisticated and complex tests for non-randomness have been devised by Royaltey *et al.* (1975).

We can summarize thus: classification of geographical individuals can be considered as pattern recognition. The prime justification for this is that classification is often carried out on the basis of how far apart the individuals are in a 'property space' (fig. 5.11) and that classification is the partitioning of this into discrete 'areas' or slices of space. This has been notably successful in many land use studies, although we noted earlier (p. 86) the limitations to the accuracy of some studies using this methodology. Comparatively little work, however, has been carried out and no satisfactory measures exist for the quantitative description of land use patterns; in geographical space this is a most complex area, as the attempts by Dacey (1970), Betak (1973) and others to formulate languages for describing patterns on maps demonstrates. Overall, then, the computer has a major role in storing, retrieving, summariz-

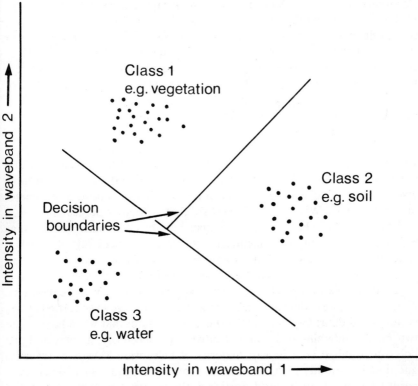

Figure 5.11 The use of 'pattern' in property space: the graph illustrates plots of intensities (e.g. in two of the four Landsat 1 wavebands) and the way in which different clusters form. Such a procedure is, conceptually at least, the basis of much classification, such as that used to produce figures 5.8 and 5.9.

ing and grouping data: at present, our analysis of patterns in space is probably still best done by human means.

COMPARING DATA FOR THE SAME AREA

We have already come across examples where land use data must be overlaid on similar data for another date – notably where up-dates have to be collected by successive 'blanket' surveys (chapter 4). Here the aim is to detect real changes over the intervening time period – and not merely the presence of clouds in different places on remotely sensed imagery! Often, however, we wish (p. 16) to overlay land use distributions on top of those of soil, of land ownership, of rock, etc. In an urban sense, we may wish to superimpose the land use pattern from one city on top of another and check for their congruence. Again, we may wish to produce composite indicators in environmental assessment, such that loadings are given to different types of land use and to other environmental characteristics and, for each geographical individual, a 'score' is calculated from these; such a procedure is being evaluated for use at a resolution of about 1 km^2 throughout the European Economic Community (Ammer *et al.* 1976). All these necessitate the ability to lay one 'map' on another, scaling and stretching where necessary to ensure a correct fit, and then to produce a map or a cross-tabulation of the extents of the area over which, say, land use A at time 1 intersects with land uses A, B, C, etc. at time 2. The process is illustrated in fig. 5.12. It is clear that such area-based schemes and the statistical measures which describe the level of coincidence, are really appropriate only to land cover data. Given this, various other possibilities are available by 'sieving' different data sets. Fig. 5.13 illustrates one example.

In the past, such overlay has often been carried out by photographic means where two different data sets have occurred on maps of similar scale – making a negative film image of each map and superimposing these on a light table gives the area of coincidence which can then be measured using a planimeter or similar means. Webster (1977) has used these yes/no or Boolean maps in a variety of ways. The use of computers greatly eases such comparisons especially if the data are in identical raster form (as in LUNR, Tomlinson *et al.* 1976) or can be made such. Several land use packages convert their zone-based data stored as vectors to this form purely for ease of overlay: all that is required is a pixel-by-pixel comparison between the two or more data sets. Numerous technical difficulties attend the overlay process when carried out on vector-based data: Goodchild (1978) has pointed out that when he overlaid two maps containing 478 and 150 polygons respectively, a total of 1,503 polygons resulted and the vast majority of these were 'slivers' of (usually) questionable validity along the edges of other polygons; such slivers may result from mis-digitizing or distortion in the source document. The level of data produced even by such a simple overlay of only two variables is thus 2.4 times greater than the sum of the two and much more serious problems exist when additional overlays are performed! In practice, then, trading off accuracy by moving to artificial units such as grid squares may be very helpful; in some circumstances, the slivers are, however, of great importance and could not be retrieved from a coarse-resolution raster data base.

A quite different approach to the comparing or linking of data is taken in various other schemes, such as the Durham and Northumberland Land Use Surveys (Rhind and Hudson 1980) and the Joint Information System (Spicer *et al.* 1979). In the first of these especially, different files of data are linked

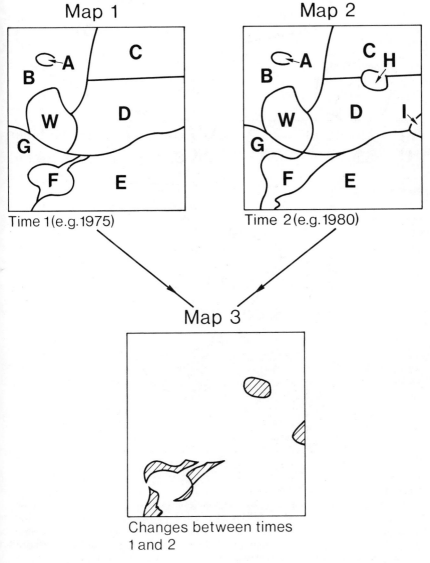

Figure 5.12   Overlay of two maps: land use at different moments in time, 1 and 2, and the difference between them (= change).

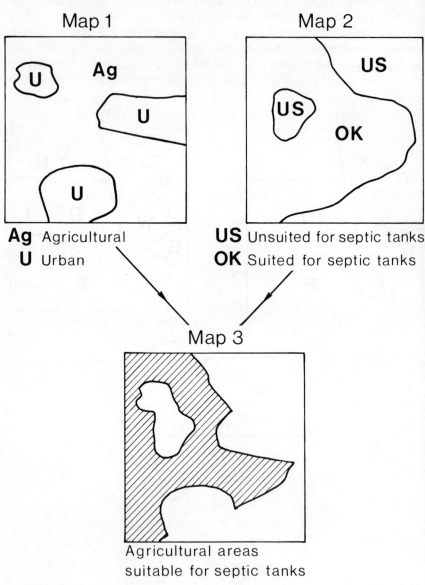

Map 1

U

Ag

U

U

Ag Agricultural
U Urban

Map 2

US

US

OK

US Unsuited for septic tanks
OK Suited for septic tanks

Map 3

Agricultural areas
suitable for septic tanks

Figure 5.13

a Sieving different data sets: by combining maps of land use (urban/rural areas) and maps of soil which is or is not suitable for septic tank emplacement, those areas which are suitable for new housing (non-urban and suitable for septic tanks – on these criteria) may be isolated. Normally, more complex criteria and more maps would be involved.

b (on facing page) Illustrates a similar procedure using coarse raster-based data.

Areas of high death rates in working age population

Areas with high risk industries

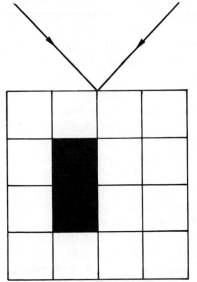
Areas with high risk industries and high death rates in working age population

together either by a unique property number, by grid reference, by location within a post-code zone or an administrative district. The method of storing the data (see p. 92) ensures that they may be aggregated to whatever area of ground is of interest. The extreme example of such flexibility is undoubtedly the Swedish Land Data Bank (Rystedt 1977) which stems from a statutory 'land ownership by parcel' record in existence for 300 years. Rystedt has indicated that, since about 50% of the properties in Sweden are grid referenced, land ownership and other data from the file may be aggregated to other units for comparison with, for example, census data. Moreover, since the population registers in Sweden relate every person to a specific property, there is a link between property number and each individual's civic registration number: all central government data relating to individuals can then be 'tied' to areas of ground and combined at will. Such a system is, of course, extremely unlikely ever to become possible in Britain or the United States.

DETERMINING OPTIMUM LAND USES

We have already mentioned the assessment procedures which can be based upon scoring individual areas on a number of criteria (such as various environmental characteristics), then summing these scores to achieve an overall measure of 'satisfaction', 'deprivation', 'appropriateness' or some other complex concept upon which the different areas are compared. It is now quite common, however, to go beyond this and to experiment with the effects of different choices of land use for different areas. In the extreme case, some calculation of the 'best' arrangement of land uses in terms of some overall objectives is derived. An example of the latter approach is the study reported by Cocks and Ives (1978). They and other officers in CSIRO were involved in a pilot study of resources in a 6,000 km² area of the south coast of New South Wales, with the aim of providing a rational methodological basis for planning decisions on a wide variety of land uses. Following the assembly of very substantial volumes of data on the physical environment and socio-economic characteristics of the population, experiments with the 'optimization' of the land use pattern were carried out using a linear programming model. In essence, they provided a specification of the preferred use of each planning zone and a specification of the permitted uses for each zone. Generally speaking, permitted uses would only be those with a low reversion cost of conversion to the preferred land use: once a zone is urban in character, this is also usually the only practicable and hence permitted use! The preferred land use for each zone was found by maximizing an objective function containing 'party preferences' (expressed as voting weights) for a number of land use policy constraints (36 in their case, represented by rating weights) for each land use on each planning zone.

The first step was to define a set of planning zones from their rudimentary, spatial building blocks: 3,854 basic units of land or geographical individuals were aggregated together on various criteria into 360 planning zones. The policy constraints were then formulated, based upon general factors which should be taken into account in defining the land use: one such constraint was to give preference, in accordance with agricultural capability, to the agricultural option when choosing preferred land use. Another of the 36 constraints was an upper bound – to limit the total area of urbanized land to 2,500 ha. Having defined such constraints, alternative objective functions can be maximized based upon changing the weights assigned to different results: if a decision-maker felt that equal achievement in any of the policies was of the same value to him, all his voting weights would be equal. On the other hand, if he was interested solely in maximizing the achievement of one preference, the weight given to that would be unity and zero to all the others. Clearly any intermediate position is possible and as many different decision-makers as are necessary may take part. The result is the best compromise allocation of land uses which meets the desires of those decision-makers involved.

Such approaches are academically interesting and also have the advantage of replicability – the same preferences and other parameters and data will give the same result. They are also flexible in that preferences can be altered simply. On the debit side, they are so complex as to be rarely understood readily by those who must use the output and, as formulated, they still have technical shortcomings, e.g. they are partly aspatial when carrying out the optimization: the location of allocation to urban uses, for instance, is forced next to existing urban uses only by considerations such as minimizing transport costs. To some extent, the Cocks and Ives approach also takes a deterministic attitude towards land use allocation – they point out that it 'fails to recognize that preferred land use might be different for different dates, might differ with the time taken to realization and might differ according to contingencies' (Cocks and Ives 1978, p. 99). Despite all this, it will be obvious both that such modelling is relatively easily accomplished from pre-existing data bases – especially if these sit within a geographical information system (see p. 124) – and has considerable merit, not least in so far as the mapped results will often force a reassessment and refinement of the decision-makers instincts and preferences.

Displaying the data

Perhaps the greatest benefit of the recent developments in computer methods of handling land use (and other geographical) data is the ease with which the same data may be analysed statistically, then portrayed. Since the data are stored in numerical form (rather than, say, in analogue form as a map) manipulation is easy and further analysis after study of the display of the data usually amounts to little more than a few instructions.

Examples of such systems are discussed in the next section but almost all of them provide some capabilities for mapping, producing histograms, scatterplots or other graphical display of the data.

Rhind (1977) has reviewed the principles, methods and equipment types through which maps are made by computer. In essence, maps may now be made to any desired level of accuracy and graphic quality – subject to the quality of the original data, and the availability of appropriate computer programs and output equipment. As in digitizing map data, two basic methods of display exist, based upon vector or raster technology: a great variety of equipment exists from comparatively inexpensive pen plotters costing about £1,500 to very high precision machines recording on photographic film and costing over £100,000. It is possible to produce output directly on microfilm, ready for projection as slides or as a ciné film. Much more usually, the computer has been used to produce land use maps via the standard line printer – a typewriter-like attachment (in effect, a raster plotter) which produces symbols of varying shades by overprinting different alphabetic characters. Thus it is possible to produce land use maps and graphs without additional cost of equipment and these may even be produced in colour, as in the Ohio Department of Natural Resources system (Schneider with Amanullah 1978); fig. 5.14 illustrates part of a line printer land use map. Increasingly, however, more sophisticated graphic output devices are becoming available and the line printer map is likely to become less common because of its numerous disadvantages, offset only by its low cost (Coppock 1975).

Figure 5.14   Part of a line printer map of land use in Ohio, made by filling areas of common land use with typewriter-like symbols; in this case a hand-drawn overlay has been photographically combined with the map. Such maps are rapid and cheap to produce: they have, however, many disadvantages in practical use (from Schneider with Amanullah 1978).

Figure 5.15 A cathode ray tube (Tektronix 4014); this is capable of drawing lines at many metres per second; if a print on paper is needed, 'hard copy' may be produced at will.

A development of profound importance is the evolution of 'ephemeral' displays, notably cathode ray tubes (fig. 5.15), on which maps, graphs, etc. can be plotted extremely quickly and without making any paper record unless this is required. Such equipment is only meaningful as a computer terminal to an inter-active system (see p. 124). It is technically possible to display data on television screens and it may well be that access to land use and other data bases via telephone links and TV screens will become much more widespread in the future.

The form of the graphical display is limited only by the imagination of the user and the creator of the computer programs. Fig. 5.4 illustrates zone-type land use maps compiled from individual property records; figure 5.16 is a block diagram compiled by computer of similar data. Here the number of properties in each 100 m square have been shown by the heights of the pillars, hidden lines being removed automatically and topographic detail added to aid the user. Intersection of different data sets rapidly permutates the number of possible maps – combination of census and land use data could, for example,

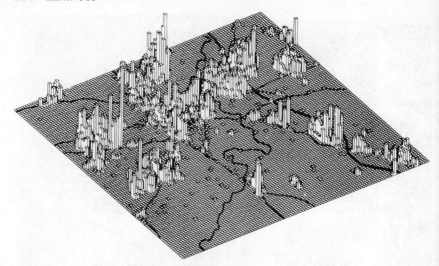

Figure 5.16   A block diagram showing the density of properties of all types (number per 100 m square) in Durham City, viewed from the southwest; the higher the block, the more the properties. Hidden lines are removed automatically; roads and rivers have been added to aid recognition. This is based on about 20,000 properties. The same data may be used to produce statistical summaries (e.g. table 5.2) or conventional or unconventional maps (figures 5.8 and 5.9).

give maps, block diagrams, graphs or tables describing variations in numbers of people within a certain distance of all or selected retail establishments, hospitals, and so on.

Geographical information systems–some examples

Frequent allusion has been made in this book to the need for computer processing of land use data – especially for the conceptually simpler tasks. Yet simply providing computer programs which carry out defined tasks is not a solution, as was found in the late 1960s and early 1970s. In recent years, the realization that a more integrated approach in which users could carry out operations in sequences which they chose, using the output from one task as the input to another and, after the initial period of loading the system, never touching the data by hand again – has led to the creation of geographical information systems. Tomlinson *et al.* (1976) have reviewed the capabilities of six of these, all handling land use and other data, while Schneider with Amanullah (1978) give a simple introduction to the whole subject and describe ten State or County systems. All of those thus described are derived from North America but equally important developments have also occurred in Britain (e.g. Duffield and Coppock 1975; ECU 1978; Harrison 1978; Rhind and Hudson 1980; Spicer *et al.* 1979; Thompson 1978) and elsewhere (e.g. Rystedt 1977, Walker and Davis 1978). Applications of such systems are widespread: Miller *et al.* (1978), for example, have described their analysis of land cover changes in Northern Thailand from Landsat images and the ways in which they have modelled the processes involved. Floyd (1978) has pointed out that land use data are handled by geographical information systems in Puerto Rico. Internally, the systems differ in the type of geographical individual they handle, the way they store the data, the ease with which the user can express and extract what he requires, and so on, but most provide the rudiments of the needs listed on pp. 16 and 101.

The systems in most frequent operational use appear to be those which collect data as an administration process and use them for a variety of purposes. Notable amongst these are the Swedish Land Data Bank (Rystedt 1977) and the Tyne and Wear Joint Information System (Spicer *et al.* 1979). But perhaps the system most specifically designed for handling land use (*ss*) and land cover data is GIRAS, under development by the United States Geological Survey since 1973. The acronym stands for Geographic Information and Retrieval and Analysis System. The early versions of GIRAS were batch-orientated, i.e. the communication between user and system was by punched cards; genuine conversational use of the system from terminals was impossible. Later developments provided such an inter-active facility.

GIRAS sets out specifically to handle the land use and land cover data which was to be available for all the USA by the end of 1982 (p. 65). The data are converted to computer form by line-following from 1/250,000 scale maps. In addition, maps of political units, census sub-divisions, hydrological units such as drainage basins, federal and state land ownership are also digitized and stored. Mitchell *et al.* (1977) estimate that this will produce some 57 km of digitized lines by 1981. In pre-processing stages, the data are checked, corrected where necessary and converted to common storage in latitude and longitude units.

Once this stage is complete, data may be inter-related and the vector-type data converted to raster images for comparison with satellite data (p. 117). The system can produce a wide variety of types of areal summary; it can, under certain circumstances, fill in data in unknown areas by interpolation from surrounding data; generalization and filtering are also possible. Selection of the data for these tasks may be carried out either (or both) by specifying an area of interest and one or more land use codes: numerous combinations of attributes may be specified such as 'select all residential areas bordering on water'. In plotting maps of the results, polygon areas can be filled in with colour or patterns specified by the user and perspective or isometric block diagrams can be generated. Finally, in being based upon data which are now being periodically up-dated and in providing a conversational mode of operàtion, the system permits the generation of land use models from data on past land use, land ownership, unit costs (if available) and so on and comparison of the results with the contemporary pattern. Such facilities permit the user to do, over a meaningfully large area, what he can do by hand with two or three land use zones: they do not, of course obviate the severe philosophical and methodological problems resulting from the considerations of data type, accuracy, etc. considered in chapter 3.

Part   3

6 Land use within Britain

Introduction

We have already pointed out that perhaps the most common fate of land use data is to provide statistical summaries which are then used for a variety of planning purposes. Such aggregations are also often the simplest task to carry out from a technical point of view. In this chapter we describe, assess and compare some of the various statements about land use in parts or all of the United Kingdom. Our discussion is based upon a selection from the major data sources (table 6.1). A much more complete guide to British data sources is given in the seminal work by Coppock and Gebbett (1978).

It is essential in reading this chapter to bear in mind two general considerations – the lack of direct comparability of the various surveys (see chapters 2 to 5) and the smoothing effect of using gross areal units. It is well known in the geographical community that, the larger the areal units, the smaller the variation between them. Consideration of land use taking, say, the county as the arbitrary and collective geographical individual in Britain would therefore give rather different results to those based on 'standard regions', administrative Districts or Enumeration Districts. Beyond this, we have a much more surprising difficulty – in establishing the percentage of the total extent of a particular land cover. We may measure or estimate the extent of the land cover by a variety of means, yet the baseline figure (the area of Britain) is obtained by an accumulating procedure which is certain to contain some errors (Coppock 1978, p. 12). Although these are likely to be small, differences in organization of the statistics may be significant. Coppock (1978) has pointed out, for instance, that the administrative areas supplied to the Registrar General of England and Wales and published in the volumes of the population census and elsewhere include both land and inland water, whereas the latter (totalling 2% of the land area) are excluded from the comparable statistics supplied to the Registrar General of Scotland! In addition, central government definitions appear to vary over time without obvious explanation; the Government Statistical Service booklet *UK in Figures* (GSS 1975) gives an area for England and Wales of 151,139 km^2; the same booklet for 1978 gives the area as 151,207 km^2. The 1975 figure has been used consistently in this book.

Table 6.1 Land use within Britain – a summary of the primary data sources utilized.

Source	Area of cover	Date of data	Classification	Basis	Change data?
Stamp survey	England and Wales	mostly 1931–34	Stamp's	Field survey	No
SLUS	Britain	1960s	Elaboration of Stamp's	Field survey	(i) by comparison with Stamp's (ii) some re-survey
Best	Britain	1947–77		Development Plans	Minor amounts
				Agricultural returns	Yes
Fordham	United Kingdom	pre-1939 to 1974	Grouping of features on OS maps	Sample from OS maps	Yes
DoE	Urban area in England and Wales	1968–69	On building form	Air photo survey	No

Throughout this chapter, all units used by the different authors have been standardized for comparison purposes; where conversions from Imperial to metric units have been made, they are based on constants tabulated by Anderton and Bigg (1972).

The extent of the urban areas in the UK

All urban land use studies have been bedevilled by the difficulty of defining what is urban (p. 49). Administrative definitions of urban areas were enshrined in the old County Borough/Rural District distinction existing between the 1880s and 1974. Even then, however, this was markedly unsatisfactory: it has been estimated (Best 1968) that 33% of the land in County Boroughs in England and Wales in the 1960s was rural. A variety of studies, such as DoE (1974b, 1975) and Goddard *et al.* (1976) have attempted to define the urban areas on different criteria ranging from completeness, contiguity and size of the built-up area to population density and journey-to-work characteristics. As a consequence, it is scarcely surprising that this problem of definition, allied to the different classifications used and to the different methods of survey, sampling or extrapolation, result in some variations. Appropriate allowance must be made for this in comparing different sets of figures (below): knowing what *is* appropriate is not a simple matter.

The first moderately reliable and complete figures for the extent of urban land in Britain were those derived from measurement of appropriate categories on the maps of the Land Utilisation Survey (see p. 62). The first post-war estimates were provided by Dr R. H. Best, together with a break-down into the component parts of urban land use.

Best's original figures for urban extent (Best 1959; Best and Coppock 1962) stem initially from the statutory obligation placed on local authorities in 1947 to carry out land use surveys and analysis before making their Development Plans. On the basis of selected maps submitted between 1949 and 1955, stratifications of settlements on the basis of population size were drawn for England and Wales and for Scotland and, using acreage and population figures for each Development Plan, a population density was calculated for each stratum. Acreage estimates for the whole country were then calculated by use of the 1951 Census of Population figures. The accuracy of the method therefore relied upon the method of measurement of land use, the approach to Development Plan sampling and the assumption that the relationship between density and land use was everywhere constant. Fordham (1974) has severely criticized these aspects of the work and Best has always acknowledged that the results – especially in areas of numerous small settlements, such as Scotland – were less than perfect (Best 1976a,b). The method of calculation (Coppock 1978, p. 51) ensured that they should be regarded as maxima. On the basis of this work, the total extent of urban land in Britain in 1951 was said to be 1.648×10^6 ha and in England and Wales, 1.458×10^6 ha. Subsequently, Best and associates calculated the urban area at the time of the

1961 Census of Population using data from later Development Plans and from reviews of those submitted earlier. Drawing also upon the Second Land Utilisation Survey (p. 63) for land use information in small settlements, the estimates for England and Wales for 1961 amounted to 1.49×10^6 ha (Best 1976a,b).

Fordham's procedures for estimating the extent of land use have been briefly described earlier (p. 57) and are elaborated in his two publications on the topic (Fordham 1974, 1975). The most important aspects of these are that they were based on a systematic point sampling from a sample survey using OS 1/2,500, 1/10,560 and 1/63,360 scale maps: because of the use of randomly selected areas within randomly selected map sheets, he was able to provide a useful measure of the likely accuracy of his results by calculating the coefficient of variation (the standard deviation of results as a percentage of the mean value). Urban land was defined as that occupied by buildings, roads, railways and immediately related open areas, such as gardens; any open areas within the urban perimeter which could not be identified as parks or playing fields were not included. Thus, although he emphasized that an objective of the exercise was to make his classification as comparable with Best's as possible, it should not be surprising if his figures are lower than Best's. Data were obtained from as many post-war 1/63,360 scale maps as were available: most were published in the periods 1948–55 and 1958–65, estimates of changes in urban areas at 1961 being obtained by interpolation. Most of the 1/10,560 scale maps used to sample rural areas dated from 1948–52; estimates of changes in urban land in these areas up to 1961 were produced via the surrogate variable of population change between 1951 and 1961. It will be seen as a consequence that there are a number of important assumptions also built into Fordham's study but that it was based upon easily exploited sources of data and, as a result, did not demand very large amounts of work in data compilation.

The methods by which the other data sources were compiled (Coleman's Second Land Utilisation Survey and the DoE Developed Areas survey) have already been described; areas of different land uses were obtained from the former by systematic point sampling of the resulting land use maps and from the latter by digitizing the boundaries of all the Developed Areas, then summing the areas and producing results using a computer. The method of obtaining changes between Stamp's survey and the Second Land Utilisation Survey is described by Coleman *et al.* (1974).

Comparisons of the extent of urban land – or some euphemism for this – are set out for the only common time period and areal unit (England and Wales in 1961) in table 6.6. This is based upon the more detailed information in tables 6.2 to 6.5. The most striking aspect of this table is the degree of correspondence between the figure interpolated from Fordham's estimates for 1969 and the DoE figure for England and Wales in 1969. However, given the method of deriving the 1969 figures from Fordham's estimates, this coincidence should not be taken as an indication that the remainder of his estimates (see below) are highly accurate. The most extreme figure is that of Coleman – ignoring the difference in dates of survey for the moment, her postulated area of 'urban' coverage is 21% larger than that of Fordham. To some extent, this is entirely predictable – Coleman's figures are for 'total settlement' rather than for 'urban areas' as such. It is remarkably difficult, however, to say how much of this discrepancy is due to the difference in definition. As an example, the Coleman figures include all airfields; these

Table 6.2 Land use in England and Wales in 1933 and 1963, according to Coleman (1978).

Category of use	1933 (ha)	% of total	1963 (ha)	% of toal
Tended open space	107,965		187,043	
Airfields	12,456		43,933	
Other settlement	971,690		1,398,166	
Total settlement	1,092,111	7.2	1,629,142	10.8
Permanent pasture	6,667,760		4,422,206	
Leys	908,555		1,937,745	
Arable land	2,977,832		3,692,348	
Orchards	105,186		111,085	
Allotments	24,628		19,784	
Total improved farmland	10,683,961	70.7	10,183,168	67.3
Woodland	856,763		1,212,525	
Other cover types	2,359,433		1,939,079	
Water	130,150		159,722	
Total cover types	3,346,346	22.1	3,311,326	21.9
Total area	15,122,418	100.0	15,123,636	100.0
Total area according to GSS (1975)			15,113,900	

Table 6.3 Land use structure of the UK and EEC in 1971, according to Best (1978).

	England and Wales Area (100 km²) %		UK Area (100 km²) %		EEC %
Agriculture	1,162	76.9	1,908	78.2	64.2
Cropland	571	37.8	732	30.0	36.2
Pasture	591	39.1	1,176	48.2	28.0
Woodland	113	7.5	193	7.9	21.6
Urban development	166	11.0	195	8.0	6.8
Other	70	4.6	144	5.9	7.4

The area figures were derived by multiplication of Best's percentages by the total areas as given by GSS (1975) and subsequent rounding.

Table 6.4 Land use in England and Wales in 1969, according to DoE (1978).

Economic Planning Region	Total 'Developed Area' (km²)	Total 'Developed Area', as % administrative area	A	B	C	D	E	A	B	C	D	E
			(as % administrative area)					(as % total 'Developed Area')				
South East	4,726	17.4	11.06	2.31	0.20	0.95	2.87	63.6	13.3	1.2	5.5	16.5
West Midlands	1,533	11.8	7.12	2.40	0.10	0.59	1.55	60.4	20.4	0.9	5.0	13.2
North West	1,594	21.8	13.08	4.09	0.21	0.98	3.42	60.0	18.8	1.0	4.5	15.7
Northern	874	5.7	3.19	1.43	0.05	0.37	0.62	56.1	25.2	1.0	6.6	11.0
Yorkshire and Humberside	1,530	9.9	5.41	1.91	0.11	0.83	1.62	54.7	19.3	1.2	8.4	16.4
East Midlands	1,405	9.0	5.11	1.90	0.06	0.97	0.93	56.8	21.2	0.7	10.8	10.4
East Anglia	853	6.8	4.10	0.74	0.05	1.31	0.56	60.4	11.0	0.8	19.4	8.3
South West	1,459	6.1	4.20	0.86	0.05	0.46	0.51	68.9	14.3	0.9	7.6	8.4
Wales	877	4.2	2.34	1.20	0.03	0.26	0.35	55.9	28.6	0.8	6.3	8.4
England and Wales	14,850	9.8	5.95	1.71	0.09	0.70	1.31	60.8	17.5	1.0	7.2	13.4

Total area of England and Wales is 151,139 km² given by GSS (1975).

A Predominantly residential use
B Predominantly industrial and/or commercial use
C Predominantly educational/community/health/indoor recreational use
D Transport use
E 'Urban' open space

Source: Derived from DoE (1978, Annex 2).

Note: Minor inconsistencies occur in the summations in the table owing to rounding effects.

Table 6.5 Estimated urban land use in the UK 1951–71, according to Fordham (1975).

	1951 (km²)	(%)	1961 (km²)	(%)	1971 (km²)[1]	(%)
South East	3,132		3,602		3,982	
West Midlands	1,336		1,501		1,671	
North West	1,615		1,756		1,963	
Northern	1,162		1,287		1,445	
Yorkshire and Humberside	1,242		1,368		1,522	
East Midlands	975		1,149		1,331	
East Anglia	417		461		538	
South West	1,554		1,704		1,976	
Wales	542	2.6	623	3.0	720	3.5
England and Wales	11,975	7.9	13,451	8.9	15,148	10.0
Scotland	2,185	2.8	2,254	2.9	2,287	2.9
N. Ireland	773	5.5	797	5.6	809	5.7
United Kingdom	14,933	6.1	16,502	6.8	18,244	7.5

The 1971 figures were obtained by extrapolating those for each urban area and then aggregating the results (Fordham 1974).

Table 6.6 Total urban land use in England and Wales in the 1960s according to various authors.

Author	Approximate date of survey	Area (km²)	% total area
Best (1976b)[3]	1961	14,900	9.9
Coleman (1978)[4]	1963	16,290	10.8
Fordham (1974)	1961[1]	13,451	8.9
Fordham	1969[2]	14,809	9.8
DoE (1978)	1969	14,850	9.8

[1] Interpolated by Fordham from information mapped at various dates.
[2] Derived by linear interpolation from Fordham's 1961 and 1971 figures.
[3] Based on Best's (1976b) figure for 1961 of 1.490×10^6 ha (rather than his grossed-up estimate). The extent of England and Wales is that given by GSS (1975), i.e. 151,139 km².
[4] Coleman's figures relate to settlement in total; they include rural roads and railways, hamlets and dispersed farmhouses, i.e. they cover a more extensive area than most of the other surveys.

were only included in the Best study in so far as they impinged on the area of land enclosed by the boundaries of the Town Map. We should note another sample survey by Anderson (1977) who has specified that urban land in 196 accounted for 9.7% of the total area ($\pm$ 1.1% as the 95% confidence limits), similar or slightly larger 'error band' due to sampling existing around th Fordham data (Anderson's base figure for the area of England and Wales i unknown). In principle, of course, the exhaustive, specially commissioned DoE study should be the most accurate: in practice, this is also likely to be th case but some slight degree of undercounting will be included owing to th exclusion of any areas less than 5 ha in size.

In theory, the relative magnitude of errors – and hence of those difference between the different studies which are not attributable to differing classifi cations of urban land – should be at a minimum at such a coarse level as th national unit and get proportionately greater at more local levels. Yet th variations in land use between different areas are of considerable practic importance. Tables 6.4 and 6.5 provide a comparison between two studies a the Standard Region level; there are eight such regions in England, bein identical to the Economic Planning Regions. It is obvious that, although th national figures are very comparable, considerable variations occur at th regional level – ignoring the 2 year difference in survey dates, the Do detected 19% more developed area/urban land in the South East region. Th surplus was largely compensated by deficits in four of the other areas. Some c the deviations are even more extreme: the Fordham (1975) figures for th Northern Region exceed the DoE ones by 65%. Apart from errors, difference may be due to two obvious factors. These are differences in definition betwee 'Developed Areas' and 'urban areas' (although the results indicate that, if the exist, the effects of these differences cancel each other out at the national level The alternative is differences in the boundaries of the so-called Standar Regions: in 1974 these were adjusted to take account of the change in th boundaries of counties after the reorganization of local authorities in Englan and Wales; the Fordham study relates to those before the reorganization, th DoE one to the counties after the regrouping and hence to the later set c regional boundaries.

The composition of land use in Britain

Variations in classification become significant as more detailed results ar compared. Thus Fordham's results itemized in table 6.7 do not compare at a closely with those obtained by DoE in table 6.4 (again the change of regiona boundaries will have some effect). Fordham considered 'buildings' to includ residential, service and industrial land, 'transport' to include roads, railway and footpaths and 'open land' to include gardens, playing fields and car parks In other words, his buildings category largely subsumes DoE categories A, and C. In the South East, buildings accounts for 24% of the total urban cove according to Fordham (1975), yet 78.1% of the total Developed Area according to the DoE! The difference is just as marked at the national level

Table 6.7 Individual land uses in Britain in 1961, according to Fordham (1975).

Standard Region	% of urban land		
	Buildings	Transport	Open land
South East	24	33	43
West Midlands	32	33	34
North West	31	44	26
Northern	20	45	35
Yorkshire and Humberside	23	38	39
East Midlands	15	51	34
East Anglia	20	50	30
Wales	20	65	15
England and Wales[1]	24	41	35
Scotland	23	59	18
N. Ireland	19	62	18
United Kingdom	24	45	31

[1] Calculated from Fordham's figures.

ndicating that these differences occur even where no effects from changes in boundaries have occurred. On the basis of the Fordham figures, only two-thirds of the urban area in 1961 was actually covered by concrete or asphalt while transport land, particularly in rural areas, dominates the figures.

Fordham (1975, p. 76) indicated that less reliance should be placed upon these data than upon his figures for the extent of urban areas as a whole. Because of this and because they result from a complete, special purpose survey, we shall concentrate on the DoE statistics for description of the different land use types (table 6.4). In passing, we might note that results of accuracy checks based upon re-survey have not been published in respect of the DoE study, although Smith (1978) has claimed high accuracy of photo-interpretation. We can consider these data in two ways: first, as originally presented by DoE, with each class as a percentage of the total Developed Areas in that region or, alternatively, as a percentage of the total adminis-trative area. On the first consideration, the greatest variation occurs in the extent of industrialization, a colossal contrast occurring between Wales and the Northern region at one extreme and East Anglia and the South West at the other. Partly as a compensation for this, East Anglia has a high percentage of its urban land devoted to transport uses – although we should note that, in absolute terms, this is quite small because East Anglia has the smallest physical extent of urban land of all the regions. The East Midlands, however, scores surprisingly highly on the transport scale, having twice as much in both

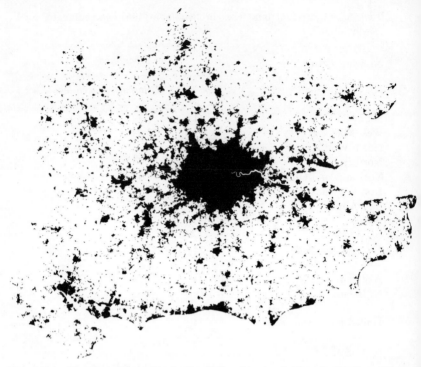

Figure 6.1 'Developed Areas' in the South East Economic Planning Region of Britain (provided by Department of the Environment; Crown Copyright reserved).

absolute and relative amounts as the contiguous region, the West Midlands – home of the British car industry. Residential uses of land are generally highest in the least industrialized areas.

Considering the other aspect of the figures emphasizes the 'rurality' or 'urban-ness' of the different regions, although the figures are highly dependent on how the regional boundaries of these arbitrary and collective geographical units are drawn. Thus the South East has by far the greatest physical extent of built up land (see fig. 6.1) but, in percentage terms, the North West is the most 'urbanized'. The low percentage figure for the Northern region reflects the concentration of settlement and industry in the eastern, coastal areas particularly around the lower reaches of the rivers Tyne, Wear and Tees; the western areas of the region are largely unpopulated. On the basis of these latter figures, all of which conceal substantial variations within the region, the two most similar regions are East Anglia and the South West or, alternatively Yorkshire and Humberside and the East Midlands. The most disparate pair is either the South East and East Anglia or the North West and East Anglia

Changes in the extent of urban land

The rate of conversion of agricultural farmland and other land to urban areas has been a matter of concern, contention, debate and high polemic for many

Table 6.8 Annual average net transfers of (specified) land to urban use in Britain.

Author	Time period	Area (1000 ha/annum)		
		England and Wales	*Scotland*	*Britain*
Fordham (1974)[5]	1951–61	—	—	15.6
Best (1978)[1]	1922–26	9.1	—	—
	1926–31	21.1	—	—
	1931–36	25.1	—	—
	1936–39	25.1	—	—
	1939–45	5.3	—	—
	1945–50	17.5	—	—
	1950–55	15.5	—	—
	1955–60	14.0	—	—
	1960–65	15.3	2.5	17.8
	1965–70	16.8	2.8	19.6
	1970–74	14.9	2.0	17.4
	1931–60[4]	17.9	—	—
Coleman (1978)[2]	1933–63	16.7	—	—
[3]	1933–63	17.9	—	—

[1] Best's figures relate to transfer of 'farmland'.
[2] This relates to a loss of 500,792 ha of 'improved farmland' over 30 years.
[3] This relates to a gain of 537,476 ha of 'settlement' over 30 years.
[4] Computed from Best's other figures.
[5] Fordham's figures relate to transfer of any non-urban land to urban uses.

years (see Best 1978; Coleman 1978; Coppock 1978). Table 6.8 sets out the various estimates produced of this rate at specified time periods.

Despite this furore and dispute, the figures correspond remarkably well – even though obtained from sources as diverse as agricultural returns collected by the Ministry of Agriculture, Fisheries and Foods (Best), comparisons of re-aggregated results from interpretations of figures produced by Stamp's Land Utilisation Survey and from point sampling of land use maps of the Second Land Utilisation Survey (Coleman) and point sampling of topographic maps and interpolation to a decennial interval (Fordham). The only possible area of disagreement centres around Coleman's assertion (Coleman 1978, p. 19) that little by way of permanent loss by transfers of land occurred for approximately one third of her 30 year period; on this basis, she scaled-up the rate cited in table 6.9 by 50%. If continued on this basis, Dr Coleman has projected that the entire farmland resource would be consumed in 400 years in England and Wales; on a continuation of Best's UK rate, the corresponding time period to Armageddon would be 900 years. Best has warned of the dangers of taking long-term averages, pointing out that the

Table 6.9 Thames Estuary: land-use changes 1962–72 (km²).

	Settlement						Farmland				Vegetation						Total losses	Area in 1972
	Residential	Industry	Extractive	Derelict	Transport	Open space	Orchards	Horticulture	Arable	Improved grass	Woodland	Scrub	Waste	Heath	Marsh	Water		
Settlement																		
Residential		1.0			4.0	6.0		2.0	1.0	0.5		2.0	1.5				18.0	188.0
Industry					1.5	0.5							2.0				4.0	30.0
Extractive	0.5			4.5		0.5				1.0			5.0				11.5	16.5
Derelict					1.0							0.5	0.5				2.0	7.0
Transport	1.0	0.5				1.5						0.5					3.0	93.5
Open space	2.0						0.5	1.5	1.0	2.0	0.5	1.0	1.0			0.5	10.0	80.0
Farmland																		
Orchards	1.0							*Rotations*					1.0				2.0	13.0
Horticulture	1.5	0.5			0.5	1.5		*90.5*					2.5				7.0	66.0
Arable	2.5	1.5	1.5		0.5	3.0							6.5				14.0	148.0
Improved grass	5.0	2.5		1.0	1.0	2.5						0.5	18.0			0.5	32.5	98.0
Vegetation																		
Woodland	0.5				0.5	0.5		1.0				1.5	1.0				5.0	19.0
Scrub	4.5	2.5	0.5		0.5	0.5					0.5		3.5				6.5	9.0
Waste		2.0	2.0	1.0		2.5		2.0				1.0					15.5	63.5
Heath													0.5				0.5	0.5
Marsh			0.5							0.5			1.5				1.5	9.0
Water								0.5				0.5	0.5				1.5	9.5
Total gains	18.5	7.0	6.5	6.5	11.0	17.5	0.5	4.5	2.0	6.5	1.0	7.0	45.0	0.0	0.0	1.0	134.5	850.5

Source: Coleman (1976, p. 414; 1978, p. 24).

Previous use

New use

Previous use	Agriculture and forestry	Health and community services	Defence	Education	Recreation and leisure	Manufacturing	Mineral extraction	Offices	Residences	Retail distribution and servicing	Storage	Transport	Utility services	Wholesale distribution	Unused land, water and buildings	Total previous use	Land use in 1978 (ha)	Land use in 1978 (%)
Agricultural and forestry				16.2					151.9			80.4				248.5	36,286	59.3
Community and health services															2.6	2.6	136	0.2
Defence																0.0	94	0.2
Education									1.4						2.4	3.8	835	1.4
Recreation and leisure									9.8							9.8	1,743	2.8
Manufacturing											0.4				0.4	0.8	3,379	5.5
Mineral extraction																0.0	70	0.1
Offices																0.0	24	0.0
Residences		1.3													13.9	15.2	8,170	13.3
Retail distribution and servicing															1.1	1.1	221	0.4
Storage															0.1	0.1	367	0.6
Transport														0.2		0.2	1,964	3.2
Utility services																0.0	1,035	1.7
Wholesale distribution																0.0	173	0.3
Unused land, water and buildings		0.3		2.8		14.0			21.3	0.8	4.9	8.3		0.2		52.4	6,731	11.0
Total new use	0.0	1.6	0.0	19.0		14.0	0.0	0.0	184.4	0.8	5.3	88.7	0.0	0.2	20.5	334.5	61,228	100.0

Source: CCDP (1978).

rate of farmland conversion in the 1930s was very much higher than in recent years. In conclusion, we may note a curious item of total dissent: the Central Statistical Office have concluded (CSO 1979, p. 167) that 1,500 ha of agricultural land were lost to other uses over the *4 years* between 1970/71 and 1974/75!

Some local studies of land use change

Little by way of generality can be deduced from the few local studies of change which have yet been published. Even so, these are important in their own local context. We shall consider only two – changes in the Thames Estuary between 1962 and 1972 (Coleman 1978, p. 24) and in Cleveland County between 1976 and 1978 (CCPD 1978). The changes are tabulated in tables 6.9 and 6.10. Since there are no obvious ways of checking the accuracy of these figures, we shall have to accept them – at least for the present purposes.

Coleman's data are derived from the Second Land Utilisation Survey and a re-survey of the area a decade later. They are interesting because of the detailed nature of the transfers shown; the significance of some of these transfers is, of course, only assessable in relation to the total figures (see Coleman 1976, p. 414). Even so, it is noteworthy that, while 18.5 km^2 changed into residential and commercial use (15 km^2 from 'farmland' or 'vegetation'), 18 km^2 passed out of such use, 7 km^2 of the latter going to 'farmland' or 'vegetation' use. Some 6.5 km^2 became derelict land and 2.0 km^2 were converted from this into other (partly other unproductive) land. Some 55.5 km^2 of farmland was lost in this area over the decade and 13.5 km^2 gained to this use. Clearly the sort of figures used earlier in this chapter – in which net changes only are shown – conceal much of interest and, especially, information giving clues to the mechanisms responsible for land use changes.

The Cleveland study is based upon statutory land use change notifications and the use of a base survey from an earlier period. No direct detailed comparison between the Thames Estuary study and that of Cleveland are possible because of the different classifications involved. The most notable characteristics of the latter results are the 2.5 km^2 converted from farmland to largely urban uses in the 2 year period and the net diminution in unused land.

The largest contribution to the creation of unused – or dormant – land is that from land formerly used for residences. Even so, the scale of the change (0.15 km^2) is rather small and the time period too short from which to generalize. Over-all, no less than 5.5% of the total land area is claimed to have changed its use between NLUC orders in this brief time and, of this change, no less than three-quarters involved the transfer of agricultural and forestry land to urban uses. These compare with a 16% change in uses (over different categories) and 30% of the transfers being a net conversion from farmland to other uses over the 10 years of Coleman's study of the Thames Estuary.

Concluding remarks

The simple analyses made in this chapter of the tabulated land use summaries llustrate that there is perhaps more consensus on the most aggregate levels of urban land in existence than is generally accepted. Even so, some important differences between authors have been indicated and some of these are unresolvable: realistic comparisons are only feasible for the situation more than a decade ago. When we focus on smaller spatial or geographical units than the national territory, considerable divergence of view exists in the few available statistics and even the most reliable are now (at the time of writing) more than a decade out of date. Considerable differences in interpretation have been made of the national 'changes in land use' figures. Finally, local studies of land use are interesting and often especially valuable where they provide data on land use transitions – rather than net changes – but are often impossible to compare because of the different classifications used. From this point of view, the adoption of the NLUC and a better response to the DoE Circular 71/74 (see p. 15) would greatly improve our land use data base – we would know 'what' has changed to 'what', even if we did not know 'where' with any degree of precision.

It is worth reiterating that many of these statistics are for arbitrary units, i.e. regions, districts. Until recently, we have had comparatively little published information on land use within functional urban units, such as towns or villages. Hitherto, the best information on such geographical units comes from *ad hoc* studies often containing maps, such as by Gautam (1976) or from detailed ones which can be aggregated to whatever geographical units are required (Rhind and Hudson 1980; Spicer *et al.* 1979): to that extent, the values of land uses by town given in table 5.2 are rather unusual. Recently, however, the Department of the Environment (DoE 1978) have offered to make available tabulations of land use in their five broad categories within each continuously developed area, i.e. for functional urban areas defined in physical terms. Such tabulations are too voluminous to publish for the whole country. The implications of this situation are important when we proceed to begin modelling land use, especially urban areas. The following part (part 4), then, reviews some of the models and theories which have been constructed to define and explain patterns of land use.

Part 4

7 Models of agricultural land use

Introduction

While from one point of view the distinction between rural and urban land use may be seen as an arbitrary one (p. 49), in view of the high proportion of land devoted to agricultural uses (see chapters 1 and 6) it is appropriate to commence a discussion of land use models with those concerned with agricultural land use. However, a major problem in comparative studies of agricultural land use is the paucity of comparable data. As we have already shown (p. 29), land use data are collected at nominal or perhaps ordinal scales of measurement; that is, in discrete classes. As Haggett (1966, p. 158; see also Haggett *et al.* 1977, p. 197) notes, despite moves set in motion at the 1949 IGU Congress in Lisbon with the intention of establishing a common international classificatory system, progress towards this goal has been slow (see also p. 35). To a considerable degree, this reflects the marked variations that are found in agricultural systems at a world scale and the consequent problems of devising a classification system which can satisfactorily encompass these variations at anything other than a superficial level. As a consequence, the most successful and significant works tend to remain regional monographs of land use in relatively restricted areas, such as Board's (1962) study of the South African Border Region.

Despite this problem of absence of strictly comparable data, sufficient empirical evidence has accumulated to suggest that a characteristic spatial pattern of agricultural land use, found in a variety of social, cultural and technical contexts and at a variety of spatial scales, is of a concentric zoning of land uses around nodal points. Several of these empirical case studies are briefly described below. Not all the available evidence, however, points to concentric zoning: for example, Jackson (1972, p. 261) argues that in tropical Africa cultivation zones of concentric rings are uncommon.

Description of agricultural land use patterns is one problem; a more fundamental problem is satisfactorily to explain these. In many ways it is appropriate to commence a discussion of land use models with von Thünen's seminal contribution of the 'Isolated State' (1826). Although it has recently been suggested that it was anticipated 37 years earlier by Adam Smith in *The Wealth of Nations* (Chisholm 1979), this has generally been hailed as the forerunner of modern location theory. It was an early attempt to explain concentric land use zones yet retains considerable contemporary relevance – provided one relaxes certain assumptions and admits the impact of technological change on agricultural location patterns. Von Thünen's account pivots on the concept of economic (or locational) rent. Related interpretations of land use patterns can be made in terms of bid rent curves, although these were mainly developed in the context of urban, rather than agricultural, land use patterns. Such interpretations are, to some extent, all predicated upon certain historically specific assumptions concerning the level of socio-economic development.

Recognizing this and, as a consequence, regarding von Thünen's model as a special, limiting case – not only from the point of view of the assumptions made concerning the socio-economic environment but also geometrically – Haggett (1966) attempted to relax these assumptions and produce a more general and ahistorical explanation. Barnbrock (1974) has recently criticized conventional interpretations of von Thünen from a very different stance, suggesting that von Thünen's principle concern was to legitimate bourgeois society by demonstrating the inevitability of the 'natural wage' of the agricultural labouring class and to re-establish the harmonic bond between classes. Thus Barnbrock suggests that the model is to be understood as part of an idealistic counter-ideology rather than as an account of reality. We consider these approaches in turn, examining not only the models but also empirical evidence as to their validity.

Von Thünen's 'Isolated State'

In his book *Der Isolierte Staat in Beziehung auf Landwirtschaft*, first published in 1826, von Thünen set out a model of agricultural land use zones arranged concentrically around a central city (fig. 7.1; see also table 7.1). In order of

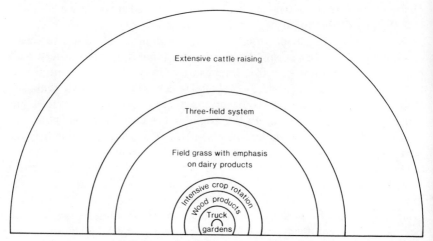

Figure 7.1   Von Thünen's Isolated State.

Table 7.1 von Thünen's land use rings: the Isolated State.

Zone	% of State area	Relative distance from centre[1]	Land use type	Major marketed product	Production system
0	< 0.1	≤ 0.1	Urban–industrial	Manufactured goods	Urban trade centre of state, near iron and coal mines
1	1	0.1–0.6	Intensive agriculture	Milk, vegetables	Intensive dairying and trucking, heavy manuring, no fallow
2	3	0.6–3.5	Forest	Firewood, timber	Sustained yield forestry
3a	3	3.5–4.6		Rye, potatoes	6 year rotation: rye (2), potatoes, clover, barley, vetch, no fallow; cattle stall-fed in winter
3b	30	4.6–34.0	Extensive agriculture	Rye	7 year rotation: pasture (3), rye, barley, oats, fallow
3c	25	34.0–44.0		Rye, animal products	3 field system: rye, pasture, fallow
4	38	44.0–100.0	Ranching	Animal products	Mainly stock raising, some rye for on-farm consumption
5	—	> 100.0	Waste	None	None

[1] Distance to the edge of the Isolated State is assumed to be 100 units.
Source: After Haggett (1966, p. 165).

increasing distance from the centre, the zones are of: intensive agriculture; forest; extensive agriculture; ranching; and waste. To understand why land uses take this particular spatial arrangement, one must consider two related issues: first, the specific historical circumstances and experiences which formed the background to von Thünen's work (see Hall 1966); and second, the specific assumptions on which the model is constructed.

With regard to the former, in 1810 von Thünen (at the age of 27) acquired his own agricultural estate at Tellow, near Rostock on the Baltic coast of Germany. For the remaining 40 years of his life he farmed this estate, meticulously preserving copious records of the costs and revenues of its operation. In his theoretical analysis of agricultural land use patterns he drew heavily upon this empirical basis: many of the assumptions and all of the values of the empirical constants which he employed were derived from this highly specific experience. Certain features of his land use model also reflected the particular historical setting in which it was derived, notably the location of forestry near to the central city. This commanded such a location in von Thünen's day because of demands for timber and firewood, demands that are today satisfied by other commodities in industrialized societies. However, there is evidence that demand for recreational woodland near to city centres in such industrialized societies may lead to renewed contemporary pressures for such an inner woodland zone, albeit for very different reasons to those which gave rise to it in 19th-century Mecklenburg. Gottman (1961) suggests that this may be the case around the intensely urbanized areas of the eastern seaboard of the USA. Again, there is evidence that in currently less technically advanced societies, such a zone may persist for similar reasons to those which held in 19th-century Mecklenburg: Waibel (1958) points out such an arrangement in South East Brazil (cited in Haggett 1966, p. 167).

Of more importance than the content of particular zones at different times and in different places are the principles underlying concentric zone formation. In this context the crucial issue is the assumptions which underlie von Thünen's model. These relate both to the environment and to the principles governing land use allocation. He made six major assumptions. First, he assumed the existence of an 'Isolated State', a discrete entity cut off from the rest of the world and surrounded on all sides by waste. Second, this 'Isolated State' is dominated by a single city which provides the sole market for agricultural commodities and the sole supply of industrial commodities; by implication the economic rent (see below) yielded by urban land use exceeds that from agriculture – to this extent the principles enunciated by von Thünen as governing land use allocation have a more general significance than merely in the agricultural sector. Third, there is an established system of exchange of agricultural for industrial commodities between rural and urban dwellers. These second and third assumptions imply a particular pattern of social relationships governing production and exchange, a particular social division of labour, and a particular level of technological attainment. From the point of view of land use, they presuppose the conversion of land in its 'natural' state or in agricultural use to urban use. Fourth, the State is located on an isotropic plain: both fertility and transport costs are everywhere equal, so that production costs (other than those of transport) for a given commodity are everywhere equal, while transport costs for a commodity are simply proportional to distance. Fifth, farmers transport their own goods to market on a dense system of routes which converge on the central city; thus transport costs are seen as a necessary cost of production. Finally, farmers act so as to maximize profit, automatically (and, implicitly, instantaneously) adjusting output to demand changes in a market which is perfectly competitive. It is this latter mechanism (which again presupposes a particular pattern of social relationships) which is in fact decisive in allocating land uses to given locations.

In the context of land use allocation it has been suggested that the key concept in von Thünen's formulation is that of locational or economic rent. Chisholm (1973, pp. 21–6) sketches out the nature of economic rent and illustrates its impact on land use patterns in relation to competitive bidding for locations. He argues that the concept of economic rent underlies all questions of competition for the use of land and, in addition, provides the means to resolve this competition into patterns of land use; thus, in a limited sense, such a conceptualization offers some understanding of why land use changes occur. In Ricardian terms, economic rent is the return that can be obtained from a particular piece of land over and above that which can be obtained at the margin of economic cultivation. Imagine a town in which the demand for wheat is met by cultivating only the best quality (grade A) surrounding land. Suppose this yields 2 tonnes of wheat per hectare. However, the population of the town expands and demand for wheat rises. It is necessary to convert additional non-agricultural land to agricultural use in order to produce this extra wheat on poorer quality (grade B) land, yielding only 1.5 tonnes per hectare; however, this requires production costs per unit area identical to grade A land. Farmers cultivating the poorer land thus receive 0.5 tonnes of wheat per hectare less than those on the better land, for an identical outlay. It is thus worth their while to offer up to 0.5 tonnes of wheat per year (assuming an annual harvest) for the property rights to a hectare of grade A land, this being the surplus product which arises because of soil fertility differences.

Now suppose a single landlord owns all the farming land. It is in the interests of tenant farmers on poorer land to offer, say, 0.25 tonnes per hectare in order to be able to farm grade A land. Their yield per hectare will rise to 2 tonnes, of which they retain 1.75, leaving them 0.25 tonnes per hectare better off than when farming with grade B land. However, farmers displaced from grade A to grade B find themselves 0.5 tonnes per hectare worse off: indeed, it is in their interests to bid up to 0.5 tonnes per hectare to retain use of grade A land. At this figure, farmers on both grades of land get the same net return for the same inputs. The surplus which accrues as a result of soil fertility differences is taken by the landlord. The economic rent of grade A is 0.5 tonnes per hectare and that of grade B land zero.

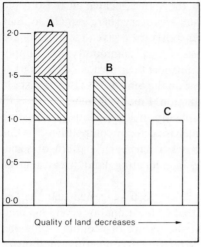

Left
Figure 7.2 Economic rent for a single crop and the quality of land.

Below left
Figure 7.3 Economic rent for a single crop and distance.

Below right
Figure 7.4 Economic rent and land use change.

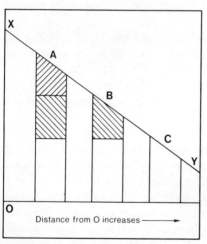

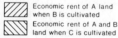

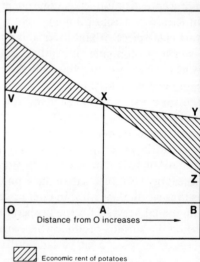

But suppose that further population growth occurs and demand for wheat rises further. All grade B land becomes cultivated and it is necessary to push grade C land into use, yielding only 1 tonne per hectare. Assuming identical production costs on all three grades of land, grade B land now has an economic rent of 0.5 tonnes per hectare while that of grade A land rises to 1.0 tonne per hectare (fig. 7.2).

While economic rent in this example arises as a result of naturally occurring fertility differences, it can also arise as a consequence of differences in the prices of inputs to the production process, including transport costs. As distance from market increases and transport cost rises, assuming a given market price, equal costs of inputs and yields per unit area, the return to the farmer from the production of a particular crop falls with increasing distance from market (fig. 7.3). This declining return is shown by the slope of line XY in fig. 7.3. The shaded portions of the columns indicate the levels of economic rent at A and B if the next most distant location is cultivated. As such, under assumptions of a perfectly competitive allocative system, these represent the limiting amounts that a farmer would pay to retain use of the land he farms.

So far only one crop has been considered but it is a simple matter to extend consideration to the case of two (or more) crops, each yielding a particular level of economic rent in differing locations. A simple (hypothetical) example might involve the cultivation of wheat and potatoes (fig. 7.4). In this case, the shaded area WXV represents the level of economic rent of potatoes in relation to wheat, YXZ that of wheat with respect to potatoes. Wheat is therefore grown between B and A, potatoes between A and 0. Rotating this line through 360° about a central town yields an inner ring of potato cultivation, enclosed by one of wheat cultivation. Given the assumptions which von Thünen made, this geometrical arrangement arises for two reasons: first, the unit price which potatoes can command in the central market exceeds that of wheat; second, unit transport costs rise more rapidly with distance from the market for potatoes than for wheat. Thus potatoes bring higher returns in the zone immediately adjacent to the market; however, this advantage is eroded with increasing distance and additional transport cost until the returns from wheat rise above those from potatoes.

More formally, economic (or locational) rent may be defined as follows:

$$E = Y(p - a) - Y.f.k.$$

where E is the economic rent, k the distance, Y the crop yield per unit area, p the market price per unit of commodity, a the production cost (excluding transport) per unit commodity, and f the transport cost per commodity per unit distance.

Lösch (1954, pp. 38–48) has argued that ring formation was not inevitable, even accepting the six assumptions which von Thünen made in deriving concentric land use zones and also such a definition of economic rent. He argued that for a pair of crops (i and j) there are 17 possible combinations in which one or other crop predominated or both were grown side by side, and only 10 in which rings were formed. Ring formation necessitates that certain conditions held which, considered simply and intuitively, guaranteed that the economic rent levels for the two crops intersect at some point away from the market (as shown in fig. 7.4). More generally, perhaps the clearest formal statement of the conditions that must hold for concentric land use rings to form is that by Stevens (1968), who recast von Thünen's model in a linear programming framework (see p. 206). One may conclude that the assumptions upon which such formal analyses depend were implicit in von Thünen's own analysis.

Clearly a key element in determining economic rent levels for different crops over space is that of the costs and ease of transport. Certain crops tend to be more expensive to transport than are others. Some of them are crops which have a relatively low value in relation to unit volume or weight. Others are crops which deteriorate or perish rapidly and for which time to market may be crucial. Although historically the relative costs of transport have been reduced as a result of technological progress (often with spectacular impacts on agricultural location patterns, as in the case of refrigeration), differences remain in the ease and costs of transport of different agricultural commodities.

Testing the validity and generalizing the land use patterns of the 'Isolated State'

A problem with attempting to assess the empirical validity of von Thünen's

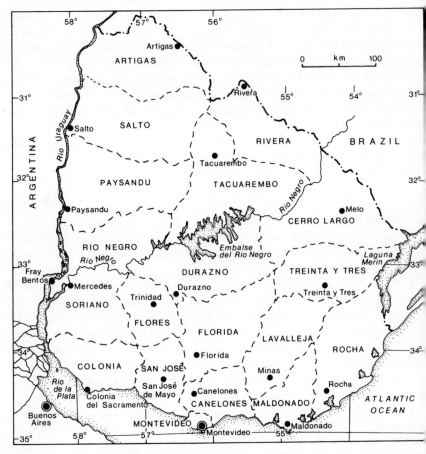

Figure 7.5   Uruguay: departmental boundaries.

concentric zone model is that this geometric arrangement depends upon a set of assumptions which, by definition and design, drastically simplify real world conditions. However, in some parts of the world these assumptions are more closely approximated than others. Griffin (1973) suggests that Uruguay's physical and cultural landscape is sufficiently uniform to serve as a test site for von Thünen's model (fig. 7.5).

Even so, Griffin notes that in two important respects the assumptions made by von Thünen are violated in Uruguay and therefore one might expect a rather more complex agricultural land use pattern than simple concentric zones. This is because both better soils and a more comprehensive transport system are to be found in the west of Uruguay and these might be expected to

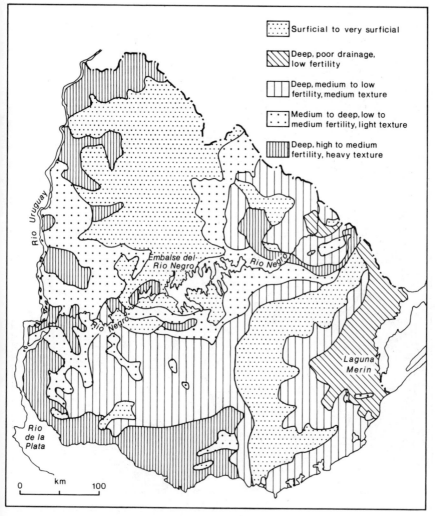

Figure 7.6 Uruguay: soil types.

attract the more intensive agricultural land uses (figs 7.6 and 7.7). Recognizing this and using information as to the actual areas dedicated to horticulture and truck farming, dairying, cereals, and stock raising, a modified model based upon the principles of von Thünen's original formulation can be constructed.

Griffin suggests that if, subject to the above assumptions, Uruguay was a perfect example of an isolated state, Montevideo (the capital city) would be surrounded by four arcs of decreasing land use intensity (fig. 7.8). In the first zone, covering 5% of the national territory, the city would be enclosed by an arc of horticultural production and truck farming, extending from southern

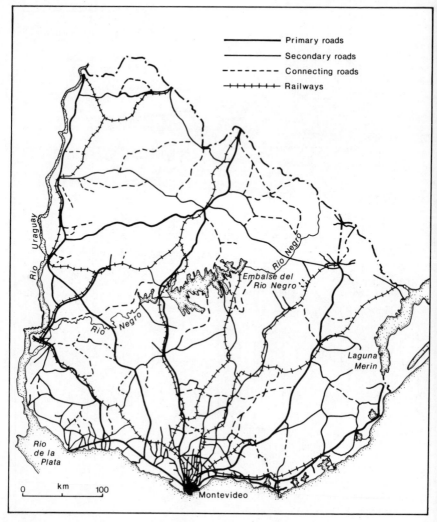

Figure 7.7   Uruguay: transport networks.

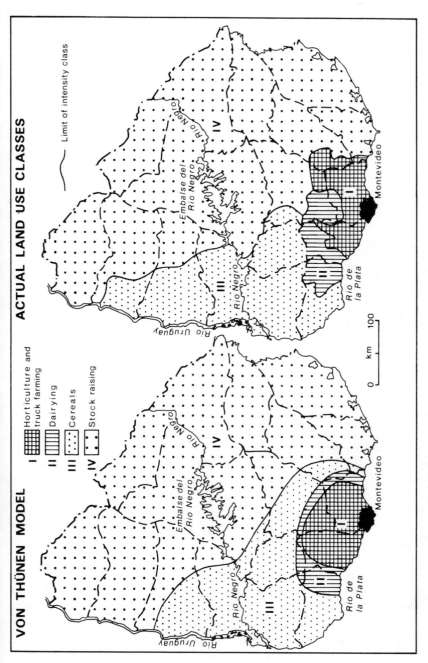

Figure 7.8 Uruguay: agricultural land use classification.

157

Canelones through Florida and much of San José. Next would be a dairying zone, to supply the Montevideo market. Production of bulkier, more perishable fluid milk products would be located on the southern edge of this zone; cheese and other milk products more able to withstand transport costs would be located on the northern fringe. This zone would extend from eastern Canelones and western Maldonado through southern Lavelleja and Florida and into western San José, southern Flores and Soriano, and eastern Colonia. The third zone would be a cereals region, stretching from south-eastern Canelones and western Maldonado north west into Paysandu, including an area of cereals production nearest Montevideo and cereals – livestock combinations along its outer margin. The final zone, occupying the northern and eastern two-thirds of the country, would be devoted to stock rearing; the more intensive ranching systems would be located in the inner parts of this zone, the more extensive towards the periphery.

Griffin then goes on to compare this model with the actual agricultural land use pattern in Uruguay (fig. 7.8). He concludes that, in general, the model agrees well with the actual intensity of land use and the location of different crops and that someone ignorant of the agricultural land use distribution in Uruguay would be greatly enlightened by studying the model as to how agricultural land use varies spatially over the country. He notes, however, a much better correspondence between expected and actual land use patterns in western than in eastern Uruguay.

Griffin then proceeds to examine more closely the relationship between actual and expected patterns, employing a more detailed land-use classification based upon crop–livestock combinations and intensity of production, yielding seven areal classes (fig. 7.9). In order of decreasing intensity of land use these are: orchard and vineyards; intensive crop production; dairying; cereals; cereals and livestock; cattle grazing; extensive sheep grazing. At this level of disaggregation, there continues to be some agreement between the actual land use pattern and that of the model, but significant deviations occur.

The locations of orchard and vineyard and intensive crop production continue to conform with those expected on the basis of von Thünen's model, while Griffin suggests that the location of dairying can probably be attributed to variations in transport efficiency. For the rest, land use seems largely unrelated to location. Thus, even considering differences in fertility and accessibility, the land use distribution is difficult to explain solely in terms of von Thünen's principles. Griffin goes on to suggest various factors which might be responsible for these discrepancies (a theme we take up more generally in chapter 9). For the moment, we simply note his conclusion that while von Thünen's land use model may be valid and useful up to a certain level of generalization, with a more detailed land use classification it breaks down. The level at which it breaks down depends (*inter alia*) upon decisions as to the level of disaggregation at which land use data are collected or, conversely, are available (see p. 30). As Griffin puts it, aggregation of seven land use classes into four masks profound differences in the location of

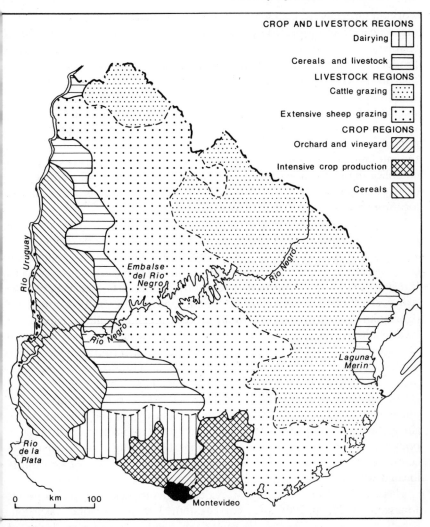

Figure 7.9 Uruguay: agricultural land use regions.

various activities with respect to intensity and distances from market. This serves to exemplify a more general point and to raise questions concerning the basis for choosing a particular classificatory system and the subsequent impact of this choice upon analysis (a point discussed more fully earlier pp. 33–48).

Further generalization of von Thünen's model

In this section we explore various ways of relaxing the assumptions made by von Thünen, while remaining *within* the general framework of variations in economic rent and profit maximization as the determining factors underlying land use patterns. Thus this section develops the point illustrated by Griffin's work on Uruguay. Relaxing other assumptions challenges the validity of the theoretical structure erected by von Thünen and these we consider below (see chapters 9 and 10). In essence, relaxing the assumptions considered here produces more complicated land use patterns than simple concentric circles, but the processes, while their manifestation becomes more complicated, remain at root those assumed by von Thünen.

First, one can relax the assumption of only a single nodal point and admit the existence of other market towns. Von Thünen himself considered the impact of a subsidiary city on the geometry of production zones. In practice, the intermingling of the production zones of different towns is the rule, a complicating factor in empirical analyses of such zones: such a situation is clearly demonstrated by Rutherford *et al.* (1966) in an analysis of agricultural location patterns in New South Wales, Australia.

Second, consider the effect of the long-period reduction in the real cost of transport on agricultural location patterns. Related to the development of world markets for agricultural commodities, the combination of technological progress and the scale economies of mass movement have reduced transport costs as a proportion of total production costs. For example, the real cost of ocean shipping fell by almost 60% between 1876 and 1955 (Chisholm 1973, pp. 163–4). As transport costs fall, one would anticipate that locational specialization in agricultural production would increase: Taafe and Gauthier (1973, pp. 34–6) have devised a simple descriptive model which relates agricultural land use change and regional specialization to improvements in transport linkages and the successive integration of initially isolated regions into national and international markets. As a corollary of this process, one would anticipate that land use rings would expand, and in relation to a single state, that peripheral land use zones might be displaced outside the state boundaries. Furthermore, rather than a single town being the regional market centre for the products of such zones, a group of towns (not necessarily located within a single state) might come to function as the market.

There is a substantial body of evidence to support such propositions. Jonasson (1925, p. 290) sees northwestern Europe as 'one vast conurbation . . . one vast geographic centre' and mapping the average decline of yield of eight crops from this centre (fig. 7.10) lends support to this notion. Related to the emergence of this centre, Peet (1969, 1972) has examined both the global expansion of commercial agriculture in the 19th century and the effect of the growth of demand for imported food in Britain in the 18th and 19th centuries on agricultural patterns in continental Europe. Prior to the development of the railways, agricultural production was mainly organized in relation to regional (rather than national and international) markets and perishable commodities were supplied on a local or perhaps national basis. However, Peet identifies a source zone for imports of semi-perishable foodstuffs which developed on the coastal fringes of the English Channel and southern North Sea in response to the opportunity for comparatively rapid and cheap movement of agricultural commodities to English coastal markets.

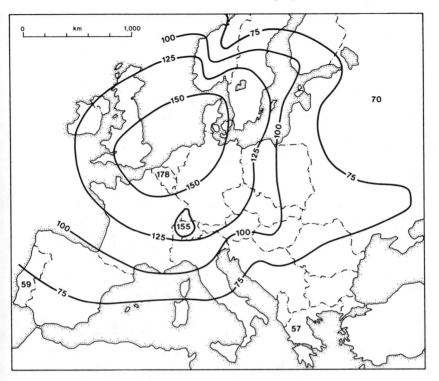

Figure 7.10 Intensity of agricultural production in Europe.

One consequence of the emergence of this pattern of production and trade was a proliferation of smaller ports on the North Sea and Baltic coasts, drawing on hinterlands of some 30 to 50 km. For non-perishable commodities, transport cost also became the dominant determinant of the location of production. By the 1860s von Thünen rings were visible on an international scale: inner northwestern Europe and the northeast United States supplied market-garden and dairy produce; southeast Europe, the Ukraine and the USA midwest supplied grain; the west of the USA, Argentina, South Africa, Australia and New Zealand supplied wool, hides and meat (table 7.2).

This global expansion of agricultural land use zones was made possible by transport improvements, notably by advances in ocean-going shipping. Analogies may be observed between this process of successive outward expansion of agricultural land use zones and Burgess' suggestions as to the processes of growth of urban areas (see p. 173).

Third, it is possible to relax the assumption that transport costs rise as a linear function of distance and, related to this, that transport to market is undertaken by the farmer. Von Thünen considered both the effects of relaxing the assumption of equal ease of movement in all directions (and thus of transport cost as a simple linear function of distance) and also the effects of this upon the geometry of his concentric zone model (fig. 7.11). In practice,

Table 7.2 Average distance (km from London) over which agricultural imports to Britain moved, 1831–1913.

Imports	1831–35	1856–60	1871–75	1891–95	1901–13
Fruit and vegetables	0	518	535	1,140	3,008
Live animals	0	1,008	1,392	5,648	7,200
Butter, cheese, eggs, etc.	419	848	2,144	2,576	4,992
Feed grains	1,376	3,248	3,888	5,184	7,728
Flax and seeds	3,432	5,200	4,432	6,528	6,240
Meat and tallow	3,200	4,640	5,984	8,080	10,000
Wheat and flour	3,880	3,472	6,720	8,240	9,520
Wool and hides	3,680	14,128	16,000	17,616	17,440
Weighted average for all above imports	2,912	5,840	6,880	8,080	9,408

Source: Peet (1969, p. 295).

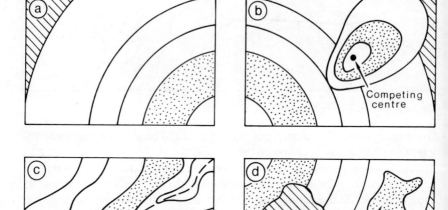

Figure 7.11 Distortions of the regular annular structure
  a of the von Thünen landscape, and
  b by a second competing centre;
  c alternative transport routes, and
  d areas of differing productivity.

there is considerable evidence that transport cost is not related to distance in any simple way but rather that transport cost–distance relationships are complex (for a comprehensive review of this, see Locklin 1966). Indeed, Griffin's work in Uruguay also pointed to this conclusion. Again, Alexander

(1944) provides evidence of directional variations in transport cost in the USA, in areas near to Milwaukee and Chicago. He has mapped the pattern of railway freight rates for grain and for livestock moved to Chicago (fig. 7.12). In c and d maps the contour interval is 2 cents per 45.45 kg (100 lb); areas over 13 cents are stippled in the case of grain, those over 18 cents in the case of livestock. Given these rate structures and considering two points equidistant from Chicago (β) in physical terms, the locational advantage with respect to alternative land uses is markedly different – γ has a locational advantage in livestock production, δ in grain production. These distortions of simple transport cost–distance relationships reflect the fact that, in general, transport to market is not the responsibility of farmers aiming to minimize their transport costs but rather that of transport companies, inherently monopolistic in their operations because of the unique characteristics of

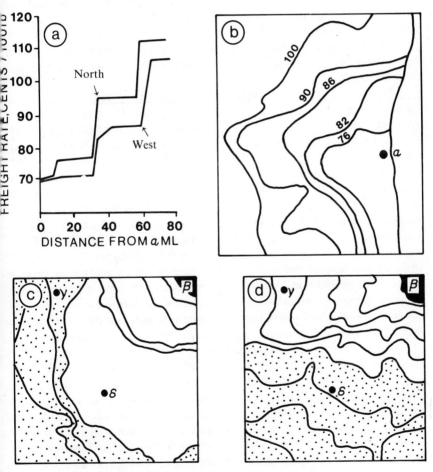

Figure 7.12 Directional variations in railway freight costs in selected areas of the USA: West of Milwaukee (a, b); Southwest of Chicago (c, d).

locations. In the case of private companies they may be more concerned to maximize their revenues, and, perhaps, in the case of State companies, to minimize total movement within an economy, rather than with minimizing the costs of movement of particular individuals.

A fourth assumption that can easily be relaxed is that of equal soil fertility. Again, von Thünen was aware of the practical implausibility of this assumption and that land use patterns are affected by differences in soil fertility, parent materials, relief, climate and related factors, as well as by transport costs, and he considered the effects of such differences on his concentric zone model (fig. 7.11). Again, there is considerable empirical evidence of the relationship between soil type and land use. For example, Griffin demonstrated a relationship between soil type and land use in Uruguay. Hidore (1963) has shown a moderate positive correlation ($r = +0.65$) between flat land, defined as slopes of less than $3°$, and the production of grain as a cash crop in a sample of 730 counties in the north central USA. It is possible that, with the erosion of transport costs as a proportion of total production costs, what we might term the natural resource endowment has come to have a progressively greater impact on agricultural land use patterns.

A further way in which a simple concentric pattern of land use is altered is by recognizing that production costs for a crop can also vary spatially as a result of using different methods of production. This can operate in two ways. One is that the method of production for a single crop can change between locations, thereby varying the non-transport element of production cost. However, if such changes are confined to within a zone, a point is reached at which economic rent is raised more by switching to another land use (or falls to zero at the margin), thus avoiding disturbing the geometry of concentric rings. A related point is that the nearer one approaches to market, the greater is the intensity of agricultural production. Von Thünen himself identified such adjustments in farming systems, showing that rye could be profitably grown at different locations at different distances from the urban market by varying methods of production. As distance increased, unit production costs are lowered by raising the portion of land left fallow. In the innermost part of the rye zone, no land is left fallow but in the outermost part, one third is left fallow each year (table 7.1). A more contemporary example is provided by Gottman (1961, p. 286). He compares the dairy farming zones of the Atlantic coast of the USA around the Boston–New York–Washington urban area with those of the Wisconsin zone in the Midwest. The former represents, in terms of von Thünen's analysis, part of an intensive inner zone, the latter a part of a more extensive outer zone. Although farms are about the same size in both areas and yields per animal are similar, the production systems in the two areas differ sharply. In the Atlantic coast zone, stocks per acre and investment in machinery are 40% higher, returns are 60% higher and the per unit output of milk and investment in land and buildings is 80% higher. In terms of land use 30% more hay is grown in the inner zone and correspondingly less grains. In part, these contrasts between the two areas reflect the returns to liquid milk as opposed to processed milk (butter, cheese, etc.) to which von Thünen drew attention.

In some circumstances, however, switching between production methods can distort the symmetry of decreasing intensity of production with increasing distance from market. Chisholm (1973, p. 26) identifies two situations in which this may be the case: first, when output per unit area is very large, despite small inputs, and is of low value per unit weight or volume. Such crops are grown near to market. An example of this in von Thünen's time was timber. Second, when large quantities of inputs yield a high value per unit volume product. An example of this would be butter production located at some distance from market. In all these cases, however, the criterion upon which is made the interdependent choice of which commodities to produce and which production system to employ is the same: that of profitability. As Lösch (1954, p. 51) noted: 'total profits are decisive; there is no additional criterion for individual crops.' If we accept this viewpoint, then it is quite consistent to produce the same crop in different locations with different production systems.

A final factor which can distort a simple pattern of concentric land use rings is to admit the existence of scale economies and their impact on agricultural land use patterns. As agriculture has become more industrialized, organized around bigger and more capital-intensive units, the importance of scale economies in shaping agricultural location patterns might be expected to increase. In addition to internal economies at the individual farm level, external economies also operate at the regional scale to affect agricultural land use patterns. Harvey (1963) demonstrated the importance of such economies, especially in relation to information about rapidly changing market conditions, in explaining the evolution of the Kentish hop industry. Chisholm (1973, p. 168) has demonstrated the importance of external scale economies with respect to Californian agriculture. Helped by favourable climatic conditions, California quickly became a major supplier of citrus fruits for the northeast of the USA. The scale of production and shipment enabled favourable rates to be negotiated with railway companies for shipping the fruit to market and enabled Californian producers to undercut those from smaller but physically nearer areas such as Florida. This advantage has subsequently been eroded by the development of motorized road transport since scale economies are of less significance in this mode of transport. This has enabled producers in Florida to compete once more with those from California. Finally, standardized marketing is becoming increasingly common as agriculture becomes industrialized in the capitalist world and this may lead to further development of concentrated production of particular crops on a regional scale. Haggett *et al.* (1977, p. 219) suggest that, in fact, such an explanation may well be appropriate to certain existing concentrations of agricultural production, such as rhubarb cultivation in the West Riding of Yorkshire.

Further evidence of concentric zones and an alternative explanation

Von Thünen argued that the concentric zone pattern would be found at the scale of individual farms as well as of regions, precisely because the same principles would operate at the two spatial scales. In addition to evidence supporting the presence of concentric ring arrangements at international, national and regional scales, a considerable body of empirical evidence has accumulated which suggests that such patterns are commonly found at farm or village level. Moreover, several of these examples are drawn from societies where the social processes of land use sorting via differential economic rent are patently inapplicable.

Prothero (cited in Haggett 1975, pp. 390–1) describes such a zoning pattern around a village in northern Nigeria. He identifies four zones. First, an inner garden zone of close interplanting, a continuous crop sequence, and intensive care. Second, a zone extending from 0.8 to 1.2 km from the village which is continuously cultivated (mainly with Guinea corn, cotton, tobacco and groundnuts) and fertilized. Third, a zone with an outer boundary at 1.6 km, which is used for rotation farming, the land being cultivated for 3 to 4 years then left to return to bush for at least 5 years to regain its fertility. Fourth, a zone of heavy bush within which there are isolated clearings, the three zones sequence being repeated in each of these.

Chisholm (1973, pp. 49–66; 1979, pp. 45–59) also cites a number of examples of zoning at this scale in countries as diverse as Bulgaria, Finland, Ghana, India, the Netherlands, Spain, Sweden and the USSR. Despite the variety of settings from which these examples are drawn, there is a tendency for inputs of both labour and fertilizer to decrease beyond a seemingly critical distance of 1 km from the farm or village.

One of the more interesting and better documented of such cases is that of land use around the Sicilian village of Canicatti (fig. 7.13). This considers the relationship between distance from the village centre and cultivation of three types of crops: vines; olives; unirrigated arable crops. Within the area considered, vines were grown on less than 6% of the area, being particularly concentrated within 4 km of the centre. Olives were predominantly grown in the zone between 2 and 6 km from the centre while unirrigated wheat dominated the outer zone. However, as the latter crop was grown over half the total area, it was also prominently represented even in those zones nearest to the centre. Other crop types also showed distinctive locational patterns: citrus fruits were characteristic of the inner zones while pasture, waste and coppice wood were concentrated in the outer zones.

An explanation of regularities at this micro-scale is hinted at by Prothero, noted by von Thünen and explicitly spelled out by Chisholm in relation to zoning around Canicatti. Using estimates of annual labour requirements per hectare for various crops, made by the Instituto Nazionale di Economia Agraria in Rome, Chisholm relates the location of crops to their labour requirements (table 7.3). Clearly those crops which are most labour-

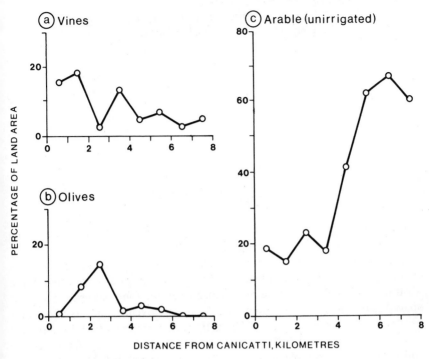

Figure 7.13 Land use in relation to distance from the village centre: Canicatti, Sicily.

Table 7.3 Land use, labour inputs and distance from Canicatti.

Land use type	Vineyards	Olive groves	Unirrigated arable
Average labour input (man-days/ha)	90.0	45.0	35.0
Modal distance from Canicatti (km)	1.5	2.5	6.5

Source: Chisholm (1962, p. 63).

demanding are, on average, grown nearest to the centre. Even for a given crop, there is some evidence that less labour-intensive methods are used as distance from the centre increases.

Similar considerations influence the behaviour of 'suitcase farmers' in Sully County, South Dakota, USA (Kollmorgen and Jenks 1958). These are farmers who reside more than 30 miles from the border of the county in which their farmland is located. Such farmers tend to devote a much larger proportion of their generally smaller farms to cash crops (table 7.4). The farms of 'suitcase farmers' are thus distinguished as areas of wheat production in counties in which the dominant local agricultural pattern is one

Table 7.4 Land use in Sully County (in 1950) in relation to the residential location of farm operators.

	Local farmers	Suitcase farmers
Average farm size (ha)	518	295
% of farm area		
cash crops	14	60
feed crops	25	21
livestock	56	11

Source: Kollmorgen and Jenks (1958, p. 34).

of diversified crop and livestock production, two-thirds of the land area being devoted to pasture and feed crops.

Consideration of this and other evidence (such as that cited previously in this chapter) led Haggett (1966, pp. 161–5) to attempt a more general and abstract explanation of these recurrent concentric zone patterns at various spatial scales, in terms of minimizing the total movement inputs needed for production of various crops (see Haggett *et al.* 1977, pp. 200–4, for a refined restatement upon which the following summary is based). Consider the following simple example, involving three land use activities (1, 2 and 3) each with their own distinctive characteristics (table 7.5): area of production (A_i); weight of production per unit area (W_i); unit transport cost to move the product of each land use type (C_i); movement resistance (r_i), defined as W_i multiplied by C_i. Assuming a circular land use pattern, the cost of movement (H) at the outer margin of the circle for each land use type may be estimated as:

$$H(d_{max}) = W_i.C_i.d_{max}(A_i), i = 1, 2, \ldots, n.$$

In fig. 7.14a, these weighted costs (H) are plotted independently on the y-axis as a function of distance on the x-axis.

Assuming that the same plot of land cannot be used simultaneously for more than one crop, then the total crop area required is 600 km² and the corresponding d_{max} is 13.82 km (table 7.5). Two issues remain to be resolved: first, will the three land uses form discrete concentric rings about the centre?; second, if they will, what will be the sequence of land uses? Since there are $N!$ possible arrangements of N land use types, in this case there are six possible zonal sequences: 123; 132; 213; 231; 312; 321. The *total* effort, in terms of weighted movement costs, associated with each of these is shown graphically as a cross-section by the shaded areas in fig. 4.14b. More formally, this may be defined as:

$$H = \int_{\Sigma A_i} A_i.W_i.C_i.d_j, \quad i = 1, 2, 3,$$

Table 7.5 Derivation of net movement inputs.

Land use activities	Area required, $A_i (km^2)$	Max. radius, d_{max} (km)	Weight, W_i $(tonnes/km^2)$	Cost of movement, C_i $(unit/tonne)$	Movement resistance, r_i	Net movement inputs at radius $H (d_{max})$
Type 1	100	5.64	3	1.0	3.0	16.92
Type 2	200	7.98	2	0.5	1.0	7.98
Type 3	300	9.77	1	2.0	2.0	19.54
All types	600	13.82	—	—	—	—

Sources: Haggett (1966, p. 162).
Haggett *et al.* (1977, p. 201).

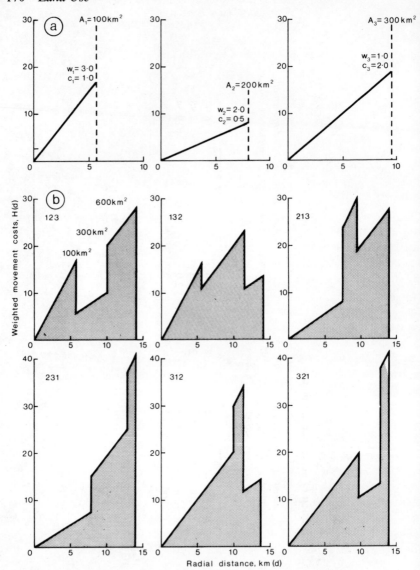

Figure 7.14 Stages in the analysis of hypothetical movement inputs for land uses.

where j is the location of the jth point within a circle with an area equivalent to 600 km² (of the areas A_1, A_2, A_3) and focused upon a section through 360°. On this basis, the minimum movement solution is given by the sequence 132. This places crop 1 nearest the centre (since it has the greatest movement resistance value: table 7.5) and crop 2 furthest from the centre (this having the least movement resistance).

Concluding remarks

We began this chapter by considering von Thünen's model of the 'Isolated State' and the theoretical framework from which this agricultural land use model arose. A number of studies were briefly discussed which demonstrated that, in certain circumstances, this model retains considerable value in helping to account for agricultural location patterns. However, the theoretical account it offers is based upon certain historically specific premises concerning the processes which govern agricultural location patterns. A further complication is that there is evidence (in addition to that cited above, see, for example, Horvath 1969) that even when these postulated processes are not dominant, concentric land use patterns may still be observed – to borrow Harvey's (1969) terminology, the model is over-identified.

Recognizing the historically specific character of the processes invoked by von Thünen, Haggett suggested a solution to the dilemma posed by the historically limited character of the land use allocation process central to von Thünen's model. Reflecting the locational analysis approach to understanding spatial patterns, which rose to prominence in North American and British geography in the 1960s, this involved constructing a general explanation of concentric agricultural land use zones in categories which abstract from and cut across particular social relationships which govern agricultural production. Haggett (1966, p. 165) makes this quite explicit with respect to his own formulation and that of von Thünen: 'Our concept of movement input is perhaps simpler in that it avoids specific consideration of market and production constants, p and a, and substitutes for them assumptions about the demand for products in terms of area (A).'

More recently, however, the aim of producing general theory of this sort has come under attack, precisely because of its high level of abstraction and deliberate neglect of the specific social relationships that underlie land use patterns. This issue we take up in chapter 10. For the moment, however, it seems reasonable to conclude that an explanation of concentric agricultural land use zones in terms of minimizing movement inputs is perhaps most appropriate when applied to societies possessing simple technology and in which small scale subsistence production rather than large scale production for a market continues to hold a decisive position.

8 Models of urban land use

Introduction

There is a well-developed intellectual tradition of studying urban land use patterns, in part a reflection of the increasing importance assumed by urban areas in social and economic affairs in the last two centuries. Moreover, cities form relatively easily identifiable and mappable units for some of which a flood of comparatively uniform data have been available for the last century and a half (Haggett *et al.* 1977, p. 8) – in some, if not all, of the world. Thomas Milne, for example, produced a land use map of London in 1800, using seventeen land use categories (Hodgkiss 1977, p. 110). In some senses, therefore, the patchy nature of urban data has rendered it more suitable for intellectual modelling exercises than for very practical purposes: we have already seen (p. 8) that Best, Coppock and others have bemoaned the lack of comprehensive data for urban areas.

A number of models have been proposed which attempt to describe and account for intra-urban land use patterns. Perhaps reflecting the complexity and variety of forces at work shaping these patterns, such models of urban land use have arisen in a variety of social science disciplines; sociologists, economists and human geographers have all contributed to attempts to answer vexed questions concerning urban land use patterns, perceiving these from their own particular disciplinary standpoints. More recently, approaches to urban land use patterns have been developed which cut across and challenge these conventional disciplinary boundaries.

While heterogeneous in respect of their disciplinary origins, there are also certain unifying influences at work which provide common threads linking the various, older models. Particularly important in initial attempts to understand urban socio-spatial structure was the context of cities in the USA in and before the inter-war period. For it was from empirical studies of these cities that the pioneering models of urban land use were developed. This context was to have a profound impact on subsequent attempts to understand urban patterns in other historical, cultural and spatial settings.

In this chapter, we seek briefly to review the various 'general' models of urban land use structure which have been suggested, critically examining both their conceptual basis and empirical fit in various contexts (for a much fuller review see Johnston 1971). Leading on from this, we consider more recent attempts to understand urban socio-spatial structure, which have arisen in response to critiques of the models proposed by people such as Burgess (1925), Hoyt (1939) and Harris and Ullman (1945). In addition to these 'general' models of urban land use, models have also been developed of the location of one particular land use within cities. We conclude by examining one such type of 'partial' model – models of intra-urban retail location.

Burgess' concentric zone model

The central thesis embodied in Burgess' (1925) model is that urban land use patterns conform to a concentric zonal pattern. He conceptualized urban areas in terms of five rings of different types of land use (fig. 8.1). First, the most central area of the city is occupied by the central business district (CBD), the focal point of commercial, civic and social life in the city. Within this area are to be found the main shops and offices. Transport routes converge on the CBD which is thus the most accessible location within the urban area. The second zone is the transition zone, an area characterized by blighted conditions and the penetration of commercial and industrial uses into residential areas. This is the area of lowest residential quality, inhabited by immigrant groups and those most disadvantaged and powerless. The remaining three rings are purely residential, the quality of residential areas increasing with distance from the centre of the city, in response to the

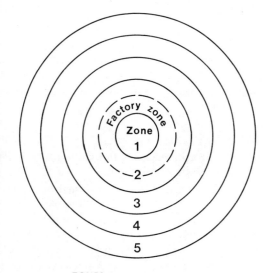

ZONES
1 Central Business District
2 Zone in transition
3 Zone of working men's homes
4 Residential zone
5 Commuters' zone

Figure 8.1 Burgess'
Concentric Zone Model.

differential ability of groups of people to be able to afford the cost of travel to work. In order of increasing distance from the CBD these zones are: multiple-occupancy working-class housing; single-family dwelling; and, finally, a peripheral zone with both suburban areas and satellite towns.

Burgess' model thus represents an extremely simple representation of urban land use patterns; in essence, an ideal-typical model of land use and also of urban socio-spatial structure. Moreover, it is a model which links with some conception of process and land use change, both in terms of the internal structure of cities and the conversion of rural land to urban use. Reflecting his association with the human ecology approach to the study of urban areas, Burgess postulated that the concentric circle structure reflected the annular expansion of urban areas via a progressive movement outwards of commerce, industry and people, the successive invasion of particular areas by differing activities and groups of people. While prepared to concede that the form of the concentric zone pattern might be altered in particular cases by transport routes or terrain, he nevertheless maintained that the basic logic of growth as a result of colonization of successive outer rings would remain valid. This conception of the processes governing urban growth and land use allocation and structure, particularly the 'sub-social' process of competition for location, is based upon analogy with succession in plant communities.

A number of criticisms can be levelled at Burgess' model. These are comprehensively reviewed by Carter (1976, pp. 175–93). The criticisms can be categorized into three broad types: first, those which reject the conceptualization itself; second, those which extend the conceptualization; and third, those which follow from a deductive reformulation of the model. The first and third are considered below (pp. 180 and 190, respectively), the third being most conveniently dealt with in the context of the relationship between land value, rent and land use. For the present we focus upon the second class of criticisms which are essentially positive in their intent. In essence these amount to attempts to relax some of Burgess' tacit assumptions, introducing new variables into the model or allowing what were previously treated as constants to vary. They are changes which can be incorporated within Burgess' original (partly implicit) conceptualization and without departing from the logic of the original model. One such modification involves replacing the notion of a two-dimensional city with that of a three-dimensional city, thereby giving recognition to the fact that accessibility declines vertically as well as horizontally from the centre (fig. 8.2). A second modification is to recognize that cities do not grow equally in all directions, a point which is considered below in the context of Hoyt's sector model. Related to this, urban expansion does not proceed smoothly by the conversion of agricultural to residential land; rather, the expansion is uneven, involves the conversion of agricultural to non-residential as well as residential uses (see p. 214), and is linked to wider cyclical economic movements (see, for example, Whitehand 1972). A third modification is to recognize that there may be more than one functional centre within a city, Burgess assumed a unicentred city and also,

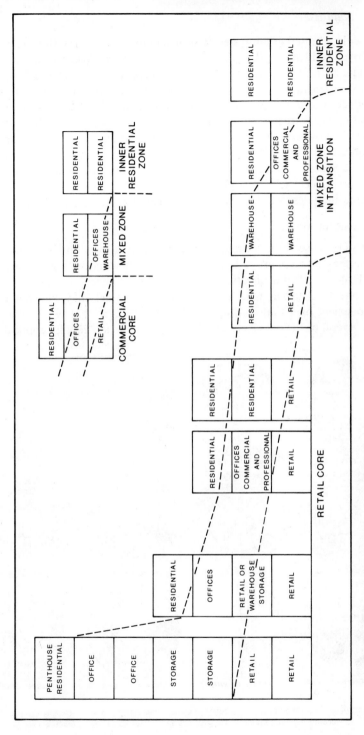

Figure 8.2 The relationship of land use to building height.

175

implicitly, a closed urban system with all employment in the CBD and with all employed residents of the urban area working there. Attempts to introduce consideration of the existence of multiple nuclei are considered below in the context of Harris and Ullman's model. Finally, attempts have been made to introduce a size variant, which raises questions about the nature of the transition from uni- to multi-nuclei forms in the course of urban growth. There is, however, some confusion in this respect in Burgess' original formulation. While on the one hand claiming to describe patterns in the largest USA cities, Burgess' model assumes only one functional centre within urban areas. Yet such an assumption has greatest validity for small towns and is increasingly less valid as urban areas grow larger.

Hoyt's sector model

Hoyt's (1939) sectoral conceptualization of urban form and growth can be seen as a direct response to Burgess' work and the concentric zone model. In that Hoyt specified a directional as well as a distance from the city centre component to urban land use patterns, his model may be seen as an improvement over that of Burgess (Haggett 1966, pp. 178–9). At the same time, several of the criticisms levelled at that model are equally applicable to

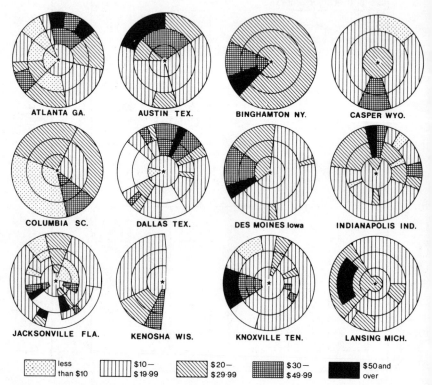

Figure 8.3 Generalized rent patterns in selected US cities.

Hoyt's sector model. For example, on the one hand, what we may call technical criticisms and, on the other, criticisms of lack of universality may be applied as well to Hoyt's as to Burgess' model.

Like Burgess, Hoyt developed his model of urban form and the processes of the development of this form on the basis of evidence taken from quite specific historical circumstances. The empirical basis of Hoyt's conceptualization was detailed historical study of residential rent levels in 25 cities of the USA (fig. 8.3). On the basis of these (*op. cit.* pp. 73–6), he concluded that, despite differences between individual cities,

> there is, nevertheless, a general pattern of rent that applies to all cities. This pattern is not a random distribution. It is not in the form of sharply defined rectangular areas, with blocks in each rental group occupying completely segregated segments. It is not in the form of successive concentric circles . . . . Even when the rental data are put into a framework of concentric circles there is revealed no general gradation upward from the centre to the periphery. From the evidence presented, therefore, it may be concluded that the rent areas in American cities tend to conform to a pattern of sectors rather than of concentric circles. The highest rents of a city tend to be located in one or more sectors of the city. There is a gradation of rentals downwards from these high rental levels in all directions. Intermediate rental areas or those ranking next to the highest rental areas, adjoin the high rent areas on one or more side, and tend to be located in the same sectors as the high rental areas. Low rent areas occupy other entire sectors of the city from the centre to the periphery.

Hoyt's generalized model is shown in diagrammatic form in fig. 8.4.

The quality of the data upon which Hoyt's model was based has never been seriously questioned (Everson and Fitzgerald 1972, p. 36). This point is of some importance when evaluating the relative merits of a sectoral as compared to a concentric zone model, even in the very specific circumstances of the growth of American cities in the early 20th century. A comparison of Burgess' rather subjective description of land use patterns in Chicago with Hoyt's more firmly grounded description of rent patterns (fig. 8.5) suggests considerable disagreement as to the land use pattern within the same city in broadly the same period. Purely on empirical grounds, there are good reasons to prefer Hoyt's version. Note that for the moment we assume what is demonstrated below: namely that land use will reflect, *inter alia*, rents and land values.

If we accept this relationship between land use and rents, the key to understanding the distribution of the former is to account for the sectoral pattern of the latter. Hoyt assumed an initial distribution of types of residential areas around the centre of a growing city. The initial distribution reflected the prior operation of a variety of factors, including chance. In other words, Hoyt assumes away the problem of accounting for this initial

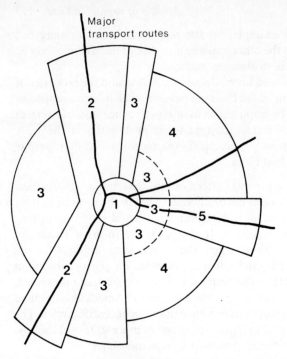

1 Central Business District
2 Wholesale and light manufacturing
3 Low-class residential
4 Medium-class residential
5 High-class residential

Figure 8.4 Hoyt's Sectoral Model.

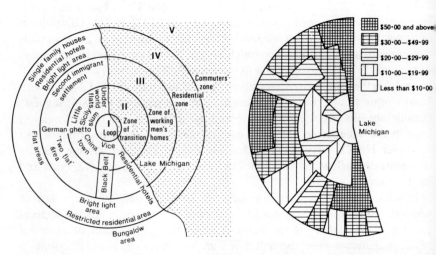

Figure 8.5   Burgess' and Hoyt's models of the urban structure of Chicago.

locational pattern and also (as did Burgess) that of explaining the processes of producing urban growth. This is important in so far as the internal spatial organization of the city reflects those processes which in the first instance produced urban growth (see Aglietta 1978).

Nevertheless, given this initial assumption, Hoyt postulated that land uses will migrate out from the centre in wedges. The key to the evolving land use and rent patterns is the location of the highest status residential area; fig. 8.6 illustrates the changing location of such areas within Boston over the period 1900–36. Hoyt (1939, p. 114) argued that the changing locational pattern of such areas did not skip about at random in the process of movement but rather followed a definite path in one or more sectors of the city. He suggested a number of factors which would influence the location of high status residential areas. Perhaps the most important of these was the location of major arterial routes into the city. In addition, however, several other factors were seen as important in determining the location of such residential areas: waterfronts not used by industry; high ground free from flood danger; open countryside; the houses of community leaders; existing nuclei of buildings or commercial centres; and the operation of real estate promoters.

The last factor is of particular importance because American housing and property markets have been and continue to be usually organized to protect existing areas of high property values and exclude undesirable land uses, such as unsightly or polluting heavy industry, from these and adjacent locations. Property markets in other capitalist countries are similarly organized. Of course, rent levels alone may be sufficient to screen out land uses which are considered undesirable and which would threaten existing property values. Furthermore, there may be advantages in such other activities agglomerating in common locations. The net result of these various processes mediated through and structured by property institutions is a sectoral organization of rents and land use within the city. Hitherto we have assumed that if the organizational processes are structured sectorally, then so will the land use pattern. This is not necessarily so, however, for the resultant land use pattern

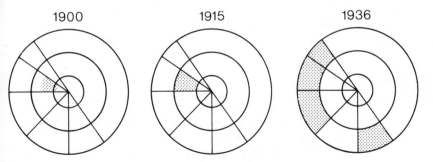

Figure 8.6 The changing location of fashionable residential areas (shaded) in Boston, Massachusetts.

may show evidence of concentric zones, as sectors migrating out leave behind partial zones of homogeneous land use (consider, for example, fig. 8.6).

Mann's fusion of the Burgess and Hoyt models

Taking up the point that sectorally structured processes may still produce partial concentric zonal patterns, Mann (1965) has attempted a fusion of Burgess' and Hoyt's models. While adhering to a unicentred city, he also attempted to modify the resultant model in a way which makes it more appropriate to the historical context of British cities in the post-Second World War period rather than to American cities of the inter-war years (fig. 8.7). For example, Mann's model takes account of State intervention in the provision and location of housing (a point we amplify in chapter 9).

Harris and Ullman's multiple nuclei model

The models of urban land use patterns considered thus far have, despite many

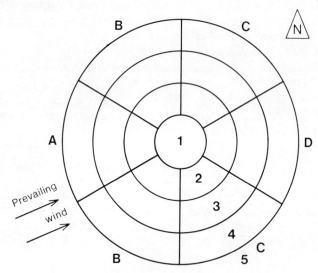

1 Central Business District
2 Transitional zone
3 Zone of small terrace houses in sectors C and D; larger bye-law housing in sector B, large old houses in sector A
4 Post-1918 residential areas, with post-1945 development mainly on the periphery
5 Commuting distance 'dormitory' towns
A Middle-class sector
B Lower-middle class sector
C Working-class sector (and main council estates)
D Industry and lowest working-class sector

Figure 8.7 Mann's model of urban structure.

other differences, shared one feature in common. This is the assumption of a single focal centre for activity in the city. Harris and Ullman (1945) relaxed this assumption. In essence, the model of urban structure which they propose is an amalgam of those of Burgess and Hoyt together with the addition of multiple nuclei (fig. 8.8), which display functional specialization. The presence of such nuclei reflects the internal differentiation of the city in the course of growth. Rather than being located in relation to any general distance or directional variable, these nuclei reflect the effect of the interaction of several variables. Four such variables were specifically identified by Harris and Ullman.

First, certain activities require specialized facilities. For example, high order retail facilities require the most accessible location within the city, a location which may be radically different from the geometrical centre of the

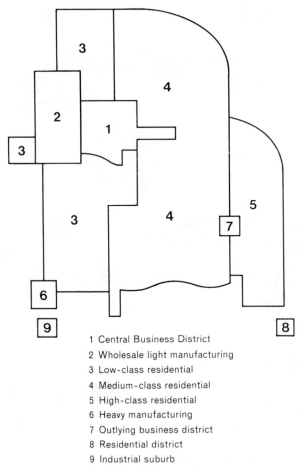

1 Central Business District
2 Wholesale light manufacturing
3 Low-class residential
4 Medium-class residential
5 High-class residential
6 Heavy manufacturing
7 Outlying business district
8 Residential district
9 Industrial suburb

Figure 8.8 Harris and Ullman's Multiple Nuclei Model.

city. Second, some activities group together because they reap benefits from agglomeration. For example, those involved in the legal profession character-istically locate in close proximity to one another; likewise those involved in banking and related activities. Third, some activities repel one another; for example, there are pressures which tend to push heavy industry into areas

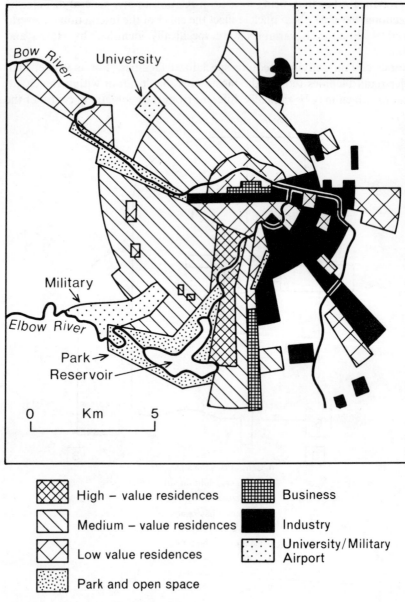

Figure 8.9   The structure of Calgary, 1961.

located away from existing high status residential zones. Fourthly, some activities are unable to afford the rents necessary to occupy the most accessible locations – a point we amplify below.

There is no doubt that, in pointing out that most major cities are multi-nucleate rather than uni-nucleate, Harris and Ullman were doing no more than recognizing a fact of life that is well-known to inhabitants of such cities. Consequently, their model of urban form has been applied with some success to particular cities; for example, Smith (1962) has done so with respect to Calgary (fig. 8.9). Nevertheless, evaluations of the utility of the multiple-nuclei model differ widely. Everson and Fitzgerald (1972, p. 38) make the point that it 'is certainly the most flexible of all the theories and can be fitted to any city'. This is perhaps true but only serves to raise the question of whether the model is so descriptively general as to lack any real explanatory content. Carter (1976, p. 188) hints at this when he concludes that: 'It is based on well-known statements regarding uses and makes no marked contribution to their complex association in area in a location sense.'

Syntheses of the individual models

At different times and in different places, claims have been made as to the validity of the various models discussed above. For example, Blumenfeld (1949) has claimed that a concentric land use pattern was present in Philadelphia; Jones (1960) has argued that the pattern of high status residential areas in Belfast is consistent with the sector model. Each model would thus seem to have a limited descriptive value, to apply in some but certainly not all circumstances. Put another way, one consequence of the changing character of the processes giving rise to land use patterns is that any given pattern, analysed at one point in time, reflects the joint effects of these varying processes. Investment in property and land tends to be written off over relatively long periods and hence there is a certain fixity and inertia in land use patterns.

In preceding sections we have shown how the model proposed by Hoyt arose in reaction to that of Burgess, and that those proposed by Harris and Ullman and Mann essentially combine the Burgess and Hoyt models, while extending these in various ways. In other words, the models are not independent of one another: successive models have arisen in response to those previously formulated. Haggett (1966, pp. 180–1) makes precisely this point. He suggests that the models (specifically, those of Burgess, Hoyt and Harris and Ullman) are not mutually exclusive and that, moreover, one might expect any given urban land use pattern to show traces of the patterns proposed in all three models. Smith (1962), on the basis of a study of Calgary, reached a similar conclusion. Robson (1969) has shown how the northern part of Sunderland displays elements of a concentric zone pattern while the southern part of the town shows evidence of a sectoral pattern, although superimposed upon this are some elements of concentric zoning. Garrison *et al.* (1959, p. 144) had in fact previously made a similar suggestion to that of

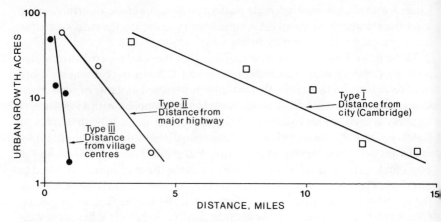

Figure 8.10   Growth – distance relationships in urban conversion of land in southern Cambridgeshire, England.

Haggett in advocating a fused growth model in which growth proceeds concentrically, not only from the main urban centre but also from various sub-centres, and is intersected by a radial growth pushing outwards along transport lines from the main centre. Furthermore, progressive sorting of differing land uses into distinct social, economic and technical zones is envisaged within the model.

Haggett cites evidence from fieldwork around Cambridge (England) by Keeble and himself which suggests that the views of Garrison *et al.* may be correct. This shows that the spread of residential development around Cambridge in the post-1945 period exhibits three distinct gradients (fig. 8.10). First, a gentle gradient around the city centre – in accord with the Burgess model. Second, a steeper gradient along main highways – in accord with the Hoyt model. Third, a still steeper gradient around outlying villages – in line with the Harris and Ullman model. Haggett (1966, p. 181) concludes: 'Clearly all three models, rather than any one are useful in explaining the growth of this land use zone; suggesting that an eclectic rather than selective use of locational models may be the better policy in analysing geographical distributions.'

While in terms of descriptive accuracy Haggett makes a valid point, in terms of analysis and understanding a retreat into eclecticism poses considerable problems. In particular, eclecticism may lead into empiricism and a viewpoint which suggests the total independence of empirical from theoretical investigation. That this danger exists is illustrated in comments made by Gittus (1964, p. 13):

> The former theories and techniques of urban analysis have lost much of their validity. There is need for new emphasis on the variability of urban structure and this involves the need for an empirical rather than a theoretical approach to the situation . . . . It is conceivable that it . . .

might fail, but in view of the impasse that has been reached in this field from the starting point of general theory, it is well worth making.

Indeed, views similar to those expressed by Gittus have attracted considerable support; these are reflected in the numerous factorial ecologies of the socio-spatial structure of urban areas. This is neither the place to review the statistical basis of factorial ecology (for this see King 1969, pp. 165–92) nor to recount in detail the substantive results of such studies (for this see Taylor 1977, pp. 254–84). Such studies have introduced technically more sophisticated methods of describing urban socio-spatial patterns and hence yielded some important insights into these, but empiricism cannot offer a solution to a theoretical impasse. Indeed, it is rather naive to imply that one can measure urban structure without at least some tacit theoretical conceptions concerning this. While theoretical and empirical research remain inseparably related, it is the latter which must be given primacy.

If the theoretical content of existing models is inadequate, then rectification of this weakness necessitates the development of more adequate theory. While more detailed empirical investigation may well be a necessary part of such development, it cannot in itself be sufficient. Everson and Fitzgerald (1972, p. 40) conclude that the various urban models discussed above are useful descriptive tools which describe the land use that can be seen in a city but do not explain the reasons for the growth of these land use patterns. While one might object that this is perhaps too sweeping a dismissal, it is difficult to deny the general point that they make. This suggests the need for more powerful theoretical statements which subsume, within a coherent framework, the variety of urban land use forms suggested by the various models. As a first step in this, we consider more fully the various critiques of these models that have been advanced.

Criticisms of the models

Carter (1976, pp. 175–93) summarizes a number of criticisms which can be levelled at Burgess' model. These can be categorized into three broad types: those which extend the conceptualization, which have been considered above in the discussion of the models suggested by Hoyt, Mann and Harris and Ullman; those which follow from a deductive reformulation of the model which are dealt with in the context of the relationship between land value, bid-rent curves and land use (see p. 191); and those which reject the conceptualization. Many of these latter, however, can be as well applied to the models of Hoyt, Mann and Harris and Ullman, as to that of Burgess. We consider these latter criticisms in a preliminary manner here, returning in later sections to some of the specific points raised.

Criticisms which reject Burgess' concentric zone model are of two types. First, those which reject the model on technical grounds – such as the difficulties encountered in defining parcels of land that are homogeneous with respect to use (see p. 23). One form of such a criticism is that rather than there being discontinuities and distinct steps between zones, values of various variables decline more or less continuously from the city centre. A second, related form of this criticism is that intra-zone variations are as great as those between zones. Note, however, that such criticisms are equally applicable to other urban land use models which have been proposed as alternatives to that of Burgess. Indeed, these intra-zone variations are merely specific expressions in the context of urban land use models of general problems that arise in any spatial analytic study which involves regionalization and the partitioning of space into areas that are in some sense homogeneous. To some extent these problems can be alleviated if land use data are available on a highly disaggregated basis, both spatially and by land use type (see chapters 3 and 5). Unfortunately, such data are rarely available on a comprehensive basis (although see Rhind and Hudson 1980).

The second type of criticism which rejects the concentric zone model is more serious for it is not met by the collection of better data; it questions the appropriateness, validity and generality of Burgess' conception. Again, though, similar criticisms can be made of other urban land use models. The model is claimed either to be anachronistic or to lack universality. With regard to these charges, however, it is pertinent to bear in mind that Burgess himself intended the range of application of his model to be the largest, most rapidly growing and industrializing cities of the USA in and up to the 1920s. As Castells (1976, p. 40) has pointed out, to conceive of the city (as Burgess did) as an ecological complex (the interdependent system of population, environment, technology and social organization) is equivalent to analysing it as the product of the social dynamics of a particular historical and geographic formation. Castells (1976, p. 41) goes on to argue that 'where Burgess errs is in (*implicitly*) presenting as a universal feature a social process which is found only under particular conditions. Thus his analysis accounts for a particular kind of urban growth . . . ' (emphasis added). If Burgess is to be criticized, then, it is on the ground that he failed to spell out with sufficient precision the historical and geographical specificity of the processes that underlay his land use model. However, as Castells is forced to admit, Burgess made no explicit claims as to the generality of his model – rather the contrary. Such modesty has not deterred others from subsequently attempting to apply the model in time and space contexts other than that in which it was devised.

The criticism that the model is anachronistic reflects social and political changes which have affected Western society since Burgess devised his concentric zone model. A particularly important change has been the rise of State intervention in various forms which has affected land use patterns; for example, in provision of public sector housing and more generally in land use and development control (see chapter 9). In the USA, prior to and during the 1920s, such intervention was minimal; land use was mainly determined through a market, albeit an imperfect one (and in some places this is still the case today). Not surprisingly, the impacts of State intervention are not reflected in the geometry of concentric land use and social status zones. As distance from the city centre increased in the model, so the status of residential areas rose.

Increasingly, however, in Western cities this simple equation of rising status with increasing distance from the centre has been disturbed as a result of the operation of a rather different set of socio-political forces to those operating before and during the 1920s in the USA. Rather than urban land use allocation being governed purely by the imperatives of the market, it is either constrained by various forms of State intervention or, in some cases, removed entirely from the sphere of market forces. One result of this is that public sector housing is frequently found on the periphery of Western cities (for example, see fig. 8.11).

In a sense, the particular charge of anachronism can be subsumed under the

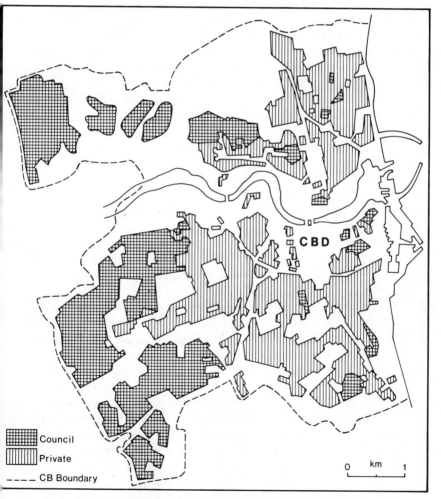

Figure 8.11 The distribution of public sector housing in Sunderland, England.

more general criticism of lack of universality: that is, concentric zone land use patterns are not found in all cities throughout history. One could equally make similar points concerning sectoral and multiple nuclei models. Again, however, this is a criticism that should be viewed in the context of Burgess' own strictures as to the intended sphere of application of his model. Furthermore, such a criticism implicitly begs the question of whether such a general model can and should be devised, thereby presupposing one particular conception of theory: that is, it presumes the validity of an analogy between land use theory and that in the physical sciences, rather than of theory based upon historically specific categories and constructs. Rather than criticize Burgess for failing to develop a universally applicable model of urban land use, we would reiterate that because of the specific socio-historical circumstances which underlie the model (but which Burgess failed to specify precisely), the geometric land use pattern which it postulates may and indeed can only be valid for a relatively circumscribed set of cities, in various times and places, developing under processes broadly similar to those implicit in Burgess' model. In other historical contexts, dominated by differing processes or different stages of the same processes, rather different land use patterns would be characteristic (although any one urban form at one point in time may bear the legacy of various changing processes).

There is, in fact, considerable empirical evidence to support these suggestions. Schnore (1965) has related the structure of Latin American cities to Burgess' model. On the basis of seven in-depth studies and a review some fifty others, Schnore concluded that while these urban areas display an inversion of the residential patterns of the concentric zone model, with high status groups in the centre and those of lowest status on the periphery, this pattern and that described by Burgess are simply two expressions of the same process: that is, rapid industrialization in a market economy, with no or little attempt to control the pattern of urban growth. Such variation in land value raises interesting questions about the locational choices of high status groups, to which we return below.

Sjoberg (1965), following Weber, draws a distinction in terms of industrialized and pre-industrialized cities and demonstrates that prior to industrialization and both in an historical and spatial context, the structural pattern of the city is a negation of the concentric zone arrangement. Specifically, the pre-industrial city exhibits three characteristics which are diametrically opposed to those postulated in the concentric zone model (Sjoberg 1965, pp. 95–6). First, the core is pre-eminent over the periphery in terms of the locational choices of high status groups. Second, there is a finer spatial segregation along ethnic, occupational and family lines (but note that evidence from factorial ecologies based on data for small areas, for example census Enumeration Districts, suggests that segregation within industrialized Western cities may be more marked than Sjoberg implies). Third, there is a low incidence of functional differentiation of land use patterns in the pre-industrial city (for example, see fig. 8.12).

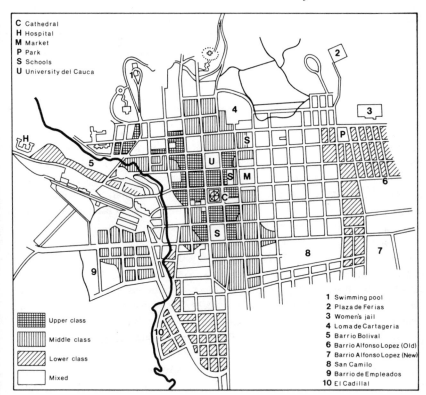

C Cathedral
H Hospital
M Market
P Park
S Schools
U University del Cauca

Upper class
Middle class
Lower class
Mixed

1 Swimming pool
2 Plaza de Ferias
3 Women's jail
4 Loma de Cartageria
5 Barrio Bolival
6 Barrio Alfonso Lopez (Old)
7 Barrio Alfonso Lopez (New)
8 San Camilo
9 Barrio de Empleados
10 El Cadillal

Figure 8.12 The social areas of Poṕyan, Colombia.

For Sjoberg the crucial issue is whether a city is industrialized. Thus he sees the crucial issue as the stage of technical development within a society. Social relations find no explicit consideration. While one can object to this, preferring a distinction in terms both of technical development and social relations (see chapter 10), it is more difficult to deny Sjoberg's general point that different social processes can lead to different urban forms. The net effect of his critique is neatly summarized by Carter (1976, p. 179): 'Burgess' model depended not only upon those processes which ecologists call sub-social (but which seem to have been economic competition for a scarce commodity, that is, central city land) but also upon a whole array of social and technological conditions which were never explicit and which were ignored when the model was seized upon as being universally applicable.' Burgess had little to say concerning why urban growth and form should follow the particular patterns he postulated; for example, why competition for space should be so structured. This reflected his method of argument by analogy with biological processes. We are left to conclude that the Burgess model, both as regards land use pattern and processes, has validity in certain circumstances but is one which fails to spell out with sufficient clarity and precision the historically specific premises upon which it is tacitly based. For example, competition is seen as natural and inevitable, rather than there being some historically specific conception of competition as a social process. Equally, however, as we have stressed, similar criticisms can be made of other urban land use models.

Land values, rents and urban land use patterns: neoclassical formulations

Carter (1976, p. 179) suggests that implicit to Burgess' model is land use allocation through the market; he goes on to argue (p. 190) that the more the concept of sub-social competition for a scarce resource is examined and refined, the more the ecologist is taken directly into the field of land economics and that is particularly so when a deductive model of land use patterns, which excludes cultural and social influences, is desired. One is forced to conclude that 'sub-social' is merely another name for 'economic'. Such economic processes are also central to Hoyt's model. Furthermore, since models such as those of Harris and Ullman and Mann essentially combine and extend in certain ways those of Burgess and Hoyt, it is reasonable to postulate that such processes are also important in shaping the land use patterns which these display. Thus the mechanisms of land use allocation through the market may provide a common theme which can be used to generate a variety of urban land use patterns, depending upon assumptions made as to the number of functional centres, the configuration of transport routes and so on. In one sense, this simply takes up Haggett's suggestion (see p. 183) to fuse elements from the three models into one model. However, in so far as it is necessary to specify the social, cultural and political climate in which unfettered market allocation can operate as the dominant process, it is possible to go beyond this. Specifying the range of circumstances in which such a model is valid also implies specifying the changes necessary, in terms of altering or relaxing these various social, cultural and political assumptions, in order to devise models appropriate to other sets of circumstances.

The seminal statement concerning the relationship between land values, rents and urban land use patterns is generally regarded as being that of Hurd (1903). Reduced to its most elemental form, Hurd's key thesis is that land value depends upon relative location. This was later taken up by Haig (1926) and by Ratcliff (1949) and reformulated in terms of transport costs which thus became the measure of relative location. Later, more mathematically sophisticated versions of such models were produced, particularly in relation to residential land use patterns, such as those of Alonso (1964) and Muth (1969). What these more mathematically sophisticated versions made clear was something implicit in the earlier models: that is, that these drew on marginalist, neoclassical economics as a source of theoretical inspiration. Central to this form of economics is a particular conception of value and rent, (the latter seen as a monetary return to a scarce factor of production that was qualitatively no different to capital and labour). While peculiar to neoclassical economics, such a conception is by no means the only possible interpretation of value and rent (see p. 231).

For the moment, however, we set aside such qualifications. Garner (1968, pp. 335–6) provides a clear, simple and non-mathematical summary of the main points of the reformulated statement of the relationships between land value, rent and land use patterns. For each type of activity, a location has utility which is measured by willingness to pay rent for use of that location. Activities bid competitively in a land market for use of different locations. In the long run, this competitive allocation process results in a tendency for the overall land use pattern to adjust so that each location is occupied by the activity which can pay the highest rent. This yields an ordered pattern of land use in which all activities are optimally located, in the sense that utilities are maximized.

A key issue concerns the determinants of rent levels, the rents which different activities are able to offer for various locations. While acknowledging that various other attributes of a location may influence the rent that it can command, the key systematic determinant of rent levels is postulated to be accessibility. As the latter is equated with transport costs, this presupposes that rents can be represented as transport cost savings. Since competitive allocation of location maximizes rents, it simultaneously minimizes aggregate transport costs. It follows that higher rents can be substituted for transport costs to ensure use of a particular location. Consequently, those activities which derive greatest benefit from accessible locations are able to outbid those which derive less benefit. In brief, the land use pattern reflects the land value surface, the land value surface reflects rents, and rents reflect accessibility. Using these concepts, it is possible to deduce models of urban land use patterns.

To begin with the simplest case, let us consider the derivation of a model of urban land use broadly analogous to that of Burgess (see Berry 1959). To derive such a model necessitates first making explicit certain assumptions which Burgess implicitly makes (Quinn 1950, p. 120; Schnore 1965, pp. 353–4). These are: a heterogeneous urban population in terms of culture, occupation and social class; a commercial–industrial city with a single, most accessible centre; no directional bias in access to and from this centre (equivalent to assuming the existence of a transport system with many evenly spaced radial routes (Hartman 1950) if not quite an isotropic plain); cheap land available at the city periphery; private ownership of property; and land use allocation via an unfettered market. Finally, we assume a broad disaggregation of activities into categories which broadly correspond with those proposed by Burgess. Each activity is associated with a characteristic rent paying ability, both in terms of the maximum at the centre and in terms of the decline from this maximum in response to the relative advantages to be gained from various locations (fig. 8.13). Assuming a process of competitive bidding for locations by different uses, the various bid-rent curves can be superimposed, the points of intersection of the bid-rent curves indicating

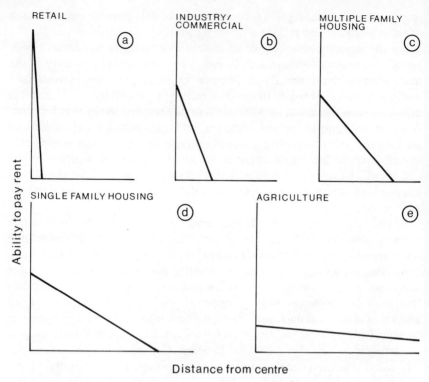

Figure 8.13   Bid-rents of different users of urban land in relation to distance from the city centre.

change in land use (fig. 8.14). Rotating this through 360° yields a model of urban land use which replicates that of Burgess, although predicated on rather more explicit assumptions as to the processes which organize land use patterns.

One of the paradoxical aspects of this model is that high status, high income groups live on the periphery on low cost land, while low status, low income groups live near the centre on high cost land. This pattern reflects the bid-rent curves of different status groups. For the poorest group, the bid-rent curve is characteristically steep since such people have little to spend on transport. Therefore, their ability to bid for the use of land declines rapidly from the centre, the assumed source of employment. On the other hand, as status and income rise, bid-rent curves become progressively more shallow as the ability to bid becomes progressively less affected by consideration of transport costs. Since locations are allocated competitively, as incomes rise so does the distance of residential areas from the centre. The poor are forced to live on high value land. The only way that they can do this is to save on the quantity of space they consume and so residential densities progressively rise as one approaches the centre.

The key to this pattern is the bid-rent curve of high status, high income

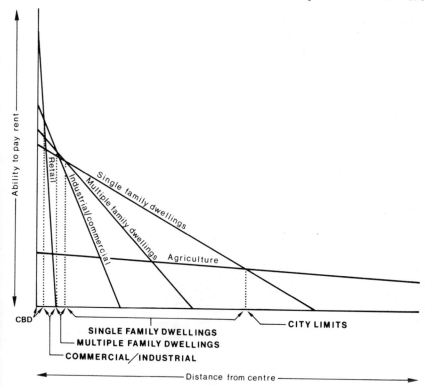

Figure 8.14   Intra-urban land use allocation in relation to bid-rents.

groups since the shape of this curve is an expression of their preference for space relative to transport cost. Lave (1970) points out that the spatial residential structure of the city will change if the preferences of this rich group change. For example, the rich might alter the form of their bid-rent function and move into the city centre in response to increased fuel costs or rising congestion costs which lead to delays and frustration in commuting. More generally, various city structures can be derived, depending on assumptions made as to the shape of these bid-rent curves and it is quite feasible to find the rich in the centre, the poor on the periphery as a result of market allocation forces. This was precisely Schnore's (1965) conclusion from a study of Latin American cities (see p. 188). Harvey (1973, p. 135) neatly summarizes the point:

> All that this actually means is that the rich group can always enforce its preference over a poorer group because it has more resources to apply either to transport costs or to obtaining land in whatever location it chooses. This is the natural consequence derived from applying marginalist economic principles (the bid-rent curve being a typical marginalist device) to a situation in which income differentials are substantial.

This echoes Schnore when he argues that a necessary condition for the Burgess arrangement is that high status social groups must be able to pre-empt newer and more desirable areas, or at least have relatively greater choice than lower status groups. As the shape of the bid-rent curves of such groups alters, so the spatial residential structure of the city alters, even given the restrictive assumptions outlined above.

One consequence of land use allocation by competition in a market is to generate an over-all rent or land value (defining this as capitalized rents) surface for the city, characterized by a central peak value with land values declining with increasing distance from this (fig. 8.15a). There is considerable empirical evidence for the existence of a major central land value peak in Western cities although this is generally not located in the geometric centre of the urban area (for example, see fig. 8.16, taken from Knos, 1962).

a Small single centre town

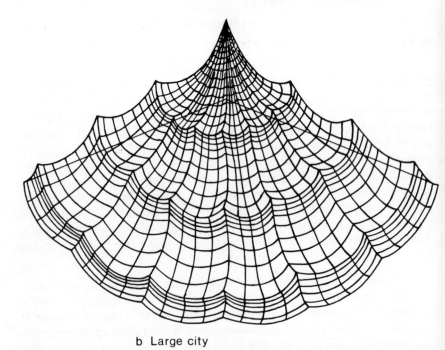

b Large city

Figure 8.15 Models of urban land value surfaces (from Berry *et al.* 1963).

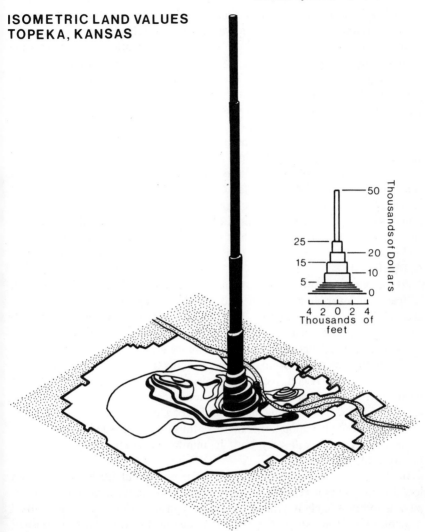

**ISOMETRIC LAND VALUES
TOPEKA, KANSAS**

Figure 8.16 The distribution of land values in Topeka, Kansas.

Moreover, by relaxing the assumptions initially made as to the existence of only one functional centre of the city and of equal access from all directions to centres, a more complex and realistic model of the urban land value surface can be produced. Thus as well as a 'grand peak' representing the point of maximum accessibility within the urban area, for a given distance from this point, land values will be higher adjacent to or near major routes and will form 'mini-peaks' at route intersections. Again, there is empirical evidence to support these propositions, much of it relating to cities in the USA. For example, in addition to Hoyt's pioneering study (fig. 8.3), both Seyfried (1963) for Seattle and Yeates (1965) for Chicago demonstrate the importance of a sectoral component in urban land value surfaces, reflecting the influence of radial routes. Berry *et al.* (1963) have shown a relationship between the relative importance of road intersections and localized peakings in land value in Chicago. Combining spatial variations in land use as a result of the operation of these influences with that of a decline from an absolute central peak value yields a more complex generalized land value surface within the city (fig. 8.15b).

Clearly the land use pattern associated with this generalized land value surface would be considerably more complicated than that associated with a model which admitted only variation in land value from the central, most accessible point. Indeed one would expect such a model to include elements of concentric zone, sectoral, and multiple nuclei models. As we have previously noted, several authors have pointed out that actual urban land use patterns show traces of patterns from each of these models. The point that we wish to make here is that there are theoretical grounds as to why such hybrid patterns will be found.

At the same time, however, we would stress that this theoretical framework is itself an over-simplification and requires elaboration. For example, accessibility is defined in terms of the transport system; however, considerable technological change has characterized transport in the last two hundred or so years and such changes re-define accessibility surfaces. Schaefer and Sclar (1975) discuss the relationship between changing transport and urban form in cities in the USA. Again, recall that accessibility has been defined solely in terms of transport cost and is assumed homogeneous for different activities and users. It is worth recalling that the utility of a location depends not only on accessibility but also upon 'other factors', thus far disregarded. Furthermore, these other factors will vary both in number, character and importance between differing uses.

In the case of retailing activities, revenue and profit levels depend upon location at points accessible to customers. Accessibility in relation to rent-paying ability is likely to remain the central consideration shaping locational distributions. However, in the case of residential location, both the desired size of residential plot and incomes interact with transport costs to shape location patterns (Alonso 1960) while factors such as proximity to open countryside, green belts (Richardson 1971), or to existing high status residential areas may be important. Put another way, the bid–rent functions of different residential groups may not and usually will not solely be the product of access to the city centre. With respect to manufacturing industry, Hamilton (1968, pp. 408–10) has proposed a model of the spatial industrial structure of a metropolis which distinguishes between four types of manufacturing activity, each with distinct locational requirements. First, those activities which occupy central locations to give access either to skilled labour drawn from the whole urban labour market or to the CBD. Essentially these are small manufacturing units which, of necessity, agglomerate in or near to central areas, the advantage of external scale economies offsetting high rents. Examples of such groupings include the metal plating, printing machinery, printing works, typesetting, lithographic plate-making and ancillary trades in the Clerkenwell–Fleet Street area of London and the jewellery and gun quarter of Birmingham (see Wise 1951). The second and third categories of activity are those which locate along radial or ring transport routes, seeking some combination of cheaper land, a good location for raw material or component assembly and product distribution, and access to less skilled labour. Examples of these include the factories located along the North Circular Road around London – in general this is a diverse group mainly of consumer goods industries. Finally, there are those activities which locate on the fringe of the city or at locations such as estuarine marshes, because of their need for large amounts of space or because their production processes are dangerous and/or obnoxious. Examples of these would include petro-chemicals complexes (such as those at Teesside and Grangemouth), iron and steel complexes (for example, Newport and Redcar), and motor vehicle assembly (for example, Ford at Dagenham).

These different locational requirements begin to raise questions concerning the adequacy of the very broad land use categories conventionally used in general urban land use models. In turn, this raises the issue of the need for more finely disaggregated land use data, both sectorally and spatially (see chapters 3 to 5). While to some extent residential use is disaggregated by type, there is perhaps a need to further disaggregate other land uses according to their locational requirements. To some extent, this is accomplished in the various partial land use models which have been proposed and it is to a consideration of these that we turn in the next section.

Partial land use models: the case of retailing

On the basis of studies of cities in the USA, Berry *et al.* (1963) have suggested a typology of retailing configurations, classifying these as nucleated shopping centres, ribbon developments and specialized areas. Each of these basic categories is further sub-divided (fig. 8.17). The classification thus encom-passes not only morphology but also function and different types of retail land use. The various types of retail configuration can also be related to the generalized urban land value surface.

Around the point of peak land value and maximum accessibility is the CBD while at non-central peaks in the land value surface other centres will be found. Berry arranges these centres in a hierarchical order, drawing on analogies with central place theory and the distribution of retailing facilities at an inter-urban scale (see also Berry 1967). As one ascends the functional hierarchy, centres progressively include functions which require increasingly large thresholds which, in turn, require increasingly accessible locations in order to be viable. Ribbon developments are located on land value ridges associated with radial routes, while specialized areas may be either of a nucleated or ribbon form.

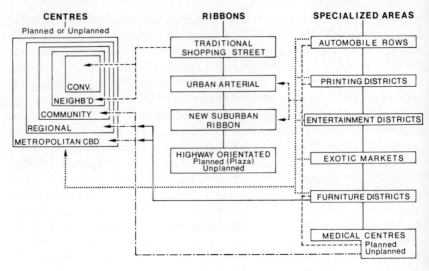

Figure 8.17   Berry's classification of urban business configurations.

One can also analyse the spatial arrangement of land uses within retail configurations in terms of land value surfaces and bid-rent curves associated with different types of retailing activity. Garner (1966), drawing on empirical studies of Chicago, argues that land uses within retailing centres will be arranged in concentric zones. He assumes three hierarchically ordered types of retail function, each with differing thresholds and distinct bid-rent curves: neighbourhood; community; and regional. Paralleling these, are three levels of centre (below the level of the CBD), each defined by the highest order function located therein. Within each centre, the functions are located in concentric zones around the point of peak accessibility, this horizontal spatial organization reflecting the vertical hierarchical ordering of functions (fig. 8.18). Davies (1972) suggests that such a model is appropriate in describing the retailing structure of the central area of Coventry. Despite its origins in an American context, the possibility thus exists that Garner's model may have a more general validity.

Indeed, Garner's model represents a considerable conceptual advance in our understanding of the internal spatial arrangement of retailing areas. Despite a wealth of empirical studies (several of which are reviewed in Carter 1976, chapter 10), the only previous substantial, generalized statement configurations in terms of land value surfaces and bid-rent curves associated (1959) rather simplistic model of the CBD. Influenced by Murphy *et al.* (1955), this dichotomized the CBD into a core and frame, each characterized by particular functions (fig. 8.19). While undoubtedly of some limited descriptive value, the principal problem of the core-frame model is the absence of a convincing theoretical account of why land use should be so arranged. A corollary of this is that it is difficult to relate this systematically to more general urban land use models. In this respect, Garner's conceptualization in terms of

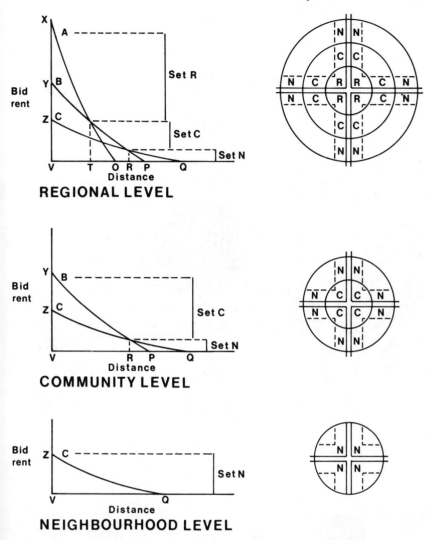

Figure 8.18 Garner's model of the internal structure of shopping centres.

the forces operating to organize the internal spatial structure of retailing centres is clearly preferable.

However, as originally formulated, Garner's model is also in need of modification. An anology may be drawn between this and models of the over-all urban land value surface. For while considering intra-centre variation in land value and use in relation to decline from a central peak land value, Garner ignores sectoral variation and also the existence of other localized land value peaks within each centre. While one might perhaps reasonably discount such influences in the case of small neighbourhood centres, as centres become

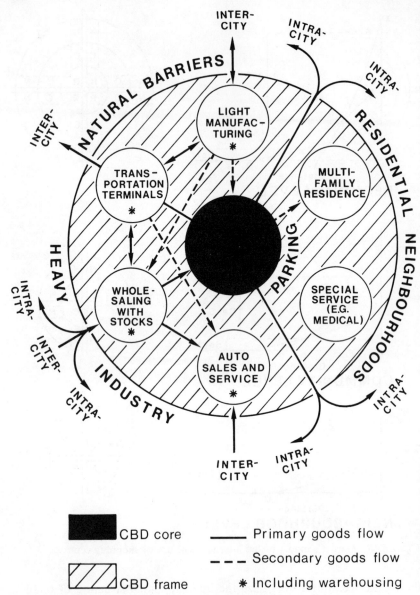

Figure 8.19   Horwood and Boyce's central area Core-Frame Model.

physically larger and functionally more complex, this becomes increasingly untenable, particularly in the case of major metropolitan CBD's.

It is possible to modify Garner's original conceptualization to take account of these other influences. Davies (1972, pp. 74–9) has produced such a modified model, although drawing on an analogy with Berry's classification of retailing configurations throughout the city rather than by structuring this

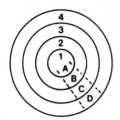

NUCLEATED CHARACTERISTICS

SHOP TYPES
1 Central area
2 Regional centres
3 Community centres
4 Neighbourhood centres

EXAMPLE CLUSTERS
A Apparel shops
B Variety shops
C Gift shops
D Food shops

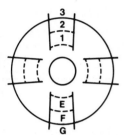

RIBBON CHARACTERISTICS

SHOP TYPES
1 Traditional street
2 Arterial ribbon
3 Suburban ribbon

EXAMPLE CLUSTERS
E Banking
F Cafés
G Garages

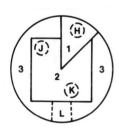

SPECIAL AREA CHARACTERISTICS

SHOP TYPES
1 High quality
2 Medium quality
3 Low quality

EXAMPLE CLUSTERS
H Entertainments
J Market
K Furniture
L Appliances

THE COMPLEX MODEL

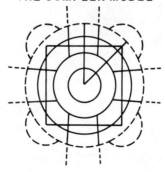

Figure 8.20 Davies' model of the structure of central area retailing facilities.

explicitly in terms of relationships between land use and values. As we have already suggested, however, it is possible to relate Berry's typology to the land value surface of the city. Thus, superimposed upon a concentric zone arrangement of different types of retail facility, Davies adds components representing ribbons and special areas, introducing the added sophistication of differences in quality as well as in type of retail establishments (fig. 8.20). This yields a 'complex model' of the internal structure of the CBD which shares some features in common with the core–frame model. Davies goes on to show that the model may be applied to the specific case of retailing configurations in the Coventry central area (figs 8.21 and 8.22).

Whereas Garner's model assumed a single central peak, from which land values decline evenly in all directions with increasing distance, Davies' model implicitly presupposes ridges of higher land value along the routes as well as

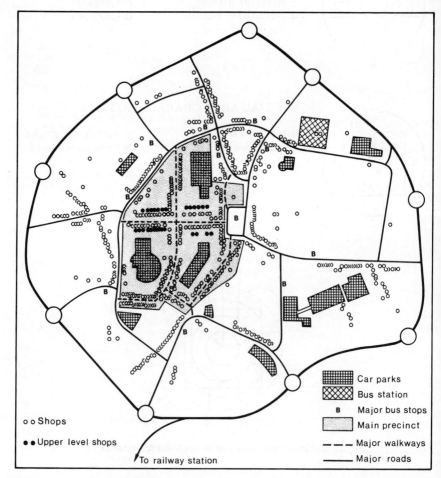

Figure 8.21   Retail configurations in the Coventry central area: actual distributions.

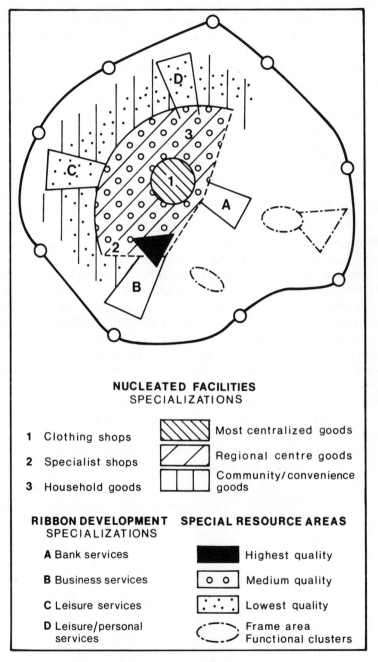

NUCLEATED FACILITIES
SPECIALIZATIONS

1 Clothing shops

2 Specialist shops

3 Household goods

⬚⬚⬚ Most centralized goods

⬚⬚⬚ Regional centre goods

⬚⬚⬚ Community/convenience goods

RIBBON DEVELOPMENT
SPECIALIZATIONS

A Bank services

B Business services

C Leisure services

D Leisure/personal services

SPECIAL RESOURCE AREAS

■ Highest quality

⬚ Medium quality

⬚ Lowest quality

⌇ Frame area Functional clusters

Figure 8.22 Retail configurations in the Coventry central area : theoretical distributions.

local, non-central value peaks. In essence these are analogous at an intra-centre level to the simple and generalized land value surfaces for the whole urban system (fig. 8.15). As such, these models of retailing are quite consistent with explanations of the over-all urban land use pattern in terms of accessibility and competition for locations and differential advantage to be gained by activities from the same location. In essence, such models of retailing structure merely involve a finer disaggregation of land use categories. These modifications, together with those which entail consideration of factors other than transport in determining the utility of different locations, do not challenge the over-all explanatory framework but, rather, can be incorporated within it. Other modifications are not so easily contained, however. It is to these that we turn in our next chapter.

Concluding remarks

In the course of the chapter we have reviewed both a number of models of intra-urban land use and various criticisms of them; we have also suggested a possible account of the processes giving rise to land use patterns via neoclassical economic theory. Before proceeding to consider further criticisms and reformulations of these models and alternatives to them, we would point out that these models, both in their original and revised forms, may be more widely applicable than simply in the context of intra-urban land use patterns. As we pointed out above (see, for example, p. 174), it is perhaps unwise to regard the distinction between urban and rural land use as a rigid one; Haggett *et al.* (1977, pp. 227–30) briefly review a number of studies which suggest that models proposed initially in the context of intra-urban land use (specifically, those developed by Burgess, Hoyt and Harris and Ullman) can be fruitfully applied in the context of the conversion of rural to urban land and the evolution of rural land use patterns. Equally, however, criticisms which are made of these models in their original intra-urban context may remain equally valid if these models are applied more generally.

9 Reforming land use models

Introduction

We have shown that agricultural land use patterns may be interpreted in terms of economic rent (chapter 7). Similarly, we have argued that urban land use models can and have been formulated in terms of the relationship between land use, rent and land value, mediated by freely competitive allocation through a market. Indeed, at one level of abstraction the distinction between agricultural and urban land use models is a false one: both are merely manifestations of a common set of mechanisms through which locations are allocated to particular uses. Implicit in such interpretations, however, are some quite stringent assumptions concerning both the basis on which decisions concerning land use are taken and the social and cultural environment in which these take place. One point is that such models (often implicitly) make rather heroic assumptions concerning the knowledge and objectives of decision-makers. Attempts have been made to modify these models by relaxing some of these assumptions and reintroducing variables originally omitted.

Again, to present such models as deductive micro-economic models necessarily omits consideration of social, political and cultural influences on land use patterns. Put another way, to formulate models in these terms is tacitly to assume a particular pattern of social, political and cultural relationships (which may or may not have empirical validity in particular situations). Attempts to reintroduce such variables have broadly taken place on two levels. One is simply to recognize that, for example, cultural values which are not adequately expressed through the market *do* influence land use patterns: Firey (1945) demonstrated this with respect to Boston. At another level, there have been attempts to specify the broader social, political and cultural forces which constrain or permit the operation of market forces and to identify those situations for which a conceptualization of land use allocation dominated by market forces is appropriate. The corollary of this is then to identify other influences on land use allocation in situations where such a conceptualization is not appropriate.

More realistic postulates concerning individual behaviour

As we have pointed out, models of agricultural land use based upon the maximization of economic rent are predicated upon quite specific and restrictive assumptions concerning individuals' knowledge, objectives and behaviour. Implicit in a model which accounts for land use patterns as the outcome of a competitive process, which in the long-run results in each location being occupied by the activity which will pay the highest rent, are a similar set of sweeping assumptions concerning the aims and knowledge of individual decision-takers (whether these be individual people or organizations).

Included in these assumptions are those of perfect knowledge and common objectives on the part of classes of buyers and sellers regarding the use of land: that is, sellers who wish to maximize revenue and buyers who wish to maximize their profits or satisfaction. These assumptions become most explicitly stated when such models are written as linear programming models, maximizing a given objective function subject to certain constraints (see Stevens 1968; for a comprehensive treatment of linear programming and its extensions, see Dantzig 1963). Abler *et al.* (1972, pp. 458–64) have demonstrated via a (fictitious) simple example how linear programming models can be used in analysing agricultural land use patterns. A Kenyan farmer in the Kikuyu Highlands wishes to maximize his total money income. Two crop choices are available to him: to grow a cash crop for export (Arabica coffee) or a subsistence crop for the local market. Coffee production results in a monetary yield of 100 cents/kg, and production of the subsistence crop 86 cents/kg; 1 kg of the former requires 0.0015 ha to produce, of the latter 0.0012. However, certain constraints exist which limit the absolute and relative amounts of the two crops which he can grow. First, he has a finite amount of land on which he can grow crops, some 9 ha. Second, he has a finite amount of labour available to him, that of himself and his wife, totalling 4,500 person-hours/year. Third, because of an international coffee agreement, a maximum of 6.6 ha can be devoted to growing coffee. Each constraint may be expressed graphically and the individual graphs superimposed to yield both the range of feasible solutions and the optimal solution (figs 9.1 to 9.5). The optimal solution (that combination of crops which yields the farmer the maximum income) is given by that point on the boundary of the feasible solution which is furthest from the origin. This reveals that the farmer's money income is maximized if he produces 3,600 kg of coffee and 3,000 kg of the subsistence crop; thus to maximize his income the farmer must devote 5.4 ha of land to coffee, 3.6 ha to the subsistence crop.

Heady and Egbert (1964) employed linear programming methods to derive optimal production patterns, both by agricultural sector and region, for the USA, while Wolpert (1964) has employed such programming methods to derive the potential maximum productivity of farm labour in Sweden. Furthermore, Wolpert went on to demonstrate that actual productivity as revealed by Swedish government statistics fell much below potential productivity and, moreover, that within Sweden there were regional variations in the magnitude of this discrepancy (fig. 9.6). While in northwest Sweden, the

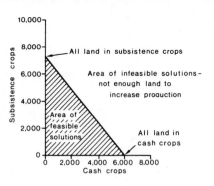

Figure 9.1 The land constraint on the production of the African farmer.

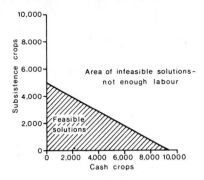

Figure 9.2 The labour constraint on the production of the African farmer.

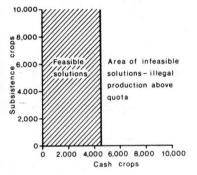

Figure 9.3 The coffee quota constraint on the cash crop production of the African farmer.

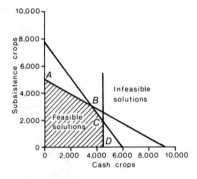

Figure 9.4 The land, labour and coffee quota constraints combining to delimit the area of feasible solutions.

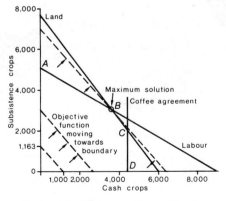

Figure 9.5 The constraints, objective function and optimal solution.

207

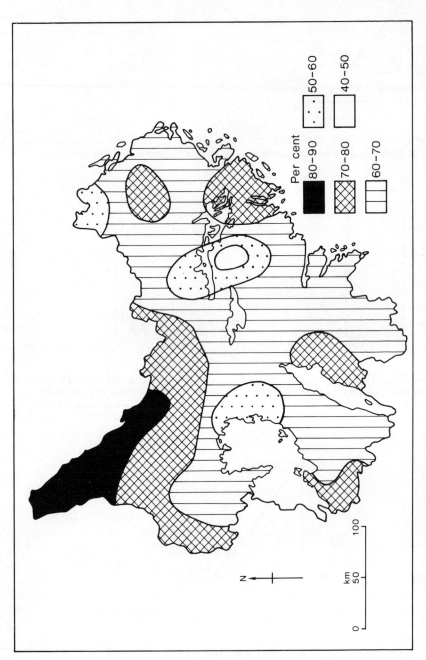

Figure 9.6 The relationship between actual and maximum possible productivity of farm labour in middle Sweden.

actual return on labour was 80% of the potential return, in small areas of the east it fell to less than 50%. The clear implication of these differences was that farmers' aims differed from those assumed and/or their knowledge was less than perfect. In fact, it is most probable both that their aims differed and that their knowledge was imperfect. Moreover, because of the spatial pattern of information diffusion, there were regional differences in the degree of imperfection. Crucially, however, Wolpert's study unambiguously revealed that agricultural land use patterns diverged considerably from those which should occur if the behavioural assumptions of the linear programming model were actually valid.

More generally, there is a considerable body of evidence to suggest that individuals and organizations have incomplete knowledge and motives other than those assumed within neoclassical models of the land market. As Turner (1977, p. 37) has argued, sellers and buyers generally enter the land market with a very limited and often highly distorted view of market conditions. However, some organizations are better informed than others, notably life insurance companies, pension funds, property companies and (in Britain) the Church Commissioners, all of whom are heavily involved in the land market. Three examples will serve to exemplify these points of varying motives and imperfect but variable knowledge. Massey and Catalano (1978) have shown that the assumption that land-owners in Britain are guided solely by the imperatives of the market in deciding how to use their land is untenable. They identify three classes of land-owners in contemporary Britain: former landed property; industrial land-owners; financial land-owners (such as property companies, pension funds, etc.). Only the latter are governed by a purely capitalist calculus of rent maximization as regards use of their land. In a rather different context, Harvey (1973, pp. 173–6) identifies six major groups of 'actors' in the USA housing market, all of whom come to the market with differing aims. These groups (residents, realtors (estate agents), landlords, developers, financial institutions, government institutions) are all active in the housing market in pursuit of different goals. Finally, in a very different context, an analysis of the arrangement of agricultural land use zones around Addis Abbaba, Ethiopa (Horvath 1969, pp. 322–3) has demonstrated that different ethnic groups vary in the degree to which their behaviour conforms to the motives attributed to Economic Man. While for some (the Gurage) this concept provides a reasonable description of their motives, for others (the Amhara and Galla) this is certainly not the case. More generally in an African context, Jackson (1972) suggests that the rationale governing agricultural land use patterns in tropical Africa is in general very different to that assumed by von Thünen; in particular it is concerned with maximizing returns to labour rather than land.

Consequently, reflecting the emergence of such evidence, attempts have been made to devise more realistic behavioural postulates as a basis for models of the decision processes which give rise to land use patterns. These attempts particularly concentrated on relaxing assumptions as to certainty and perfect knowledge; however, a corollary of relaxing these key assumptions is that simple assumptions as to maximizing, say, rent also became untenable and assumptions as to objectives necessarily change.

One way, in principle, to relax assumptions as to perfect knowledge and to incorporate uncertainty and differing objectives into an analysis of land use patterns is to adopt a game theory approach (for the seminal statement on game theory, see von Neumann and Morgenstern 1944). The purpose of the 'game' is to select a strategy or combination of strategies (in this case land use patterns) which are 'best' in relation to an assumed objective, based on the notion that a whole range of strategies are open to players which yield, depending upon other players' choices, various outcomes.

Game theory models may be categorized in terms of whether they involve two persons or *n* persons, whether they are zero sum games (that is, one player's gains are another's losses) or non-zero sum games. Equally, different players' aims and strategies may vary. The simplest type of games are two-person zero sum games, the most complex *n*-person non-zero sum games. Abler *et al.* (1972, pp. 486–8) demonstrate how such game theory models may be used in understanding land use patterns, both urban and agricultural (see also Found 1974, pp. 106–23).

With respect to agricultural land use patterns they illustrate how these may be analysed as a two-person zero sum game between Man and his Environment. The notion of personifying the Environment in this way may initially seem incongruous but it is argued that this is highly apposite in situations where there is great uncertainty about the environment and in which it is, therefore, astute to assume the worst about the environment, to represent this as a malevolent opponent. Again, they present a simple example to emphasize the point, involving a farmer in the barren Middle Belt of Ghana, a zone of high environmental variability in which rainfall is particularly uncertain. This farmer can grow five crops, the yields of which vary depending on rainfall; the latter – the Environment's choices – is dichotomized into wet and dry years. The relationships between rainfall and yield can be set out as a pay-off matrix, which shows the varying yields of crops in wet and dry years, and are as follows:

	Wet	*Dry*
Yams	82	11
Maize	61	49
Corn	12	38
Millet	43	32
Hill rice	30	71

The farmer's aim is to choose that strategy which yields him the minimum possible disadvantage, assuming that the Environment does its worst, i.e. his objective is to select a minimax strategy. This strategy (crop or land use combination) may be found graphically in the case of this simple example (fig. 9.7). The outcome associated with growing each crop in a wet and dry

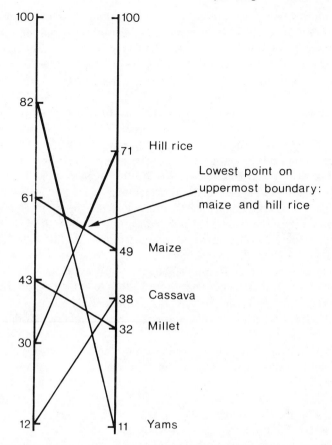

Figure 9.7 Locating the optimal strategy combination.

year is represented on a scale with two axes, calibrated from zero to 100. The lowest point on the uppermost boundary formed by the inter-sections of individual strategies indicates the crops which the farmer should grow to satisfy his objective. This indicates some combination of hill rice and maize, the relative proportions of land given to each crop being determined by their relative yields in wet and dry years: 77.4% of land for maize and 22.6% for hill rice (see also Gould 1963, 1965). Gould (1963) in fact found that actual land use patterns in Jantilla in the Middle Belt of Ghana approximated to this optimal pattern, a correspondence reflecting learning and adaptation by the resident population.

Abler *et al.* (1972, pp. 512–15) go on to show how more sophisticated game theory models may be used in helping to throw light on urban land use situations characterized by conflict. This might involve the location of a new urban motorway, airport location, or the location of nuclear power stations. They illustrate how the Prisoners' Dilemma, a non-zero sum game, may be useful in explaining the outcome of such conflicts. An important feature of such models is that central to the conceptualization of processes underlying land use decisions which they embody is the varying bargaining power of differing groups and individuals. Nevertheless, game theory models continue to make rather restrictive assumptions concerning knowledge, decisions and the determinants of behaviour, essentially remaining within the same theoretical fold as linear programming models.

However, to study decision processes directly is extremely difficult. In practice, studies designed to focus directly upon the knowledge and motives of decision takers have usually involved a study of environmental images, the image being taken as a surrogate for the decision process. The image may be thought of as a mental representation of the actual environment, comprising three components: designative; evaluative; and prescriptive. Thus attention is directed towards individuals' or groups' environmental knowledge, evaluations and preferences and temporal variations in these, in the belief that these underpin behaviour. Not only are decisions based upon less-than-perfect information but, given the impedance of distance, it is inevitable that this will be the case. Land use patterns are thus seen as a product of individual or corporate decisions taken on the basis of less knowledge and more complicated objectives than those assumed in models based upon neoclassical economics (for an extended review of urban image studies, see Pocock and Hudson 1978).

A related approach to that of focusing upon the links between images and behaviour as an explanation of land use patterns is Chapin's (1965) conceptualization of urban land use structure in terms of activity systems. He defined these as behaviour patterns of individuals, institutions and firms which occur in spatial patterns (Chapin 1965, p. 244). He saw certain individual or group-held values concerning the use of a particular parcel of land or area setting in motion a four-fold cycle of behaviour which culminates in a parcel or area being put into a particular use (fig. 9.8). Chapin recognized that culturally determined values influence individual and group behaviour and ultimately, therefore, land use patterns.

However, while clarifying some issues, the consideration of more realistic behavioural postulates for land use models is, in itself, inadequate. The limits of attempts to explain land use patterns simply in terms of individual or corporate decisions are soon reached. Individuals (both people and organizations) exist in a social context and their knowledge, values and beliefs are socially influenced, their behaviour socially constrained. Chapin recognized this but the emphasis within his conceptualization remains firmly on the individual. A more comprehensive theory of land use must take account of these social and cultural influences.

In a sense, we have now come full circle. For these are precisely the social and cultural influences originally (partially) recognized by the human ecology school and which were omitted from neoclassical models of the land market and land use in favour of the analytic precision to be gained from focusing upon 'economic' or 'sub-social' determinants of land use patterns. Castells

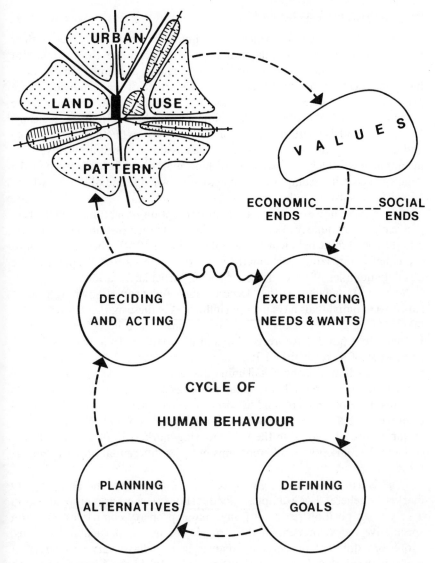

Figure 9.8 Urban land use change: the sequence of action and influence of values.

(1976, p. 40) makes the point that to conceive of the city as a product of the action of an ecological complex (the interdependent system of population, environment, technology and social organization) is equivalent to analysing it as the product of the social dynamics of a particular historical and geographical formation. The problem is to reintroduce such variables, to reintroduce historical and geographical specificity, but in a more powerful analytic way than by an appeal to 'moral order' (Park 1925) as the over-all organizing force governing the socio-spatial order of society.

More realistic markets for land

Models of the land market which, either implicitly or explicitly, derive their theoretical bases from neoclassical economics postulate the existence of markets in which individuals compete freely, equally and impersonally. Each individual decision has no effect on the ruling price of land: individuals are price-takers, not price-makers. Classes of individuals are assumed to be guided by comparable objectives, fashioned by the logic of market efficiency. Moreover, land use patterns are postulated to adjust to fluctuations in supply and demand (the adjustment process is also assumed, albeit implicitly, to be instantaneous). Such a conception of land markets is dependent upon the validity of certain assumptions as to actors' knowledge and objectives which, as we have shown in the previous section, lack empirical validity. More fundamentally, however, this particular conception of land markets is itself predicated upon quite restrictive assumptions as to their institutional structure and the social influences which shape these (Form 1954). These assumptions are equally untenable, particularly given the finite nature of land and the absolute qualities of space associated with particular locations.

An important factor is that various land- and property-owning organizations and individuals have unequal influences in these markets. Rather than taking ruling market prices, some are in a position to influence their level. Indeed, Hoyt pointed to precisely this in his analysis of the reasons for the emergence of sectoral urban land use patterns (see p. 179). We have also pointed out that Prisoners' Dilemma game theory models emphasize the importance of differential bargaining power as a central element in attempts to explain the outcome of land use decisions characterized by conflict. As an example of this unequal influence, Harvey (1973, pp. 173–6) identifies six major groups of 'actors' in the USA housing market, all of whom not only come to the market with different aims but with differential power to pursue these.

What is true of the housing market is true *a fortiori* of land and property markets in general. For example, individual house owners are competitively in a very weak position relative to, say, major property companies intent on speculative redevelopment in the struggle for use of particular locations. Moreover, different property companies in turn have varying degrees of power in the market. For example, in September 1974 Land Securities Ltd, the largest British property company, had assets of £166.3 million whereas the tenth largest, Haslemere Estates, had assets of £23.7 million (Ambrose and Colenutt 1975, p. 39). Nevertheless, Haslemere Estates clearly stood in a much more powerful position than individual house owners.

A second point is that to postulate an equilibrium (particularly an instantaneous one) of supply and demand for land via land use change is to ignore a fundamental characteristic of land and land markets. In the context of urban expansion, Sinclair (1967) has shown how land on the urban fringe is bought up and held speculatively, in anticipation of future urban development (a corollary of this is that, contrary to von Thünen's conceptualization, the intensity of agricultural production falls in the immediate environs of urban areas, as such land is taken out of agriculture or let on short-term leases which are not conducive to agricultural investment). As the early pioneers of urban land use study (such as Burgess, the ecological school, and Hoyt) well appreciated, urban areas grow sequentially, albeit primarily as a result of competitive allocation processes, and, as a corollary, people and activities locate within the city in sequence. Once located they tend to be relatively immobile. In part this immobility reflects the absolute qualities of location (that is, the fact that locations are not perfectly substitutable), in part the institutional arrangements for the renting and use of land. Harvey (1973, p. 168) argued that monopoly in absolute space is a condition of existence, not something experienced as a deviation from the spaceless world of perfect competition. Recognition of this thus poses a challenge to the theoretical structure of models based on neoclassical economics, a point we amplify below (chapter 10). Harvey went on to argue that, in capitalist society, this characteristic of absolute space is institutionalized through the private property relation so that 'owners' possess monopoly privileges over 'pieces of space'. The formation of these institutional arrangements to guarantee property rights reflects the emergence of the State in a general sense. More specific State policies have also been evolved, intended to intervene in land use allocation, to modify the context of market allocation, or even to remove some land use decisions entirely from the scope of the market. It is to a description of the role and character of State policies in relation to land use that we now turn.

State intervention in land use

To pretend that land use decisions are and for some time have been reached in an environment free of State intervention is, in many instances, perhaps the greatest myth of all. This is true of countries at a variety of levels of economic development and with various dominant socio-political organizations. For example, the collectivization of agriculture in the USSR and China had considerable impacts on rural land use patterns. In the countries of the capitalist world, rather than being an infrequent occurrence which can be treated as an occasional lapse from 'normal' market conditions, State intervention *is* today the norm. State action sets the constraints within which land markets operate or even removes certain land use decisions from the bounds of the market.

The land use planning system in Britain is often regarded as the most sophisticated in the Western World, held up as an example of comprehensiveness and effectiveness for the rest of the world to emulate (the definitive review of this system is that of Hall *et al.* 1973; see also Hall 1974). It is appropriate, therefore, to consider State intervention in land use decisions in Britain as an exemplary case study, to illustrate the character, extent and limits of the

State's role. This involves intervention both at national and local government levels as well as through various *ad hoc* bodies: moreover, supra-national organizations also affect land use patterns, for example, the EEC influences agricultural land use patterns via the impact of the Common Agricultural Policy. Such interventions may be dichotomized into those which affect land use directly, physically affecting the supply of a given type of land by allocating particular parcels of land to particular uses, and those which influence land use indirectly by affecting demand for various land uses and so land value and use. Our principal concern here is with the former but we also briefly consider the latter.

DIRECT STATE INTERVENTIONS

The attempt at a unified systematic control of land use in Britain originates from the provisions of the 1947 Town and Country Planning Act. However, the roots of this system of control can be traced back to 19th-century legislation to ameliorate living and working conditions in the newly emerging industrial urban areas of Britain. More specifically it can be traced to the first Town Planning Act of 1909 and the 1932 Town and Country Planning Act, which linked up rural and urban planning. The character of such legislation was essentially permissive and it was ineffective: by 1942 only 5% of land in England and Wales was affected by it (Turner 1977, p. 12). The social and economic circumstances of the 1930s were not conducive to the emergence of a more effective system of land use control, although the requirements of the war-time economy in succeeding years suggested the need for such controls.

At the same time those circumstances were crucial in shaping the 1947 Act and to understand the origins and import of that Act requires some brief, more general, consideration of the history of the inter-war years and the period 1939–45. The 1930s were, *inter alia*, characterized by widening regional inequalities and an increasing recognition of the costs and potential dangers associated with these and hence of the need to counter such inequalities. Growth, based on new consumer goods industries, continued in the South East and West Midlands (see Aldcroft and Richardson 1969). A consequence of this was urban expansion but, at the same time, increasing problems of urban congestion and living conditions, particularly in London. At the same time, the peripheral regions of Scotland, Wales and northern England remained profoundly depressed, characterized by very high unemployment rates and deteriorating living conditions as levels of effective demand for the products of their 'traditional' industries remained very low, only recovering with rearmament just prior to the Second World War (see Carney *et al.* 1977). The problems of these latter areas led to their being designated 'Special Areas' and a Commissioner being appointed to investigate their problems and possible solutions to these. Furthermore, a Royal Commission was set up under the Chairmanship of Sir Montague Barlow to inquire into the causes of and solutions to the problems of unbalanced regional growth. In 1940 this Commission produced its Report, on the

Distribution of the Industrial Population, which, reflecting the growing acceptance of Keynesian economic policies, suggested State intervention to stimulate fresh industrial growth in peripheral regions and dampen growth in the South East and Midlands. This echoed the views of Sir Malcolm Stewart who, in his Third Report as Commissioner for the Special Areas, argued that further development of the congested areas, notably London, must be controlled if the problems of the Special Areas were to be solved (see Carney and Hudson 1978a). The theme of restricting the physical expansion of London was central to the 1944 Abercrombie Report, a plan for Greater London, which suggested a policy of decentralization to newly built satellite towns, cut off from London by a green belt – a suggestion with very important land use implications. In fact, the general theme of the necessity for some form of land use control had also been featured prominently in the Reports of two Committees produced in 1942 concerned with rather different issues: the Scott Committee (of which Sir L. Dudley Stamp was vice-chairman, see chapters 3 and 4), set up to inquire into land utilization in rural areas, and the Uthwatt Committee. The Report of this latter group contained quite radical proposals for land management and recommended the establishment of effective machinery to implement land use planning. These various Reports and White Papers formed some of the important background to the burst of legislation in the post-war years which was to have important ramifications for land use at a variety of spatial scales.

However, equally critical to an appreciation of the 1947 Town and Country Planning Act and the various other pieces of legislation which made up this reformist package, is the broad social and political context of that period. For the 1947 Act represented but one expression of the reforming fervour of the post-war Labour government, intent on pushing through a radical legislative programme to create a more socially just society (involving a commitment to full employment, the extension of public ownership, the creation of a National Health Service, etc.). In fact, and seemingly paradoxically, many of the main elements of this radical package were consensus measures, already agreed by the war-time coalition government (such as the commitment to full employment) or with the private interests involved (the nationalization of the coal mines and railways). Essentially – as Elliott (1978, p. 18) has pointed out with respect to the 1947 Act – the 'consensus' character of these measures represented a temporary alliance of fundamentally divergent interests: on the one hand, those genuinely committed to reform and on the other conservative elements seeking to preserve the interests of rural landowners from urban encroachment. Both groups saw the 1947 Act as a route to what in fact were incompatible goals (see also Hall 1974, pp. 395–7 on this). A recognition of this point is crucial to a proper appreciation of the subsequent history of land use planning under the 1947 Act.

The 1947 Town and Country Planning Act repealed all previous relevant legislation (except the 1943 Act of the same name, which provided for the appointment of the Minister) and established for the first time comprehensive and compulsory land use planning in England and Wales (separate legislation was passed for Scotland). Although part of an attempt, informed by genuinely reformist sentiment, to tackle pressing urban and regional problems, many of the stronger measures suggested in the 1930s and 1940s as means of moving towards positive regional planning failed to find a place in the legislation, as did the radical suggestions for land management policies made in the Uthwatt Report. Rather, the legislation focused on land use control and at its heart were two inter-related threads.

One of these was the necessity to obtain planning permission prior to change of use. This alone, in fact, has defined the over-all framework of State intervention with regard to land use in the post-war period. However, in the 1947 Act it was linked with an attempt to channel to the State the benefits of changing land value arising from permitted changes of the designated use by a development tax on such windfall gains. The tax was repealed in 1953 by the Conservative government – a crucial precondition for the massive burst of speculative office and commercial redevelopment in the mid-1950s, particularly in London. More generally, by abolishing taxation on windfall gains while simultaneously encouraging rural Counties to resist pressures for land (especially housing land requested by the urban County Boroughs) and at the same time encouraging the latter to push through rehousing and slum clearance schemes, the Conservative government compounded the pressure on land with planning permission and hence land prices. The establishment of the Land Commission in 1967 (until its abolition in 1970) and the passing of the 1975 Community Land Act and 1976 Development Land Tax Act by successive Labour Governments attempted to reintroduce the principle of taxing windfall gains but to little effect. The continuation of powers to regulate change of use in the absence of effective mechanisms for taxing windfall gains characterizes most of the post-war period and, indeed, recognition of this is critical to a proper appreciation of the effects of land use planning in this period.

The Planning Authorities – based on County and County Borough Councils – which were established in the 1940s were given responsibility for implementing the terms of the 1947 Act. Each Authority was charged to draw up a Development Plan, a broad statement in the form of a Written Analysis and maps of present and future land use within its area. As part of this process, a more detailed land use statement in the form of Town Maps was also to be prepared. In principle, all Planning Authorities were to prepare a Development Plan within 5 years of the legislation being enacted, setting out broad proposals for the 'foreseeable future' – in practice interpreted to mean about 20 years. This plan was to indicate the manner and stages by which the Planning Authority proposed that land would be used and land use change result. These proposals, together with any amendments, were to be available for public inspection prior to submission to the relevant Minister (then of Housing and Local Government) for approval. Submission was followed by a Public Inquiry at which objections to proposals could be formally made. Each

Plan was intended to be reviewed every 5 years but in fact much longer periods often elapsed before a full review. For example, the Durham County Development Plan was first published in 1951 but the first review did not appear until 1964, (County Council of Durham 1951, 1964) although various Town Map proposals had previously provided revisions of parts of the plan. Parenthetically, we may note that these Plans and Town Maps and their Reviews were the data sources from which Best (1968, 1978) quarried many of the most valuable national land use statistics.

On a day-to-day basis, development control proceeds by granting or refusing permission for specific proposals submitted by individuals and organizations: that is, proposals involving land use change which technically is defined as change of use (see also p. 35). In practice, emphasis is at the level of tactical rather than strategic decisions concerning land use patterns. Obsession with detailed land use proposals rather than broad strategic considerations formed one of the main criticisms levelled at planners by the Planning Advisory Group (PAG) in a report published in 1965. The PAG was set up in 1964 to advise on planning in England and Wales, in part in response to the muddles which had been created in the 1950s by the policies of the then Conservative administrations. The PAG suggested drawing a distinction between policy and strategic decisions on the one hand and detailed and tactical decisions on the other. Only plans dealing with the former should be submitted to the Minister. Specific allocations of land for particular uses and details of implementing these should be the responsibility of Planning Authorities alone.

The suggestions made by the PAG were substantially incorporated into the 1968 Town and Country Planning Act (since consolidated in the 1971 Act of the same name). Broadly speaking, this replaced Development Plans by Structure Plans, Town Maps by Local Plans. Structure Plans were intended to deal at county level with the distribution of jobs, people, major communication routes, recreation, conservation, green belts, and overall development policies for towns and villages. Not surprisingly, the fundamental restructuring of the counties in the 1974 reorganization of local government in England and Wales caused delays and difficulties in formulating these plans. Structure Plans are also intended to link up with regional (economic) strategies; together with Local Goverment reform, this linking was intended to avoid the conflicts between cities and rural counties which emerged in the 1950s. Thus Structure Plans are essentially seen as that stage in the planning process at which the effects of economic policies on land use, environmental development and associated transport systems are integrated (Burns 1977, p. 41). There is evidence, however, to suggest that this integration is not taking place as intended (see Carney and Hudson 1976b, 1977, 1978b). At a more local level, Structure Plans are to form the basis upon which Planning Authorities go on to prepare Local Plans to serve as guidelines for development control and provide a framework for more positive attempts at environmental management. However, rather than await their completion, the preparation of Local Plans tends to proceed in parallel with that of Structure Plans.

The 1968 Act also laid down legal requirements for a greater element of participation by the Public in plan preparation and so, in principle, the determination of land use patterns. However, in practice, participation has been defined in such a way as to minimize the contribution of the wider public in this respect (see Simmie 1974; Stringer and Plumridge 1974). For example, only 6% of households in County Durham responded to a questionnaire intended to elicit their views as to desirable development patterns for the county.

Moreover, it is important to remember that Structure Plans are constrained in precisely the same way as Development Plans as a means of achieving desired land use patterns. While statements of intention as to land use patterns can be drawn up by Planning Authorities and subsequently approved by Ministers, implementing these proposals implies co-operation with and the co-ordination of a wide variety of public and private bodies and individuals. While a Planning Authority can refuse permission for changes in land use which do not conform to its Plan, acting alone it is generally powerless to promote in a positive way those changes which enable the Plan's intentions to be realized.

As well as this formal framework of land use control, there has been and continues to be considerable further State involvement in directly determining land uses. Often this has been 'inadvertent' land use planning in the sense that State actions and involvements (both before and after 1947) in diverse areas such as housing, transport, industry, regional development, open space provision (via the early provision of municipal parks: Clout 1972, p. 85) and National Parks, etc., had and continue to have important implications for land use patterns and changes. While much of this intervention has echoed the essentially negative tone of the controls of the Town and Country Planning Acts, and to some extent overlaps with these, some of it has been of a more positive nature. Three examples of very different character will be given to substantiate this point.

One important set of influences on land uses resulted from the 1945 Distribution of Industry Act and subsequent legislation intended to influence the regional distribution of industry. Following the Barlow Report, this was primarily concerned with the regional balance of economic activity but, as a consequence of this, has some specific land use implications (McCrone 1969, pp. 111–12). In relation to pursuing the aim of narrowing regional inequality, the Board of Trade could build factories in Development Areas, buying land by compulsory purchase if necessary, and reclaim derelict land. The 1945 Act also gave the Board powers, which had originated in the years of the war economy, with respect to Industrial Development Certificates (IDCs). These were incorporated in the 1947 Town and Country Planning Act. Any new industrial development of more than 5,000 ft^2 required an IDC; in this way it was intended to steer manufacturing industry to Development Areas and prevent further growth in London and the South East. This size limit has subsequently been varied by legislation: for example, in 1964 it was reduced to 1,000 ft^2, in 1966 raised to 3,000 ft^2 and 5,000 ft^2 outside the South East and the Midlands. Reflecting the switch to service activity in the post-war economy, the 1965 Control of Office and Industrial Development legislation extended control to offices. New offices of 3,000 ft^2 or more floorspace needed an Office Development Permit (ODP) if located in the London Metropolitan Region. In August 1965 this requirement was extended to Birmingham and in July 1966 to the whole of the South East, East Anglia, and East and West Midlands Planning Regions (McCrone 1969, pp. 130–1). Again the limits have subsequently varied, later being raised to 10,000 ft^2 and being substantially relaxed after 1969: in December 1973 a freeze was placed on all ODPs in the South East (Ambrose and Colenutt 1975, p. 76). Thus, although affecting very specific types of land use, this legislation concerned with the regional distribution of economic activity has influenced land use patterns. Although the effects have varied spatially, in general these have attempted to encourage particular sorts of development in Development Areas and restrict these in the South East. A corollary of this has been the attempt to encourage certain sorts of land use change in the former areas and to prevent these in the latter (although with limited success).

Another important legislative influence which has affected land use patterns relates to National Parks. The possibility of National Parks in Britain was placed firmly on the agenda in 1929 when the Addison Committee was established (Clout 1972, pp. 85ff.). Such parks already existed in other countries: for example, the first in the USA was set up in 1872 at Yellowstone, the first in Canada in 1885 at Banff. The Addison Committee reported in 1931, recommending the establishment of British National Parks. Not surprisingly, in the context of the social and economic conditions of the 1930s, these recommendations were not taken up. However, in 1942 the Scott Committee supported proposals for a central authority to delimit National Parks and recommended that a separate executive body be set up both to plan and control their use and development. In 1944, the White Paper on Land Use included proposals for National Parks. In 1945 the Dower Report appeared, the recommendations of which were included in the 1947 Hobhouse Report of the National Parks Committee. This suggested setting up twelve National Parks in England and Wales. These were defined in a basically conservative way, directed at preservation of existing land use patterns and against change. A National Park was conceived as an extensive area of beautiful and relatively wild country in which, for the nation's benefit and by appropriate national decisions and actions, the following should be the main aims: first, preservation of characteristic landscape beauty; second, ample provision of access and facilities for public open-air enjoyment; third, suitable protection of wildlife, buildings, and places of architectural and historic interest; fourth, efficient maintenance of effective farming. The implication of the basis of decisions being the national interest was that land use decisions in National

Parks ought not to be the responsibility of Planning Authorities, because of their primary local responsibilities.

Legislation in 1949 created ten National Parks (fig. 9.9), omitting the South Downs and Norfolk Broads from the Hobhouse proposals. However, responsibility for land use decisions was given to the Planning Authorities, the principal powers as regards regulation of land use thus being negative: that is,

Figure 9.9   National Parks, Areas of Outstanding National Beauty and long-distance footpaths in England and Wales.

the power to veto change perceived as undesirable. While a National Parks Commission was set up, its powers were largely advisory. Subsequent attempts to achieve a more centralized and specific control have largely been thwarted. Generally, administration of the Parks involves various *ad hoc* arrangements and joint committees drawn from interested organizations. In 1968 the Countryside Act replaced the National Parks Commission by the Countryside Commission, the general emphasis switching from preservation to conservation and use of the countryside. However, National Parks administration remained substantially unchanged. Clout (1972, p. 86) provided a succinct summary: 'With the exception of the Peak, and partially of the Lakes, National Parks are run by Local Authorities. In short, the administration of the ten parks, covering 9% of England and Wales, is a muddle and a negation of the National Parks ideal.'

Perhaps the most striking State intervention of a positive character affecting land use has resulted from implementation of the 1946 (and 1965) New Towns Acts (this is a form of intervention by no means limited to Britain: for example, see Rubinstein 1978). While the effects of this legislation have been considerable, they have nevertheless failed to reach the proportions envisaged by Abercrombie, Reith and others in the 1940s and, at least temporarily, the New Towns programme is currently (1979) being run down. While the idea of new towns, of achieving social progress by acting on the built environment, is an old one, the specific context of the 1946 Act was given by the 1944 Abercrombie Plan and proposals to deal with overcrowding and housing shortages in London. However, after 1963 New Towns came increasingly to be used as an instrument of regional policy (see Hudson 1976, pp. 1–25). To date some 33 New Towns have been designated, although Stonehouse (designated in 1971) has since been abandoned. New Towns policy has affected land use at two levels:

(1) in terms of the conversion of rural to urban land use, although increasingly New Towns have been designated which encompass in part already built-up areas rather than purely green field sites. At this scale, the impacts of the New Towns policy have been most pronounced in a ring around London and in the Development Areas;

(2) in terms of the arrangements of differing land uses within the New Town Designated Area.

Under the New Towns Act, non-elected Development Corporations are appointed by the Minister with powers to acquire land, determine the use of that land, and undertake various kinds of development: housing; industrial; commercial; etc. Detailed land use proposals, in the form of a Master Plan, are drawn up and if there are objections to these, a Public Inquiry is held before the Plan is submitted to the Minister (formerly of Housing and Local Government, now the Secretary of State for the Environment) for approval. Similar schemes have operated under the 1952 Town Development Act but with Local Authorities rather than Development Corporations as the developing agency.

INDIRECT STATE INTERVENTIONS

These, too, are of a positive and negative character, encompassing such diverse areas of legislation as that covering landlord–tenant relations (Turner 1977, pp. 101–9), land and property tax, rating procedures, and various pieces of legislation affecting agriculture (see, for example, Bowler 1976). In the latter context, the agricultural price-support system has both affected the total quantity of agricultural land, maintaining this above the area that would otherwise be given over to agriculture, and altering areas devoted to different crops. In addition, the derating of agricultural land from 1919 has had a similar effect, raising the total agricultural acreage by raising the value of agricultural land relative to other uses (Goodall 1970, pp. 20–1). Finally, agricultural price-support schemes are by no means limited to Britain: numerous other national governments and supra-national organizations (notably the EEC) operate similar schemes with varying effects on agricultural land use both in Britain and elsewhere.

In an urban context, another example of indirect State intervention is provided by the 1944 Town and Country Planning Act since the advent of which Local Authorities outside London have possessed powers (taken into the 1947 Act) to participate with developers in town centre redevelopment schemes on condition that they own at least part of the land involved. Originally these partnership schemes were intended to facilitate redevelopment of bombed-out city centres. They have since been important in producing land use changes in urban central areas. The usual practice has been for Local Authorities to grant 99 year leases to developers at a fixed ground rent (Ambrose and Colenutt 1975, p. 68), thus effectively raising the rate of return over time to developers. In this way many major city centres which had been bombed have been rebuilt, including Bristol, Coventry, Exeter, Plymouth, Portsmouth and Southampton. However, these powers have also been used to redevelop other city centres. An important recent example has been the 4 ha Eldon Square scheme in central Newcastle, a joint development between the City Council, Capital and Counties and, latterly, the Combined Petroleum Companies Pension Fund. The experience of such schemes was important in shaping the provisions of the 1975 Community Land Act. Indeed, on opening phase one of the Eldon Square development in March 1976, the Minister of Planning commented that 'This development is an excellent example of what can be achieved by constructive partnership between public authorities and the private sector ... the Eldon Square development is an example of a method which, I hope, will be extensively followed under the Community Land Act provisions' (Carney and Hudson 1976a, p. 18).

Summary

In the preceding three sections, we have outlined some of the ways in which land use models based on a neoclassical conception of competitive land use allocation through a market may be modified. However, incorporation of these various modifications destroys the simplicity of the land use patterns yielded by these models in their original form. More fundamentally, it challenges the validity of the theoretical basis of these models – the particular abstractions from real social and economic processes which are encapsulated in neoclassical theory. Rather than these modifications being merely deviations from the neoclassical conceptualization of processes of land use allocation, which nevertheless can be easily incorporated into that conceptualization, they suggest the need for a radical re-interpretation of underlying processes.

10 Land use models: alternative interpretations

Introduction

Consider the following characterization of the relationship between land use patterns and social processes in the contemporary USA city (Harvey 1973, pp. 174–5):

> The evidence suggests that the dynamics of land use change remain fairly constant under the capitalist mode of production. The consumers' surplus (the difference between what a consumer pays for a good and would be willing to pay rather than go without it) is diminished by producers of housing services transforming it into producers' surplus (rents and profits) through quasi-monopolistic practices (usually exercised on the basis of class monopoly power). Also the poorest groups generally live in locations subject to the greatest speculative pressure from land use change. In order to realise an adequate future return on investment in existing commercial urban renewal schemes . . . financial institutions have a vested interest in expanding commercial redevelopment geographically; by this process spatial externalities are created through which new commercial development enhances the value of the old. New commercial development will usually have to take place over land already in housing. Housing in these areas can be deliberately economically run down by the withdrawal of financial support for the housing market – 'red lining' by financial institutions is a common practice in the United States, although it is generally explained away as risk aversion: this is but part of the story, however. Landlords are forced under these conditions to maximise current income over a short-term time horizon, which means a rational business-like milking of a property for all it is worth. The physical obsolescence, generated by this economic obsolescence, results in social and economic pressures which build up in the worst sections of the housing market and have to be relieved, at some stage or other, by a 'blow out' somewhere. This 'blow out' results in new construction and the taking up of new land at the urban fringes or in urban redevelopment – processes which are both subject to intensive speculative pressure. New household formation and in-migration supplement this dynamic.

The same financial institutions which deny funds to one sector of the housing market stand to gain from the realisation of speculative gains in another, as land use is subsequently transformed or as suburbanisation proceeds. The impulses which are transmitted through the urban land use system are not unconnected. The diversity of actors and institutions involved makes a conspiracy theory of urban land-use changes unlikely (which is not to say that conspiracy never occurs). The processes are strongly structured through the market exchange system so that individuals, groups and organisations operating self-interestedly in terms of exchange value can, with the help of the 'hidden hand', produce the requisite result.

The character of the processes which Harvey here describes, using an eclectic selection of categories, can at best be only partially grasped within the conceptual confines of the categories of the principal approaches on which land use models to date have been constructed: ecological analogy or neoclassical economics. While both these approaches yield models of land use patterns which have some descriptive validity, the processes which they invoke as giving rise to these are found wanting as adequate explanations (irrespective of attempts to modify them). In order better to understand past and contemporary land use patterns (both rural and urban), in so far as they are determined by processes the same as or similar to those outlined by Harvey, it is necessary to adopt a different theoretical approach, focused upon the specific relationships between land use patterns and the social processes which are dominant in societies under the sway of the capitalist mode of production: both ecological analogy, with its appeal to the 'moral order', and the conceptions of process inherent in neoclassical economics offer, at best, restricted perspectives.

Economics is, however, a theoretically heterogeneous discipline. Neoclassical theory is not the only basis for interpreting land use patterns. Explanations of these can be sought in other types of economic theory: in Ricardian or Marxian political economy, for example. Recently, primarily as a result of the lead given by Harvey (1973), a radical attack has been mounted on existing land use models, challenging the theoretical bases on which these are erected, reformulating the scope of the debate over land use by drawing upon classical and modern political economy and thereby attempting to reconstruct the theoretical basis of land use models on a historically specific basis. Others have since joined the debate, either by way of extension or criticism of Harvey's seminal contribution, while he himself has further elaborated his initial statement (Harvey 1974, 1975; Harvey and Chatterjee 1974). While we briefly comment upon these contributions below (p. 235), for present purposes – an introduction to these alternative approaches to analysing land use patterns – we confine ourselves mainly to Harvey's initial (1973) contribution.

The aim of Harvey's work is to uncover the real nature of those processes which shape the contemporary city, as a necessary first step in altering these; the problem in essence is to abolish the limited empirical validity of existing urban land use models, a validity which reflects an iniquitous social order. Noting that Engels (1845, pp. 46–7) observed concentric land use zoning in English cities in the 1840s but sought to interpret this in economic class terms, Harvey adds that it seems a pity that contemporary geographers have looked to Park and Burgess rather than Engels for their inspiration (Harvey 1973, pp. 132–3). He then goes on to sketch out the ground for a theoretical interpretation of land use in capitalist cities, drawing mainly but by no means exclusively (as the quotation cited above illustrates) on concepts drawn from Marxian political economy. In particular he focuses attention on two issues: the relationship between use values and exchange values and the conceptualization of rent (Harvey 1973, chapter 5).

Harvey comments briefly upon the role of the State in relation to land use allocation but does not develop this issue. However, State intervention is – as we have shown in the preceding chapter – characteristic of contemporary land use allocation. We consider interpretations of such intervention in a later section, pointing to its paradoxical character and drawing on recently developed theories of the State to help explain these paradoxes.

Use values and exchange values

Intuitively, the distinction between use value and exchange value is easy to grasp: a house, for example, is simultaneously a use value (a place in which to live) and an exchange value (a commodity that can be exchanged either directly or indirectly, via money, for other commodities). Harvey begins by discussing Jevons' (1871) obliteration, except in a formal sense, of the distinction between use value and exchange value. This distinction had been an issue of continuing concern to preceding generations of political economists. The significance of Jevons' redefinition of use and exchange values in relation to the use of land is that this provided the basis for the development of marginal analysis and, in due course, neoclassical models of the land market and land use patterns.

While resolving certain inconsistencies in Smith's and Ricardo's discussions of the relationship between use and exchange values, Jevons' redefinition obscured certain problems which are important to an understanding of land use. Marx provided an alternative solution to these inconsistencies but in a way, Harvey suggests, that does not draw a veil over these problems and which indicated a very different path for analysis and action to that implied in Jevons' solution. Harvey therefore proposes that it may be relevant to resurrect the classical debate on use and exchange value in order to understand better contemporary urban problems. In particular, he suggests that Marx's treatment of use values and exchange values offers a key to deeper understanding of the forces producing particular land use configurations within capitalist cities (a good general introduction to Marxian political economy is contained in Desai 1974).

A key distinction between neoclassical economics and Marxian political economy is that whereas neoclassical marginalist analysis is conducted principally in technical terms, central to Marxian political economy is the concept of mode of production. Simply defined, this refers to a particular combination of forces of production (technology) and social relations of production. Marx was mainly concerned with analysing the development of the capitalist mode of production. One of the main characteristics of this mode of production is generalized commodity production for exchange, with the (exchange) value of each commodity defined by the socially necessary amount of labour required for its production. Every commodity thus has a two-fold aspect, as use value and exchange value. Marx therefore saw these aspects as dialectically related through the form they assume in the commodity, a relationship which is not merely 'a thing' but which also expresses a set of social relationships between different classes. Harvey cites a long passage from Marx (1859, pp. 41–3) which we reproduce here, illustrating the relational nature of the categories of use value and exchange value:

> The commodity, however, is the direct unity of use value and exchange value and at the same time it is a commodity only in relation to other commodities. The *exchange process* of commodities, is the *real* relation that exists between them. This is the social process which is carried on by individuals independently of one another, but they take part in it only as commodity owners . . . . The commodity *is* a use value, but as a commodity it is *not* a use value. It would not be a commodity if it were a use value for its owner, that is, a direct means of satisfaction of his own needs. For its owner it is on the contrary a *non-use value*, that is merely a physical depository of exchange value or simply a *means of exchange*. Use value is an active carrier of exchange value for its owner only in so far as it is an exchange value. The commodity therefore has still to become an exchange value . . . a use value for others. Since it is not a use value to its owner, it must be a use value to other owners of commodities. If this is not the case, then the labour expended on it was useless labour and the result accordingly is not a commodity . . . . To become a use value, the commodity must encounter the particular need which it can satisfy. Thus the use values of commodities become use values by a mutual exchange of places: they pass from the hands of those for whom they were a means of exchange into the hands of those for whom they serve as consumer goods. Only as a result of the universal alienation of commodities does the labour contained in them become useful labour . . . . To become use-values commodities must be altogether alienated; they must enter into the exchange process; exchange however is concerned merely with their aspect as exchange values. Hence only by being realised as exchange values can they be realised as use-values (emphases in original).

Harvey argues that contemporary attempts to account for urban land use patterns one-sidedly focus attention either on the use value aspects of land (through the study of houses as places in which to live) or on the exchange value characteristics (the market exchange system) but with little conception of how the two might be related. Thus, for example, various models of land use patterns (Burgess, etc.) while varying in their relative sophistication, are essentially descriptive of aspects of use value. While valuable, they cannot yield up a theory of urban land use. Use value may provide the conceptual underpinning of these traditional geographical and sociological analyses of urban land use patterns, but the concept is used in such a way as to exclude such analyses from the sphere of investigation of political economy. Again, land use models generated from neoclassical economics focus on the exchange value characteristics of land to the exclusion of use value, except in so far as this is represented in the formal relationship between these proposed by Jevons. Harvey cautions us not to allow this 'crude assumption' concerning the relationship between use and exchange value to deceive us into thinking that real problems have been resolved. Rather they have been obscured. Amplifying this point in a discussion of the inadequacy of neoclassical models of the urban housing market, Harvey (1973, 166) continues 'if a commodity depends upon the coming together of use value and exchange value in the social act of exchange, then the things we call land and housing are apparently very different commodities depending on the particular interest groups operating in the market'. If such a conclusion is valid with respect to the housing market, then it is true *a fortiori* for the urban land market in general, characterized by competition between different uses, and hence to urban land use theory as a whole.

The conclusion which Harvey draws from his critique of existing approaches to urban land use is readily anticipated: if the problem with these is their one-sided treatment of land use, what is required is a Marxist analysis which brings together use value and exchange value in a dialectical relationship. In Harvey's view, an adequate theory of urban land use can be based on nothing else. He (1973, p. 160) suggests that for a theory to emerge 'we must focus attention upon those catalytic moments in the urban land use decision process when use value and exchange value collide to make commodities out of land and improvements thereon' and that it is particularly important in understanding what happens at such moments to bear in mind the 'very special characteristics' of both land and the improvements to it.

He pays considerable attention to these 'very special characteristics', identifying six of these. Several of these have been recognized by others at various times in relation to the land market, without their full significance being wholly appreciated. These have been seen more in the context of relaxing the assumptions of neoclassical models, rather than as indicative of the need for an alternative theoretical basis to neoclassical economics (see, for example, Turner 1977, pp. 35–41; also see p. 209).

The first of these special characteristics is that, unlike other commodities, land and improvements on it cannot be moved around at will. Their location is fixed. Absolute location confers monopoly privileges upon the person who has the rights to determine use of that location. No two people can occupy exactly the same location, a principle which, when institutionalized as private property, has very important ramifications for urban land use theory.

Second, land and improvements on it are commodities which all individuals need. Some of these are indispensable. This places strong constraints on consumer choice. Indeed, one can question the degree to which a conceptualization in terms of choice rather than constraint is appropriate.

Third, land and improvements on it change hands relatively infrequently. However, the frequency of exchange varies in differing sections of the urban economy: for example, privately owned housing generally changes hands more frequently than do factories.

Fourth, land is permanent and the life expectancy of improvements often considerable. As such, land and improvements to it and the rights attached to these provide an opportunity to store wealth. Moreover, most land continues its potential for use even in the absence of upkeep. Thus land and property have a current and future use value, a current and future exchange value.

Fifth, while exchange occurs at a particular point in time, use stretches over an often considerable period of time. Rights of use over a relatively long period are purchased at one point in time for large outlays of capital. As a result, financial institutions take a crucial role in the land and property market (for amplification of this point, see Ambrose and Colenutt 1975; Boddy 1976). Turner (1977, p. 143) points out that, whereas in 1965 insurance companies invested £89 million and pension funds £22.8 million in land, property and ground rents in Britain, by 1974 their annual investments had risen to £352.6 million and £112.8 million, respectively. Moreover, this investment is not limited to urban land. It has been estimated that in 1971 financial institutions such as insurance companies, unit trusts and pension funds owned about 400 km^2 of farmland in Great Britain but that by 1976 this had risen to over 1500 km^2 (CSO 1979, p. 167).

Sixth, land and improvements to it have numerous different uses which may to some extent be compatible to the user (see p. 48). Taken together, these various uses constitute use value.

Harvey concludes that a reconstruction of urban land use theory will not be easy, especially given these 'very special characteristics'. Nevertheless, he sketches out an outline of such a possible reconstruction with sufficient clarity as to make it clear that the effort involved in this task is a worthwhile one. However, whether this can be best achieved via an eclectic blending of categories drawn from often incompatible theoretical positions, as Harvey in this instance attempts, is open to doubt.

The conceptualization of rent

A further key issue in this reconstruction concerns the way in which rent is conceptualized. Harvey remarks on the seeming paradox of the relative success of models based on micro-economic theory in describing land use patterns at the same time as the process postulates on which these models are based are so patently unrealistic. He suggests that the key to unravelling this paradox lies in the role and meaning of rent as an allocative device within the urban system. Rent, in fact, fulfils a key allocative function within neoclassically based models, serving to sort land uses into locations via competitive bidding. Rent-paying ability becomes the common yardstick before which all land uses are equal. Rent is seen as the return to a scarce factor of production, land being seen, in principle, as no different to capital or labour; rent is thus determined by the marginal productivity of land.

However, this is but one conception of rent and one which ignores the long and controversial history of the concept in political economic thought. As Harvey puts it, rent enters into urban land use theory in an innocent state, as if there were no serious problems attached to its interpretation. In particular, the assumed symmetry between land and other factors of production is untenable. Land is fixed in location, finite in supply; to deny this and maintain the neoclassical fiction that it is neither, is a trap which can easily lead us into a misinterpretation of the forces determining urban land use. We neglect the realities of absolute, relative and relationally determined time and space at our peril.

What is needed then is a concept of rent that can meet the challenge of these realities. Harvey suggests turning to the 'earthy richness' of classical political economy to elucidate the nature of rent and in particular to a close examination of Marx's categories of rent (although these themselves have been subject to considerable critical scrutiny, as Harvey points out). Marx saw rent as contingent upon mode of production and his categories of rent cannot be understood without brief reference to some aspects of his conceptualization of the capitalist mode of production. Marx saw the source of value creation as living labour. In a capitalist mode of production, society is divided into classes: from the point of view of production these are the capitalist class, who own the means of production, and the working class, who own their labour power, their capacity to work. The latter are compelled to sell their labour in order to obtain the necessities of life. However, as they sell the capacity to labour for a period of time, rather than a fixed quantity of labour, they produce commodities to a greater value than those (in the form of money) for which they exchange their labour power. Thus at the end of a period of production, the owners of the means of production not only recoup the capital (value) advanced to purchase means of production and labour power but also the surplus value, the difference between the value originally advanced and that resulting at the end of a production period. This surplus value can then be distributed in the form of profits, dividends, rents, etc.

Rent is the economic form in which landed property is realized. While landed property predates the rise of the capitalist mode of production, the latter cannot afford to destroy landed property because its own existence presupposes private ownership of the means of production. Rather the impact of capitalism is to both preserve and partially transform a class of landlords creating 'modern' landed property. Capital, as it were, must pay a tax on production (rent – a portion of total surplus value) as the price for perpetuating the legal basis of its own existence; in turn this may enter into production costs. At this point it is important to consider different categories of rent which Marx considered could arise in a capitalist mode of production: differential rent; monopoly rent; and absolute rent.[1]

First, let us consider differential rent: this arises simply from the difference between an individual firm's production price for a commodity and the general production price of that commodity in a given sphere of production.[2] Thus differential rent cannot enter into the price of production or of products as its origins lie in the excess (i.e. above average) profits accruing to certain producers because of their location. These can be claimed by landowners in the form of rent. Whereas Ricardo (1817) discussed differential rent only in rather limited circumstances (as arising in agriculture from fertility differences with diminishing returns to successive inputs of labour and capital), Marx (in Part vi of *Capital, Vol. III*, 1894) discusses this more generally, in the context both of fertility differences, differential application of variable and constant capital, and locational differences. Harvey (1973, p. 181) summarizes thus:

> differential rent takes on its meaning in a relative space which is structured by differentials in productive capacity at different locations and which is integrated spatially through transport cost relations. Differential rent, it seems, cannot be conceptualised without projecting a relative space. But differential rent is created . . . through the operation of the capitalist mode of production in the context of the institution of private property.

Monopoly rent arises because it is possible to charge a monopoly price for a commodity. That is, a price independent of either the price of production or the value of the commodity.[3] Harvey suggests that such rents arise only through substantial imperfections in spatial competition.

Absolute rent is distinguished from monopoly rent in that, of itself, it gives rise to a monopoly price, in contrast to an independently determined monopoly price arising from conditions of monopoly within a sector of production, which allows a monopoly rent to be gained. A necessary condition (among others) for the existence of absolute rent is some barrier to the over-all equalization of the rate of profit between sectors; while this may take the form of legislative restrictions (see pp. 215–24), more generally in late capitalism (for an outline of the features of late capitalism, see Mandel 1975) these barriers simply take the form of a requirement for a certain minimal return by landowners before they will release their land.[4] However, as Harvey notes, there has been considerable controversy surrounding the concept of absolute rent (see also pp. 235–6).

Harvey goes on to discuss the usefulness of Marx's categories of rent in understanding the dynamics of urban rent surfaces and land use patterns; Marx himself, while hinting at the application of these categories in analyses of cities, mainly developed his concepts of rent in relation to agricultural land use (see also Murray 1977, 1978). In the course of this, he claims to resolve the paradox of the predictive accuracy which accompanies the conceptual poverty of models based upon a neoclassical conception of rent – although as Ive (1975, p. 22) points out, this predictive accuracy appears less paradoxical if one recalls that neoclassical models reflect a conception of theory which has predictive accuracy as one of its chief goals. Harvey argues that the high rental value of land in central cities ought not necessarily to be interpreted purely in terms of differential rent and the marginal productivity of land. Rather, absolute and monopoly rents at such locations enter into the determination of rents. If such rents are dominant in the determination of the price of the land at these locations, then the price determines land use; if differential rents dominate, use determines price. In practice, over-all rents reflect combinations of each of these three types, although it is often difficult to determine empirically their precise proportions.

In the new commercial and industrial cities of the 19th century (such as Chicago), the combination of the structure of the transport system and character of production probably resulted in the dominance of differential rent as the main source of rents. However, in contemporary metropolitan centres as well as in older commercial and administrative centres, such as London in the 19th century, absolute and monopoly rents are of much greater significance. Since these types of rent necessarily enter production costs, only those firms with production functions which enable them readily to absorbe these costs will be found in such locations. One consequence of this is that central city areas are characteristically occupied by commercial and governmental activities whose productivity cannot be easily measured: for example, government offices, banks, insurance companies, stockbrokers, travel agents and various forms of entertainment.

Hence arises the paradox of 'unproductive' activity on land supposedly of the greatest marginal productivity by virtue of its location. The solution to this paradox lies in recognizing that rent levels and land value in central city locations do not reflect differential rent alone but also processes which permit absolute and, more important, monopoly rents to be charged. Likewise, this insight contains the key to understanding the relative success of neoclassical micro-economic models in replicating urban land use patterns. These generally assume a (more or less complicated: see fig. 8.15) cone of differential rent distributed around the city centre. However, Harvey argues that the actual central peaking of rents and land values reflects forces which have no necessary connection with differential rent or the marginal productivity of land: rather these reflect forces generating absolute or monopoly rents. In essence, therefore, the link between assumed processes, assumed and actual land use patterns is merely one of association, not cause and effect. Competitive bidding is undoubtedly significant but it assumes that land use determines value whereas in practice the reverse determination is more prevalent in most capitalist cities.

Harvey (1973, pp. 188–9) concludes that neoclassical, micro-economic models

> rely exclusively upon the concept of differential rent and generally set their analytics in a relative space. They also abstract . . . from the power of private property although individual monopoly control over individual land parcels is always presumed. These models must therefore be viewed as special cases, which describe conditions when absolute and monopoly rents are insignificant, when absolute and relational concepts of time and space are irrelevant, and when the institution of private property is notably quiescent in the land and property markets. It is helpful, of course, to have the analytics spelled out for these restricted conditions, but it is dangerous to regard these models as a foundation for a general theory of land use.

However, by way of conclusion to this section, we note that Harvey's views on rent have not gone unchallenged by others who accept his critique of neoclassically based models and his general point that what is required to promote understanding of land use patterns in cities is historically specific concepts of rent (see, for example, Breugel 1975; Clarke and Ginsburg 1976; Edel 1976; Ive 1975; Scott 1976 – who adds a rather distinctive contribution to this debate, arguing for a neo-Ricardian approach which owes much to Sraffa 1960; and Walker 1974, 1975). However, perhaps the most cutting indictment of Harvey (1973) and indeed of several of Harvey's critics is provided by Murray (1977, 1978). In a spirited defence of the Marxian approach to rent, he vigorously argues the need to regard issues of distribution (including rent) as subordinated to those of production. Murray (1977, pp. 119–20) argues:

> it is only through starting from value, and never losing its thread, that we can adequately understand the determination of distribution by production, and the contradictory development of their forms.
>
> It was for this reason that Marx was so virulent against analyses which lost this thread, and which started not from value but from prices of production.
>
> Unfortunately much of the recent Marxist [sic] work on rent has been marred by taking this starting point. This is true of all those who adopt monopoly rent in preference to absolute rent.
>
> In urban theory, for instance, the dominant approach is barely distinguishable, save in terminology, from traditional monopolistic competition and bilateral monopoly theory. Thus Harvey analyses cities as aggregations of sub-markets, strategically separated by landed proprietors. He likens these to man-made islands and calls the rent earned from them absolute rent. This is an utter confusion. He is no way seeking to connect rent to value . . . . The resulting rent is merely a version of monopoly rent. His confusion on value is equally clear when he

attacks neoclassical theories of differential rent as being based on distance and neglecting utility. Distance, with its implicit differential labour times embodied in the costs of transport, is the one hard basis for an adequate theory of urban rent.

Clearly much remains to be resolved in satisfactorily relating Marxian concepts of rent to contemporary urban land use patterns.

New perspectives on the State

State intervention in land use is widespread and both the ideology associated with this and the actual impacts of intervention require consideration for a more complete understanding of the determinants of land use patterns. We restrict our comments on the State to countries with developed capitalist societies, in particular Great Britain.

The characteristic image of planning (much of which in practice means land use planning, although State intervention is by no means restricted to this sphere), in Britain and similar countries is that this is organized to better some version of the collective good, formulated for example in terms of the national interest or community interest. Planning is seen as a medium of redistribution, at worst neutral in its distributive effects but at best socially progressive. This image, indeed, forms the main basis of the claims to legitimacy of planning as a social activity. However, it is an image which strongly reflects planners' self-conceptions of their roles and also the stated intentions of planning legislation, planners themselves, and so on (see chapter 1).

However, in practice, planning in capitalist societies has often been socially regressive. Elliott (1978, p. 19) concludes that in Britain the struggle between the progressive and conservative elements was an unequal one so that, by the mid-1950s, planning in Britain was firmly established as a conservative force despite the progressive ideology of the immediate post-war years. As he puts it: 'The last thirty years are the years of a novel and massive intervention by the State and by local authorities [sic] in the organisation of space. But they are also years of unattained hopes and unredeemed promises.'

Thus one principal characteristic of State interventions in land use patterns and the organization of space is that these tend to have effects in addition to or other than those originally intended. Stated goals frequently remain unrealized or, if they are realized, are done so only partially and/or are accompanied by unintended and undesirable side effects. Despite, or perhaps because of, State interventions, precisely those changes perceived as undesirable which planning intervention was intended to check and reverse have, in fact, often been encouraged. Alternatively, old problems have not been solved but rather displaced to appear in new guises. More generally, the actual effects of State interventions have been somewhat at variance with the intended, stated goals, as the following examples demonstrate.

Consider, for example, the case of British National Parks (Clout 1972, p. 90). Since their designation, a ballistic missile early warning station has been built on the North York Moors, a nuclear power station in Snowdonia, and an oil refinery and an iron stocking ground in Pembroke. Potash is being mined in the North York Moors and kaolin in parts of Dartmoor. In several of these cases the advice of the National Parks (latterly Countryside) Commission has been overridden by ministerial decisions. Blenkinsop (1968, p. 526) notes: 'Ministers gave assurances that the designation of an area as a national park meant that effective priority would be given to the protection of its beauty . . . . Each national park has its own monument to the weakness of such assurances.' Clearly in some of these cases considerations of national defence and security have been paramount. In others, however, private commercial interests rather than some conception of the national interest would seem to have held sway.

Another example is provided by the 1965 Control of Office and Industrial Development Act. Intended particularly to check new office development and hold down prices in London and the South East and encourage new development primarily in the peripheral regions, the actual results of implementing this legislation were at variance with this aim. By restricting supply, rents for new office space and property values rose sharply; for example, office rents in the City of London rose from £5 per ft^2 in 1967, to £10 per ft^2 in 1971 and £20 in 1973. The net effect of this legislation was to make London a more, rather than a less, attractive place for property investment (Ambrose and Colenutt 1975, p. 76).

Hall *et al.* (1973) reach a similar conclusion as to the effect of the post-war planning machinery in Britain, arguing that – contrary to the intentions of planners themselves – the objective impacts of the planning system have been to raise property and land prices. These prices rose from the late 1950s at rates unprecedented in British history. Moreover, these price rises and also the unintended increase in commuting reflect the success of the planning policies in containing urban development and limiting the supply of the commodity 'land with planning permission' (Hall 1974, p. 403). Such unintended results are by no means limited to Britain: for example, Rubinstein (1978, p. 92) suggests a parallel sequence of events in France.

A consequence of this unplanned spiral in land and property prices has been a socially regressive distribution of the benefits arising from the effects of planning policies (given the absence of a progressive tax on windfall gains resulting from the granting of planning permission). As Hall (1974, p. 407) puts it, the effect of planning has been to give more to those who already had most, while taking away from the poor what little they had. The biggest gains have gone to those with the largest stake in the property market. In similar vein, Ambrose and Colenutt (1975, p. 67) conclude that the main beneficiaries of the planning system are not the general public or local authorities but the development industry. They suggest that the planning system, in fact, is largely organized around the demands and premises of developers and their professional advisers and go on to point out the 'irony' that the work that local authorities put into structure plans and development control so restricts the supply of development land in certain areas that rents and the price of land are forced to rise. Harvey (1974, p. 192) makes the same point in arguing that controlling physical growth without controlling anything else merely exacerbates scarcity and creates opportunities for extracting monopoly rent; seen in this context, the abandonment in 1953 of the measures contained in the 1947 Town and Country Planning Act to control windfall gains and the subsequent failure to reimpose these in an effective way was absolutely decisive in permitting spiralling land and property prices in Britain.

To account for these seeming paradoxes, the irony of the disjunctions between intended and actual consequences of State intervention, is a theoretical question of some importance in understanding the processes which underlie land use patterns and changes in these. Ambrose and Colenutt (1975, pp. 61–3) attempt to answer this question, beginning from a technical critique of land use planning policies. They begin by pointing out that the land use groupings used by planners are usually extraordinarily vague (but see p. 35). Broad categories such as 'industry', 'residential', 'shops' or 'commercial', each cover a multitude of different uses, many of which have totally different and even opposing social connotations. Thus, housing could include council housing, privately owned luxury flats or town houses or, at the other extreme, hostels for the homeless. Industry could include everything from a high-rent warehouse to an obsolete factory unit. The result of this vague grouping is that many changes in the use of buildings do not require planning permission from the local authority. Ambrose and Colenutt regard this as the most important weakness in the planning system. The control of development takes place with reference to maps which contain broad land use categories but these, along with physical appearance, are the only criteria of planning control. All questions of price and rent are outside the scope of planning. One consequence of this is that the developer is therefore in a very strong position compared with planners or the public. He need only justify his proposals in pure physical planning terms. In addition, Ambrose and Colenutt suggest, he will have employed a team of surveyors and valuers and ex-local authority planners, which will probably know the local area at least as well and probably better than the current local authority planners, and whose members are experts in presenting schemes to planners and councillors. They further suggest that most large developers employ surveyors and property consultants who are experienced at dealing with the local authority in which the development is located and that these people often know more about the workings of the local planning department and are more familiar with the thinking of the senior planners than anyone else inside or outside the planning department.

While the description put forward by Ambrose and Colenutt clearly has some validity, as an explanation of the contradictory character of planning activity it is inadequate. Suggesting that such an explanation can be accomplished at the level of the personalities involved or the types of land use categories and planning methods used is surely too simplistic. It begs key questions to do with why certain sorts of knowledge (land use categories, planning methods, etc.) are regarded as pre-eminent, why certain views of the world are dominant and why certain interests are regarded as pre-eminent, rather than accounting for these (see Habermas 1972; also Pocock and Hudson 1978, chapter 8).

A more adequate account of the seemingly paradoxical character of State intervention requires some overall theoretical conception of the State which encompasses the production and rise to prominence of certain sorts of ideas, knowledge and methodologies. Further, it needs to recognize the fact that decisions made within the State apparatus are governed by a more complex, less easily defined calculus than those of the private sector; that there is a tension between the generally incompatible pressures for efficient management and those for progressive social reform. Specifically, it requires consideration of theories of the capitalist State which focus upon the inherently crisis-prone character of State interventions – a result of the inability of the State to solve contradictions inherent within the capitalist mode of production. Rather, these contradictions are internalized within the State apparatus, to appear in fresh forms, for example as a rationality crisis characterized by the failure of the State to fulfil intended objectives, which in turn may lead to a legitimation crisis and a questioning of the State's sovereign authority (see Habermas 1976; Offe 1975). Such theories offer a rich source of ideas for understanding the character of State intervention in land use. It is clear that, given the scope of State involvement in decisions affecting land use, satisfactory explanations of land use patterns in capitalist societies presuppose that these theoretical questions concerning the character of State intervention be more fully explored (for a brief review of different theoretical perspectives on the State, see Dear and Clark 1978; for a fuller review, see Holloway and Piciotto 1978).

Concluding comments

At this stage, several points are worth reiterating. Since a dominant mode of production creates conditions of consumption, the evolution of urban land use patterns must be understood in terms of the general development of successive dominant modes of production. Although the argument has been developed here primarily in the context of urban land use, it could equally well have been developed with respect to agricultural or rural areas under the sway of capitalism (see Murray 1978).

Within capitalism, rent plays a crucial role in the evolution of spatial form. Harvey (1973, p. 191) attributes the relative homogeneity that exists between capitalist city forms to this and, again, similar arguments could be made in relation to agricultural or rural land use patterns. However, rent only exists in a contingent sense, being dependent upon the mode of production and certain institutions relating to property ownership. Consequently, there can be no such thing as a 'general' land use theory, for urban or rural areas. Rather, theory must be historically specific, relating urban form to different modes of roduction or stages of development within a given mode of production.

Viewed in this context, criticism of, say, Burgess's model as lacking universality (p. 186) are seen to be misplaced. Furthermore, those (such as Sjoberg, see p. 188) who suggest a differentiation between industrial and pre-industrial cities (in terms of levels of technological development alone rather than in terms of mode of production, of social relations as well as forces of production) are perceived to hold a rather one-sided view.

Thus, in order to understand land use patterns in capitalist cities, we must begin with an analysis of the inner dynamic of the capitalist mode of production. Related to this, particularly in the context of late capitalism, is the question of the theoretical treatment of the capitalist State in relation to land use patterns – for the State is not located outside of the dominant set of social relations but is rather an integral part and reflection of these. The State is unable to resolve contradictions that arise as a reflection of the predominant social relationships; instead these contradictions are displaced into the State apparatus, to appear as paradoxes between, say, the intended and actual effects of policies concerning land use control.

Furthermore, the concepts and categories relevant to an understanding of land use patterns within societies dominated by capitalism are not necessarily applicable where other modes of production dominate. Even when the same concepts are applicable they may denote sharp differences as well as similarities; for example, 'rent' in capitalism takes different forms and implies different social relationships to rent in feudalism. To understand land use patterns in such non-capitalist societies, we need theory which is specific with respect to them (and theory which we have not considered here): no universal land use theory of real merit can or does exist. The broad theoretical task for the future is to show why land use patterns take particular forms within different societies dominated by different modes of production.

Notes

[1] Marx (1861; 1894, Part vi) was concerned to show how ownership of one specific factor of production, land, gave rise to an apparently independent category of distribution despite the fact that in itself it could not be productive of value. As Murray (1977, p. 13) points out 'in capitalism, rent takes the form of surplus over average profits', part of which is siphoned off from capitalists to landlords as a tribute for use of their land. In this sense, rent paid for the use of land is a deduction from total surplus value. To understand the specific mechanisms which create rent in a capitalist mode of production would entail considering, in addition to private property rights, such issues as the differing organic composition of capital in different sectors, the formation of an average rate of profit and the transfer of value between sectors – issues that are beyond the scope of this introductory text. For consideration of these, see, for example, Desai (1974), Mandel (1968), Murray (1977, 1978).
[2] In fact, Marx (1894, pp. 640–747) distinguished between two forms of differential rent. For a brief account of the differences between these, see Lamarche 1976, pp. 100–4.
[3] While the value of a commodity is defined as the socially necessary amount of labour required for its production, prices of production deviate from values. Prices of production comprise the amount of capital advanced in production of a commodity together with a share of total surplus value. This share is proportionate to the quantity of capital advanced in producing the commodity in relation to the total capital advanced in production (of all commodities in a production period). The deviation of prices of production from values reflects a transfer of value from sectors with a low to those with a high organic composition of capital as a consequence of the tendency for equalization of rates of profit and the formation of an average rate of profit within an

economy. Again fuller consideration of these issues is beyond the scope of this text; the reader is referred to the sources cited in footnote 1.

[4] As well as these barriers to free flow of capital between sectors, the existence of absolute rent depends upon other specific factors: the presence of a low organic composition of capital (i.e. a low proportion of fixed to variable capital; of 'dead labour', in the form of machines etc., to living labour) in those branches yielding absolute rent; the reproduction of the comparative monopoly power of landed property against capital in those branches (Murray 1977, p. 109).

Part 5

11   Reality, then, is not simple . . .

Not chaos-like, together crushed and bruised,
But, as the world harmoniously confused:
Where order in variety we see,
And where, though all things differ, all agree
A. Pope, Windsor Forest

. . . the extraordinary lengths to which sheer coincidence can run
must always be borne in mind; often not one, but a whole chain of
close parallels may be involved between two unrelated sets of
circumstances. The case of Presidents Kennedy and Lincoln
provides a good example: President Lincoln was elected in 1860,
Kennedy in 1960; their successors were both named Johnson.
Andrew Johnson was born in 1808, Lyndon Johnson in 1908. John
Wilkes Booth, Lincoln's killer, was born in 1839, and Lee Harvey
Oswald in 1939; both were assassinated before their trials.
Lincoln's secretary, whose name was Kennedy, advised him not to
go to the theatre; Kennedy's secretary, who was called Lincoln,
pressed him not to go to Dallas. John Wilkes Booth shot Lincoln in
a theatre and ran into a warehouse: Oswald shot Kennedy from a
warehouse and ran into a theatre.
N. Davies, Voyages to the New World

We started on what must have seemed to many to be a straightforward and
speedily completed task: we were going to review the meaning of 'land use',
describe how to collect and manipulate information on it, summarize some
existing land use statistics in a macroscopic case study and conclude by
determining the kind of generalizations which could be made about land use in
urban and in rural areas. Unfortunately, the real world – or the image of it
that we perceive – is rather too complex for us readily to provide definitive
answers to the problems that have arisen.

What we *have* done (we hope) is to illustrate the apparent variety of needs
for different types of land use information and to illustrate that very different
views of what is 'land use' are taken – for reasons of need, available 'data
capture' technology or simply a lack of awareness of other work. We have
demonstrated that the characteristics of land use data – the way they are
classified, their geographical or temporal resolution and so on – may well
inhibit and, on many occasions, totally prevent comparisons of data collected
by different organizations. Our survey of the methods of data collection and of
manipulation and analysis showed that recently introduced methods can
produce and cope with up-to-date information for very large areas yet, on
occasions, demand that substantial assumptions be made about the relationship between the land use ss and the built form. In analysing certain

aspects of the land use in Britain as a case study, the practical difficulties with and inadequacies of the data – much of it collected ingeniously from sources never designed to serve as such – were amply demonstrated. Some surprising agreement emerged at the most coarse level of analysis but unresolvable problems appeared in comparing data in any more detail – this in the country with what is reputedly the most sophisticated planning system in the Western World. Finally, our examination of the various land use models which have been built to describe the 'general situation' indicated that these have often been built or tested on the bases of flimsy data, are often rooted in particular space–time contexts and, even more important, are in many cases so naive and simplistic (not only in terms of spatial pattern but, more significantly, in terms of generative processes) as to be counter-productive. However, to begin to build more realistic and powerful explanations of observed land use patterns is by no means easy, as we have shown.

So where does the student of land use go from here? We hold the firm view that, however often it occurs, it is undesirable if decisions related to land use are made on the basis of inadequate or totally absent data; it is clear from our survey that there is a widespread need for land use data of different kinds and we believe that only nationally co-ordinated schemes (although they may be administered locally) will provide the sort of data accuracy and relevance required for many important tasks. To some extent, the wish of the planner to have more and better information is in conflict with the desirability of limiting the cost of obtaining it (especially at a time of cuts in public expenditure) and – at least in the Anglo-Saxon world – of dispelling public concern over confidentiality, privacy and, in particular, of computer data banks.

In principle, we feel there is much about which to be optimistic so far as obtaining data is concerned: although far from ideal at present, data available from satellites should in future meet many basic requirements economically and without necessarily infringing (in our view) human rights. The advent of such systems and the general availability of raw data will permit those who need to make national and even international comparisons to do so on realistic bases. Such facilities are very necessary if we are to escape from the situation which Coppock (1978, p. 63) described as follows: 'Coverage is inadequate and patchy, there are large gaps, data are rarely collected primarily as land use records and few of the sources that are available have been properly evaluated.' Developments in the methods of handling the data by computer will make certain operations such as mapping and overlay a matter of routine.

While it is difficult for anyone to deny that substantial technological progress has been in data collection and manipulation, there is considerable disagreement as to whether similar advances have been made in understanding, explaining and predicting land use patterns. For those concerned to construct models to explain and perhaps predict land use patterns, the questions must be faced of whether it is possible to generalize about patterns of land use and at what level of spatial and temporal resolution such generalization is possible. An answer to these questions implies specifying the valid domain of particular models. To some extent – and increasingly – the necessary 'real world' land use data can be made available to compare actual with model land use patterns. However, more and better data alone can provide only a partial validation of particular models – it is quite possible, as many geographers have pointed out, that the same final results (in this case a land use pattern) may be generated by radically different processes; in short, the clear relationship between a pattern of land use and factors postulated as generating it may be nothing other than coincidence. An obvious implication is that it is wiser to begin with process and infer or deduce pattern, rather than begin by pattern and attempt to infer process from it, even though our notions as to process are likely to be shaped in part by the patterns we believe we perceive around us.

At the end of the day, then, the fundamental issue is that of the search for order and generality in land use patterns, based on a philosophical belief that order and generality *do* exist. However, the methodological question of *how* we can best go about this search appears less clear-cut than it did a decade or so ago. There is no doubt that the application of what we may generally call scientific method has led to considerable advance in the ordering of land use information both in terms of data capture, manipulation and modelling. Yet this approach, valuable as it is, is based upon a particular epistemological position which has been strongly challenged in some recent attempts to understand land use patterns: these attempts have adopted what we may generally call a Marxist stance. In general, these have been concerned to reveal the processes underlying existing land use patterns so as to provide a basis for changing them, rather than to ensure their future reproduction. The debate as to the most appropriate epistemological and theoretical framework for understanding land use patterns is one which will certainly continue.

It is our belief that considerable generality *does* exist in the way in which land use patterns are brought about and that this is both demonstrable and explicable: the weaknesses of much existing theory and the interpretational complexities do not weaken our resolve on this point. What is certain, however, is that the explanatory accounts which we build in future must be of very much greater sophistication than those which underpin many existing land use models; and also, as a corollary, that there will be a need for a variety of data – much of it longitudinal through time – on factors such as property ownership, planning restrictions, and demographic characteristics, if we are to deepen our understanding of and obtain better insights into the determinants of land use structure.

Bibliography

Abler, R., Adams, J.G. and Gould, P.R. (1972) *Spatial Organisation.* Englewood Cliffs, New Jersey, Prentice-Hall.

Adams, T. (1979) The characteristics of a national topographic digital data base. Unpublished M.Sc. dissertation, University of Durham.

Aglietta, M. (1978) Phases of US capitalist expansion. *New Left Review* (July/August) **110**, 17–28.

AGRG (1978) *The Wolfson Geochemical Atlas of England and Wales.* Oxford, Clarendon Press.

Aldcroft, D. and Richardson, H.W. (1969) *The British Economy. 1870–1939.* London, Macmillan.

Alexander, I.C. (1972) Multivariate techniques in land use studies: the case of information analysis. *Regional Studies* **6**, 93–103.

Alexander, J.W. (1944) Freight rates as a geographic factor in Illinois. *Economic Geography* **20**, 25–30.

Allan, J.A. (1978) Remote sensing in physical geography. *Progress in Physical Geography* **2** (1) 36–54.

Alonso, W. (1960) A theory of the urban land market. *Papers and Proceedings, Regional Science Association* **6**, 149–58.

Alonso, W. (1964) *Location and Land Use.* Cambridge, Mass., Harvard University Press.

Ambrose, P. (1977) The determinants of urban land use change. *Fundamentals of Human Geography, Section III: Values, Relevance and Policy*, pp. 35–79. Milton Keynes, Open University.

Ambrose, P. and Colenutt, R. (1975) *The Property Machine.* Harmondsworth, Penguin.

Ammer, U., Bechet, G., Bents, D., Rosenkranz, D. and Rosenkranz, A. (1976) *Ecological mapping of the Community. Elaboration of a scheme for the classification of the community territory on the basis of its environmental characteristics. Report and recommendations for a method.* Brussels, Commission of the European Communities.

Anderson, J.R., (1977) Land use and land cover changes—a framework for monitoring. *United States Geological Survey, Journal of Research* **5** (2) 143–53.

Anderson, J.R., Hardy, E.E., Roach, J.T. and Witmer, R.E. (1976) A land use and land cover classification system for use with remote sensor data. *United States Geological Survey, Professional Paper* **964**.

Anderson, K.E., Guptill, S.C., Hallam, C. and Mitchell, W.B. (1977) Developing and using a geographic information system for handling and analysing land resource data. *Remote Sensing of the Electro Magnetic Spectrum* **4** (4) 67–83.

Anderson, M.A. (1978) A comparison of figures for the land use structure of England and Wales in the 1960s. *Area* **9** (1) 43–5.

Anderton, P. and Bigg, P.H. (1972) *Changing to the Metric System— Conversion Factors, Symbols and Definitions*. Teddington, National Physical Laboratory.

Ash, M. (1978) Letter in *The Times*, 10 February.

Baker, W.S. (1926) Some notes on a regional survey. *Geographical Teacher* **13** (6) 451–3.

Balchin, W. (1976) Introduction to paper by A. Coleman, 'Is planning really necessary?' *Geographical Journal* **142** (3) 411–37.

Barnbrock, J. (1974) Prologomenon to a methodological debate on location theory: the case of von Thünen. *Antipode* **6** (1) 59–65.

Barr, J. (1969) *Derelict Britain*. Harmondsworth, Penguin.

Bartholomew, H. (1937) *Land Use in American Cities*. Cambridge, Mass., Harvard University Press.

Bauer, M.E., Hixson, M.M., Davis, B.J. and Etheridge, J.B. (1978) Area estimation of crops by digital analysis of Landsat data. *Photogr. Eng. and Remote Sensing* **44** (8) 1033–43.

Baxter, R.S. (1976) *Computer and Statistical Techniques for Planners*. London, Methuen.

Beard, J.S. (1941) Land Utilization Study of Trinidad. *The Caribbean Forestor* **2**.

Berry, B.J.L. (1959) Ribbon developments in the urban business pattern. *Annals, Assoc. Amer. Geogr.* **49**, 145–55.

Berry, B.J.L. (1967) *The Geography of Market Centres and Retail Distribution*. Englewood Cliffs, New Jersey, Prentice-Hall.

Berry, B.J.L. and Baker, A.M. (1968) Geographic sampling. In Berry, B.J.L. and Marble, D.F. (eds) *Spatial Analysis—a Reader in Statistical Geography*, pp. 91–100. Englewood Cliffs, New Jersey, Prentice-Hall.

Berry, B.J.L., Tennant, R.J., Garner, B.J. and Simmons, J.W. (1963) Commercial structure and commercial blight. *Research Paper* No. 85, Department of Geography, University of Chicago.

Best, R.H. (1959) The major land uses of Great Britain. *Studies in Rural Land Use* No. 4, Wye College, University of London, Kent.

Best, R.H. (1968) The extent of urban growth and agricultural displacement in post-war Britain. *Urban Studies* **5**, 1–23.

Best, R.H. (1976a) The changing land use structure of Britain. *Town and Country Planning* **44** (3) 171–6.

Best, R.H. (1976b) The extent and growth of urban land. *The Planner* **62** (1) 8–11.

Best, R.H. (1978) Myth and reality in the growth of urban land. In Rogers, A.W. (ed.) *Urban Growth, Farmland Losses and Planning*, pp. 2–15. Rural Geography Study Group, Institute of British Geographers.

Best, R.H. and Coppock, J.T. (1962) *The Changing Use of Land in Britain.* London, Faber and Faber.

Betak, J.F. (1973) Two dimensional syntactic complexity measures: a preliminary evaluation. *Geographical Analysis* **5** (1) 1, 5–15.

Blenkinsop, A. (1968) The National Parks Commission. *Town and County Planning* **36**, 525–6.

Blumenfeld, H. (1949) On the concentric circle theory of urban growth. *Land Economics* **25**, 209–12.

Board, C. (1962) *The Border Region: Natural Environment and Land Use in the Eastern Cape.* Cape Town.

Board, C. (1968) Land use surveys: principles and practice. In *Land Use and Resources in Applied Geography.* A Memorial Volume to Sir Dudley Stamp. Special Publication No. 1, Institute of British Geographers.

Boddington, M.A. (1978) The classification of agricultural land in England and Wales. *Rural Planning Services.*

Boddy, M.J. (1976) The structure of mortgage finance: building societies and the British social formation. *Trans., Inst. Brit. Geogr.*, n.s. **1** (1) 58–71.

Bowler, I.R. (1976) The adoption of grant aid in agriculture. *Trans., Inst. Brit. Geogr.*, n.s. **1** (2) 143–58.

Breugel, I. (1975) The marxist theory of rent and the contemporary city: a critique of Harvey. In *Political Economy and the Housing Question.* Paper presented at the CSE Housing Workshop, London.

Bruton, M.J. (1975) *Introduction to Transportation Planning.* London, Hutchinson.

Bryan, M.L. (1975) Interpretation of an urban scene using multi-channel radar imagery. *Remote Sensing of the Environment* **4**, 49–66.

Burgess, E.W. (1925) The growth of the city: an introduction to a research project. In Park, R.E. and Burgess, E.W. (eds) *The City*, pp. 47–62. Chicago.

Burley, T.M. (1961) Land use or land utilization? *Professional Geographer* **13** (6) 18–20.

Burns, W. (1977) The Development Plan System. In Millward, S. (ed.) *Urban Harvest*, pp. 40–50. Berkhamsted,. Geographical Publications.

Calvocoresses, A.P. (1979). Proposed parameters for Mapsat. *Photogr. Eng. and Remote Sensing* **45** (4) 501–6.

Carney, J.G. and Hudson, R. (1976a) Newcastle: reactions to the Community Land Act in the North East. In *Lie of the Land*, pp. 18–19. London, The Land Campaign Working Party.

Carney, J.G. and Hudson, R. (1976b) *A Preliminary Report on Current*

Industry and Employment Analyses, Forecasts and Strategies for the North East: A Study of Regional and County Planning Documents (xiv + 122). Aycliffe and Peterlee Development Corporations.

Carney, J.G. and Hudson, R. (1977) *Prospects for the Northern Region: A Study of the Northern Region Strategy Team's Analyses, Forecasts and Recommendations* (vi + 57). Aycliffe and Peterlee Development Corporations.

Carney, J.G. and Hudson, R. (1978a) Capital, politics and ideology: the north of England, 1870–1946. *Antipode* **10** (2) 64–78.

Carney, J.G. and Hudson, R. (1978b) *Industry and Employment in the North East: A Report on Current Structure Plans for Hartlepool, Durham and Tyne-Wear* (vii + 100). Aycliffe and Peterlee Development Corporations.

Carney, J.G., Hudson, R. and Lewis, J.R. (1977) Coal combines and inter-regional uneven development in the UK. In Massey, D. and Batey, P. (eds) *Alternative Frameworks for Analysis*, pp. 56–67. London, Pion.

Carter, H. (1976) *The Study of Urban Geography*. London, Edward Arnold.

Carter, P., Gardner, W.E. and Smith, T.F. (1976) The use of Landsat imagery for the automated recognition of urban development. In Collins, W.G. and van Genderen, J. (eds) *Land Use Studies by Remote Sensing*, pp. 54–88. London, Remote Sensing Society.

Carter, P. and Jackson, M.J. (1976) The automated recognition of urban development from Landsat images. *Proceedings of Symposium on Machine Processing of Remotely Sensed Data*. LARS, Purdue University, Indiana, Paper 7B—15 to 25.

Castells, M. (1976) Is there an urban sociology? In Pickvance, C.G. (ed.) *Urban Sociology: Critical Essays*, pp. 33–59. London, Methuen.

CCPD (1978) *Land Use in Cleveland 1978*. Cleveland County Planning Department, Report 143.

Champion, A.G. (1975) An estimate of the changing extent and distribution of urban land in England and Wales, 1950–1970. *Research Paper* No. 10, Centre for Environmental Studies, London.

Chapin, S. (1965) *Urban Land-use Planning* Urbana, Illinois, University of Illinois Press.

Chisholm, M.D.I. (1962, 1973, 1979) *Rural Settlement and Land Use*. London, Hutchinson.

Chisholm, M.D.I. (1979) Von Thünen anticipated. *Area* **11** (1) 37–40.

Civic Trust (1977) *Urban Wasteland*. London, Civic Trust.

Clarke, S. and Ginsburg, N. (1976) The political economy of housing. *Kapitalstate* **4–5**, 64–98.

Clawson, M. and Stewart, C.L. (1965) *Land Use Information. A Critical Survey of US Statistics Including Possibilities for Greater Uniformity*. Baltimore, The Johns Hopkins Press for Resources for the Future, Inc.

Cliff, A.D. and Ord, J.K. (1975) Model building and the analysis of spatial pattern in human geography. *Journal of the Royal Statistical Society*, series B **37**, 297–348.

Cline, M.G. (1963) Logic of the new systems of soil classification. *Soil Science* **96**, 1.

Clout, H.P. (1972) *Rural Geography: An Introductory Survey*, Oxford, Pergamon.

Cocks, K.D. and Ives, J.R. (1978) Regional land use planning objectives. In Austin, M.P. and Cocks, K.D. (eds) *Land Use on the South Coast of New South Wales: A Study in Methods of Acquiring and Using Information to Analyse Regional Land Use Options*, Vol. 1, pp. 98–112. CSIRO.

Colby, C.C. (1933) The railway traverse as an aid in reconnaissance *Annals, Assoc. Amer. Geogr.* **23** 157–64.

Coleman, A. (1961) The Second Land Use Survey: progress and prospect. *Geographical Journal* **127** (2) 168–86.

Coleman, A. (1976) Is planning really necessary? *Geographical Journal* **142** (3) 411–37.

Coleman, A. (1978) Agricultural land losses: the evidence from maps. In Rogers, A.W. (ed.) *Urban Growth, Farmland Losses and Planning*, pp. 16–33. Rural Geography Study Group, Institute of British Geographers.

Coleman, A., Isbell, J.E. and Sinclair, G. (1974) The comparative statistics approach to British land use trends. *Cartographic Journal* **11** (1) 34–41.

Coleman, A. and Maggs, K.R.A. (1962) *Land Use Survey Handbook*, Second Land Use Survey [by same authors, fourth (Scottish) edition, 1965].

Collins, W.G. and El-Beik, A.H.A. (1971) The acquisition of urban land use information from aerial photographs of the city of Leeds (Great Britain). *Photogrammetria* **27**, 71–92.

Colwell, R.N. (1960) *Manual of Photographic Interpretation*. Falls Church, Virginia. American Society of Photogrammetry.

Cooke, R.U. and Harris, D.R. (1970) Remote sensing of the terrestrial environment. *Trans., Inst. Brit. Geogr.* **50**, 1–23.

Coppock, J.T. (1968) Changes in rural land use in Great Britain. In *Land Use and Resources: Studies in Applied Geography*. A Memorial Volume to Sir Dudley Stamp, pp. 118–25. Special Publication No. 1, Institute of British Geographers.

Coppock, J.T. (1970) Evaluation of land use data in developed countries. In Cox, I.H. (ed.) *New Possibilities and Techniques for Land Use and Related Surveys*, pp. 121–28. Berkhamsted, Geographical Publications.

Coppock, J.T. (1974) Contribution to discussion on paper by P. Hall. *Geographical Journal* **140** (3) 412–13.

Coppock, J.T. (1975) Maps by line printer. In Davis, J.C. and McCullagh, M.J. (eds) *Display and Analysis of Spatial Data*, pp. 137–54. Chichester, Wiley.

Coppock, J.T. (1978) Land use. In Maunder, W.F. (ed.) *Reviews of UK*

Statistical Sources, Vol. 8, part 14, pp. 1–102. Oxford, Pergamon.

Coppock, J.T. and Gebbett, L.F. (1978) Land use and town and country planning. In Maunder, W.F. (ed.) *Reviews of UK Statistical Sources*, Vol. 8. Oxford, Pergamon.

County Council of Durham (1951) *County Development Plan: Written Statement*. Durham.

County Council of Durham (1964) *County Development Plan Amendment: Written Statement*. Durham.

Crowley, J.R. (1975) *Land Use Planning*. Washington D.C., National Academy of Sciences.

CSO (1968) *The Standard Industrial Classification (SIC)*, 3rd edn. London, Central Statistical Office.

CSO (1979) *Social Trends*. London, HMSO.

Curtis, L.F. (1978) Remote sensing systems for monitoring crops and vegetation. *Progress in Physical Geography* **2** (1) 55–79.

Dacey, M.F. (1970) The syntax of a triangle and some other figures. *Pattern Recognition* **2**, 11–31.

Dale, P.F. (1977) Cadastres and Cadastral maps. *Cartographic Journal* **14** (1) 44–8.

Dantzig, G. (1963) *Linear Programming and its Extensions*. Princeton, Princeton University Press.

Darby, H.C. (1951) The changing English landscape. *Geographical Journal* **117**, 377–98.

Darby, H.C. (1973) Domesday Book: the first land utilisation survey. In Baker, A.R.H. and Harley, J.B. (eds) *Man Made the Land*, pp. 37–45. Newton Abbot, David and Charles.

Davies, R.L. (1972) Structural models of retail distribution, analogies with settlement and urban land use theories. *Trans., Inst. Brit. Geogr.* **57**, 59–82.

Dear, M. and Clark, G. (1978) The state and geographic process: a critical review. *Environment and Planning A* **10**, 173–83.

De Bruijn, C.A. (1978) Methods of converting remote sensed data. In *Proceedings of the European Seminar on Regional Planning and Remote Sensing*, pp. 118–31. Council of Europe, Ministers responsible for Regional Planning.

Denman, D.R. (1970) Proprietary patterns and land use. In Cox, I.H. (ed.) *New Possibilities and Techniques for Land Use and Related Surveys*, pp. 27–40. Berkhamsted, Geographical Publications.

Desai, M. (1974) *Marxian Economic Theory*. London, Gray Mills.

Diamond, D. (1974) Contribution to discussion on paper by P. Hall. *Geographical Journal*, **140** (3) 410–12.

Dickinson, G.C. (1979) *Maps and Air Photographs*, 2nd edn. London, Edward Arnold.

Dickinson, G.C. and Shaw, M.A. (1977) What is 'land use'? *Area* **9** (1) 38–42.

Dickinson, G.C. and Shaw, M.A. (1978) The collection of national land-use statistics in Great Britain: a critique. *Environment and Planning A* **10**, 295–303.

DoE (1973) *Manual on Point Referencing Properties and Parcels of Land.* London, Department of the Environment.

DoE (1974a) Joint Circular 71/74. *DoE Statistics of Land Use Change.* London, HMSO.

DoE (1974b) *De facto* urban areas in England and Wales, 1966. Unpublished report, available from DoE Library, 2 Marsham Street, London SW1.

DoE (1975) Definition of urban areas. *Occasional Paper* 2, London Urban Affairs Directorate, Department of the Environment.

DoE (1978) *Developed Areas 1969. A Survey of England and Wales.* London, Department of the Environment.

Doyle, F.J. (1978) The next decade of satellite remote sensing. *Photogr. Eng. and Remote Sensing* **44** (2) 155–64.

Dueker, K.J. and Talcott, R. (1973) Statewide land use analysis and information requirements. *Working Paper* 13, Institute of Urban and Regional Research, University of Iowa.

Duffield, B.S. and Coppock, J.T. (1975) The delineation of recreational landscapes: the role of a computer-based information system. *Trans., Inst. Brit. Geogr.* **66**, 141–8.

ECU (1978) *Land Use Mapping by Local Authorities in Britain.* Experimental Cartography Unit, Natural Environment Research Council.

Edel, M. (1976) Marx's theory of rent: urban applications. *Kapitalstate* **4–5**, 100–24.

Elliott, B. (1978) Social change in the city: structure and process. In Abrams, P. (ed.) *Work, Urbanisation and Inequality*, pp. 17–54. London, Weidenfeld and Nicolson.

Engels, F. (1845, repr. 1962) *The Condition of the Working Class in England.* London.

Estes, J. (1974) Imaging with photographic and non-photographic sensor systems. In Estes, J.E. and Senger, L.W. (eds) *Remote Sensing: Techniques for Environmental Analysis*, pp. 15–50, Santa Barbara, Hamilton.

Estes, J.E. and Senger, L.W. (eds) (1974) *Remote Sensing: Techniques for Environmental Analysis.* Santa Barbara, Hamilton.

Evans, I.S. (1979) Relationships between Great Britain census variables at the 1 km aggregated level. In Wrigley, N. (ed.) *Statistical Applications in the Spatial Sciences*, pp. 141–84. London, Pion.

Everson, J.A. and Fitzgerald, B.P. (1972) *Inside the City.* London, Longman.

Fegeas, R.G. and Kewer, P.M. (1977) Transfer of land use and land cover and associated maps into digital format. *Remote Sensing of the Electro Magnetic Spectrum* **4** (4) 55–66.

Field, E.E. (1930) The land utilization map of Northampton. *Geography* **15**, 408–12.

Firey, W. (1945) Sentiment and symbolism as ecological variables. *American Sociological Review* **10**, 140–8.

Fitzgerald-Lins, K. and Chambers, M.J. (1977) Determination of accuracy and information content of land use and land cover maps at different scales. *Remote Sensing of the Electro Magnetic Spectrum* **4** (4) 41–54.

Floyd, B.N. (1972) Some spatial aspects of rural land use in tropical Africa. *Occasional Publication* No. 9, Department of Geography, University of the West Indies.

Floyd, B.N. (1978) Resource inventory in the Commonwealth of Puerto Rico. *Area* **10** (5) 399–400.

Fordham, R.C. (1974) Measurement of urban land uses. *Occasional Paper* No. 1, Department of Land Economy, University of Cambridge.

Fordham, R.C. (1975) Urban land use change in the United Kingdom during the second half of the twentieth century. *Urban Studies* **12**, 71–84.

Form, W.H. (1954) The place of social structure in the determination of land use: some implications for a theory of urban ecology. *Social Forces* **32** (4) 317–23.

Found, W.C. (1974) *A Theoretical Approach to Rural Land-use Patterns.* London, Edward Arnold.

Frey, H.T. (1973) *Major Uses of Land in the United States—Summary for 1969.* US Department of Agriculture, Economic Research Service, Agr. Econ. Rept 247.

Frolov, Y.S. with Maling, D.H. (1969) The accuracy of area measurement by point counting techniques. *Cartographic Journal* **6**, 21–35.

Gallagher, D.B., Kleckner, R.L. and Lins, H.F. (1977) Applications of land use and land cover maps and data compiled from remotely sensed data. *Remote Sensing of the Electro Magnetic Spectrum* **4** (4) 117–25.

GAG (1977) *Feasibility and Design Study for a Computer Algorithms Library.* Geography Algorithms Group, Department of Geography, University College, London.

Gardiner-Hill, R.C. (1972) The development of digital maps. *Ordnance Survey Professional Paper* No. 23, Southampton.

Garner, B.J. (1966) The internal structure of shopping centres. *Studies in Geography* No. 12, Northwestern University.

Garner, B.J. (1968) Models of urban geography and settlement location. In Chorley, R.J. and Haggett, P. (eds) *Socio-Economic Models in Geography*, pp. 303–60. London, Methuen.

Garrison, W.L., Berry, B.J.L., Marble, D.F., Nystuen, J.D. and Morrill, R.L. (1959) *Studies of Highway Development and Geographic Change.* Westport, Conn., Greenwood Press.

Gautam, N.C. (1976) Aerial photo interpretation techniques for classifying urban land use. *Photogr. Eng. and Remote Sensing* **42** (6) 815–22.

Gazzard, R. (1978) Community Land Act and the environment. *Town and Country Planning* November, 493–8.

Gittus, E. (1964) The structure of urban areas: a new approach. *Town Planning Review* **35**, 5–20.

Goddard, J., Drewett, R. and Spence, N. (1976) Urban change in Britain 1951–71. *Research Report* No. 10, Department of the Environment.

Goodall, B. (1970) Some effects of legislation on land values. *Regional Studies* **4**, 11–23.

Goodchild, M.F. (1978) Statistical aspects of the polygon overlay problem. In Dutton, G. (ed.) *Harvard Papers on Geographical Information Systems, Vol. 6, Spatial Algorithms*. Distributed by Addison-Wesley, London.

Gottman, J. (1961) *Megalopolis: The Urbanised Northeastern Seabord of the United States*. New York, Krans-Thompson.

Gould, P.R. (1963) Man against his environment: a game theoretic framework. *Annals, Assoc. Amer. Geogr.* **53**, 290–7.

Gould, P.R. (1965) Wheat on Kilimanjaro; the perception of choice within game and learning model frameworks. *General Systems* **10**, 157–66.

Green, N.E. (1957) Aerial photographic interpretation and social structure of the city. *Photogrammetric Engineering* **23**, 89–96.

Griffin, E. (1973) Testing the von Thünen theory in Uruguay. *Geographical Review* **63** (4) 500–16.

Grigg, D. (1965) The logic of regional systems. *Annals, Assoc. Amer. Geogr.* **55** (3) 465–91.

Grigg, D. (1967) Regions, models and classes. In Chorley, R.J. and Haggett, P. (eds) *Models in Geography*. London, Methuen.

GSS (1975) *UK in Figures*. London, Government Statistical Service.

Habermas, J. (1972) *Knowledge and Human Interests*. London, Heinemann.

Habermas, J. (1976) *Legitimation Crisis*. London, Heinemann.

Haggett, P. (1966) *Locational Analysis in Human Geography*. London, Edward Arnold.

Haggett, P. (1975) *Geography: A Modern Synthesis*. New York, Harper and Row.

Haggett, P., Cliff, A. and Frey, A.E. (1977) *Locational Analysis*, Vols 1 and 2. London, Edward Arnold.

Haig, R.M. (1926) Towards an understanding of the metropolis. *Quarterly Journal of Economics* **40**, 179–208.

Hall, P. (1966) *Von Thünen's Isolated State*. Oxford.

Hall, P. (ed.) (1973) *The Containment of Urban England*. London, Allen and Unwin.

Hall, P. (1974) The containment of urban England. *Geographical Journal* **140** (3) 386–417.

Hamilton, F.E.I. (1968) Models of industrial location. In Chorley, R.J. and Haggett, P. (eds) *Socio-Economic Models in Geography*, pp. 362–424. London, Methuen.

Hammond, R. and MacCullagh, P.S. (1978) *Quantitative Techniques in Geography—An Introduction*, 2nd edn. London, Oxford University Press.

Hansen, V. (1960) Some characteristics of a growing suburban region. *Saertryk af Geografisk Tidsskrift* **59**, 214–25.

Harley, J.B. (1975) *Ordnance Survey Maps. A Descriptive Manual*. London, HMSO.

Harley, J.B. (1979) *The Ordnance Survey and Land use mapping: Parish books of reference and the County Series 25 inch maps, 1855–1918*. Historical Geography Research Group Pamphlet Series.

Harris, C.D. and Ullman, E.L. (1945) The nature of cities. *Annals, American Academy of Pol. and Sci.* **242**, 7–17. Reprinted in Mayer, H.M. and Kohn, F. (eds) (1959) *Readings in Urban Geography*. Chicago, Chicago University Press.

Harrison, J.C. (1978) The LAMIS system. Paper presented to Royal Institute of Chartered Surveyors, Land Surveyors Division and North East London Polytechnic conference on 'Data banks and digital mapping', November 1978.

Hartman, G.W. (1950) The Central Business District: a study in urban geography. *Economic Geography* **26**, 237–44.

Harvey, D.W. (1963) Locational change in the Kentish hop industry and the analysis of land use patterns. *Trans., Inst. Brit. Geogr.* **33**, 123–44.

Harvey, D.W. (1969) *Explanation in Geography*. London, Edward Arnold.

Harvey, D. (1973) *Social Justice and the City*. London, Edward Arnold.

Harvey, D. (1974) Class-monopoly rent, finance capital and the urban revolution. *Regional Studies* **8** (3) 239–55.

Harvey, D. (1975) Class structure in a capitalist society and the theory of residential differentiation. In Peel, R.F., Chisholm, M.D.I. and Haggett, P. (eds) *Processes in Physical and Human Geography*, pp. 354–69. London, Heinemann.

Harvey, D. and Chatterjee, L. (1974) Absolute rent and the structuring of space by governmental and financial institutions. *Antipode* **6** (1) 22–36.

Hay, A. (1978) Sampling designs to test land-use map accuracy. *Photogrammetric Engineering and Remote Sensing* **45** (4) 529–33.

Heady, E.O. and Egbert, A.C. (1964) Regional programming of efficient agricultural production. *Econometrica* **3**, 374–86.

Hidore, J.J. (1963) The relationship between cash-grain farming and land-forms. *Economic Geography* **39**, 84–9.

HMSO (1972) *General Information System for Planning*. London, HMSO.

HMSO (1975) *National Land Use Classification*. London, HMSO.

Hodgart, R. (1979) Optimizing access to public services: a review of problems, models and methods of locating central facilities. *Progress in Human Geography* **2** (1) 17–48.

Hodgkiss, A. (1977) The geographer as mapmaker: the role of cartography in recording the man-environment relationship. In Open University, *Man and Environment*, pp. 91–135. Units 1–3, D204 Fundamentals of Human Geography Course. Milton Keynes, Open University Press.

Hofstee, P. (1976) Actual space use map Enschede—urban 'land use' inventory with photo-interpretation. *ITC Journal* **4** (3) 431–55.

Holloway, J. and Piciotto, S. (eds) (1978) *State and Capital: A Marxist Debate*, pp. 1–31. London, Edward Arnold.

Hord, R.M. and Brooner, W. (1976) Land use map accuracy criteria. *Photogr. Eng. and Remote Sensing* **42** (5) 671–7.

Horton, F. (1974) Remote sensing techniques and urban data acquisition. In Estes, J.E. and Senger, L.W. (eds) *Remote Sensing: Techniques for Environmental Analysis*, pp. 243–76. Santa Barbara, Hamilton.

Horvath, R.J. (1969) Von Thünen's Isolated State and the area around Addis Ababa, Ethiopia. *Annals, Assoc. Amer. Geogr.* **59**, 309–23.

Horwood, E. and Boyce, R. (1959) *Studies of the Central Business District and Urban Freeway Development*. Seattle, University of Washington Press.

Hoyt, H. (1939) *The Structure and Growth of Residential Neighbourhoods in American Cities*. Washington D.C., US Federal Housing Administration.

Hsu, M.L., Kozar, K., Orning, G.W. and Streed, P.G. (1975) Computer applications in land-use mapping and the Minnesota Land Management Information System. In Davis, J.C. and McCullagh, M.J. (eds) *Display and Analysis of Spatial Data*, pp. 298–310. New York, Wiley.

Hsu, S.Y. (1978) Texture-tone analysis for automated land-use mapping. *Photogr. Eng. and Remote Sensing* **44** (11) 1393–404.

Hudson, R. (1976) New towns in North East England, Vols. 1 and 2. Report to the Social Science Research Council, HR 1734, London.

Hurd, R.M. (1903) *Principles of City Land Values*. New York, The Record and Guide.

Irvine, J. (1974) A description and appraisal of the CLUSTER system. *BURISA* **17**, 6–8.

Ive, G. (1975) Walker and the 'New Conceptual Framework' of urban rent. *Antipode* **7** (1) 20–30.

Jaakkola, S. (1978) Monitoring of agricultural and forest resources by remote sensing techniques. In *Proceedings of the European Seminar on Regional Planning and Remote Sensing*, pp. 99–104. Council of Europe, Ministers responsible for Regional Planning.

Jackson, M.J., Carter, P., Gardner, W.G. and Smith, T.F. (1980) Urban land use mapping from remotely sensed data. *Photogr. Eng. and Remote Sensing* (forthcoming).

Jackson, R. (1972) A vicious circle?—the consequences of von Thünen in tropical Africa. *Area* **4** (4) 258–61.

Jeffers, J.N.R. (1970) Modern statistical techniques in land use surveys. In Cox, I.H. (ed.) *New Possibilities and Techniques for Land Use and Related Surveys*, pp. 65–72. Berkhamsted, Geographical Publications.

Jensen, J.R. (1978) Digital land cover mapping using layered classification logic and physical composition attributes. *American Cartographer* **5** (2) 121–32.

Jevons, W.S. (1871, repr. 1970) *The Theory of Political Economy*. Harmondsworth, Penguin.

Johnston, R.J. (1968) Choice in classification: the subjectivity of objective methods. *Annals, Amer. Assoc. Geogr.* **58**, 575–89.

Johnston, R.J. (1971) *Urban Residential Patterns*. London, Bell.

Johnston, R.J. (1976) Classification in geography. *CATMOG* No. 6, Geo-abstracts, University of East Anglia.

Johnston, R.J. (1977) Urban geography: city structures. *Progress in Human Geography* **1** (1) 118–29.

Jonasson, O. (1925) Agricultural regions of Europe. *Economic Geography* (**3**) 277–315.

Jones, E. (1960) *A Social Geography of Belfast*. London.

Kain, R. (1977) Tithe surveys and the rural landscape of England and Wales. *Bulletin, Society of University Cartographers* **11** (2) 1–3.

Kendall, D.G. (1971) Construction of maps from 'odd bits of information'. *Nature* **231**, 158–9.

King, L.J. (1969) *Statistical Analysis in Geography*. Englewood Cliffs, New Jersey, Prentice-Hall.

King, R. (1973) *Land Reform: The Italian Experience*. London, Butterworth.

Klingebiel, A.A. and Montgomery, P.H. (1961) *Land Capability Classification*. Agriculture Handbook No. 210, Soil Conservation Service, US Department of Agriculture.

Knos, D. (1962) *Distribution of Land Values in Topeka, Kansas*, Kansas, Lawrence.

Kollmorgen, W.M. and Jenks, G.F. (1958) Suitcase farming in Sully County, South Dakota. *Annals, Amer. Assoc. Geogr.* **48**, 27–40.

Kostrowicki, J. (1970) Data requirements for land use survey maps. In Cox, I.H. (1970) (ed.) *New Possibilities and Techniques for Land Use and Related Surveys*, pp. 73–84, Berkhamsted, Geographical Publications.

Kraus, S.P., Senger, L.W. and Ryerson, J.M. (1974) Estimating population from photographically determined residential land use types. *Remote Sensing of the Environment* **3**, 35–42.

Lacoste, Y. (1973) An illustration of geographical warfare: bombing of the dikes on the Red River, North Vietnam. *Antipode* **5** (2) 1–13.

Lamarche, F. (1976) Property development and the urban question. In Pickvance, C.G. (ed.) *Urban Sociology: Critical Essays*, pp. 85–118. London, Methuen.

Landgrebe, D. (1976) Computer-based remote sensing technology—a look to the future. *Remote Sensing of the Environment* **5**, 229–46.

Lave, L. (1970) Congestion and urban location. *Papers, Regional Science Association* **25**, 133–5.

Lee, N. and Wood, C. (1978) EIA—a European perspective. *Built Environment* **4** (2) 101–10.

Lo, C.P. (1976) *Geographical Applications of Aerial Photography.* Newton Abbot, David and Charles.

Locklin, D.P. (1966) *The Economics of Transportation.* Homewood, Illinois, Irwin.

Lösch, A. (1954) *The Economics of Location.* New Haven, Conn., Yale University Press.

McCrone, G. (1969) *Regional Policy in Britain.* London, George Allen and Unwin.

McEwen, J. (1977) *Who Owns Scotland? A Study in Land Ownership.* Edinburgh, EUSPB.

McLaughlin, J.D. and Clapp, J.L. (1977) Towards the development of multi-purpose cadastres. *Journal of the Surveying and Mapping Division American Congress on Survey and Mapping,* 53–73.

MAFF (1965) *Agricultural Land Classification.* Technical Report No. 11, London, Agricultural Land Services, Ministry of Agriculture, Fisheries and Food.

MAFF (1968) *Agricultural Land Classification Map of England and Wales. Explanatory Note.* London, Agricultural Land Service, Ministry of Agriculture, Fisheries and Food.

MAFF (1974) *Agricultural Land Classification of England and Wales.* London, Agricultural Development and Advisory Service, Ministry of Agriculture, Fisheries and Food.

Mandel, E. (1968) *Marxist Economic Theory,* Vols 1 and 2. London, Merlin Press.

Mandel, E. (1975) *Late Capitalism.* London, New Left Books.

Mann, P. (1965) *An Approach to Urban Sociology.* London, Routledge and Kegan Paul.

Marschner, F.J. (1950) *Major Land Uses in the United States (Map Scale 1: 5,000,000).* Agricultural Research Service, US Department of Agriculture.

Margerison, T. (1977) *Computers and the Renaissance of Cartography.'* London, Natural Environment Research Council.

Marx, K. (1859, repr. 1970) *A Contribution to the Critique of Political Economy.* New York, International Publishers.

Marx, K. (1861, repr. 1963) *Theories of Surplus Value.* London, Lawrence and Wishart.

Marx, K. (1894, repr. 1971) *Capital, Vol. III.* London, Lawrence and Wishart.

Massey, D. and Catalano, A. (1978) *Capital and Land: Landownership by Capital in Great Britain.* London, Edward Arnold.

Milazzo, V.A., Ellefsen, R.A. and Schwarz, D.W. (1977) Updating land use and land cover maps. *Remote Sensing of the Electro Magnetic Spectrum* **4** (4) 103–16.

Miller, L.D., Nualchawee, K. and Tom, C. (1978) Analysis of the dynamics of shifting cultivation in the tropical forests of Northern Thailand using landscape modelling and classification of Landsat imagery. National Aeronautical and Space Administration (NASA) Technical Memo 7945.

Mills, D. (1973) Suburban and exurban growth. In *The Spread of Cities*, pp. 48–102, Unit 24. Open University Course D 201.

Millward, S. (ed.) (1977) *Urban Harvest*. Berkhamsted, Geographical Publications.

Mitchell, W.B., Guptill, S.C., Anderson, E.A., Fegeas, R.G. and Hallam, C.A. (1977) Giras—a geographic information retrieval and analysis for handling land use and land cover data. *Professional Paper* No. 1059, US Geological Survey.

Munton, R.J.C. (1977) Financial institutions: their ownership of agricultural land in Great Britain. *Area* **9** (1) 29–37.

Munton, R.J.C. (1978) Contribution to discussion. In Rogers, A.W. (ed.) *Urban Growth, Farmland Losses and Planning*, pp. 60–1. Rural Geography Study Group, Institute of British Geographers.

Murphy, R.E. (1966) *The American City – An Urban Geography*. New York, McGraw-Hill.

Murphy, R.E., Vance, J.E. Jr. and Epstein, B.J. (1955) Internal structure of the central business district. *Economic Geography* **31**, 21–46.

Murray, R. (1977, 1978) Value and theory of rent: part 1 and 2. *Capital and Class* **3**, 100–22; **4**, 11–33.

Muth, R. (1969) *Cities and Housing*. Chicago, University of Chicago Press.

NASA (1976) *Landsat Data Users Handbook*. National Aeronautics and Space Administration Document No. 76DS 4258.

NGPS (1974) *Memorandum 7: Coding, Digitising and Land Use*. National Gazetteer Pilot Study, Department of the Environment, Tyne and Wear County.

Niedercorn, J.H. and Hearle, E.F.R. (1964) Recent land use trends in forty-eight large American cities. *Land Economics* **9** (1) 105–9; also in Bourne, L.S. (ed.) (1971) *Internal Structure of the City*, pp. 121–7, Oxford.

Nunnally, N.R. (1974) Interpreting land use from remote sensor imagery. In Estes, J.E. and Senger, L.W. (eds) *Remote Sensing: Techniques For Environmental Analysis*, pp. 167–87. Santa Barbara, Hamilton.

Nunnally, N.R. and Witmer, R.E. (1970) Remote sensing for land-use studies. *Photogrammetric Engineering* **36** (5) 449–53.

OECD (1976) *Land Use Policies and Agriculture*. Paris, Organisation for Economic Cooperation and Development.

Offe, C. (1975) Introduction to Part II. In Lindberg, L.W., Alford, R., Crouch, C. and Offe, C. (eds) *Stress and Contradiction in Modern Capitalism*. Lexington, Mass., Heath.

Openshaw, S. (1977). A geographic solution to scale and aggregation problems in region building, partitioning and spatial modelling. *Trans. Inst. Brit. Geogr.* n.s. **2** (4) 459–72.

OS (1976) *SUSI—the Supply of Unpublished Survey Information*. Southampton, Ordnance Survey.

Park, R.E. (1925, repr. 1967) The city—suggestions for the investigation of human behaviour in the urban environment. In Park, R.E., Burgess, E.W. and McKenzie, R.D. (eds) *The City*, pp. 1–46. Chicago, University of Chicago Press.

Pattison, W.D. (1957) Beginnings of the American rectangular land survey system, 1784–1800. *Research Paper* No. 50, Department of Geography, University of Chicago.

Payne, A.D. (1975) Computer-based land transfer and registration. *Australian Computer Journal* 7 (3).

Pease, R.W., Jenner, C.G. and Lewis, J.E. (1977) Methods for analysis of the impact of land use on climate. *Remote Sensing of the Electro Magnetic Spectrum* 4 (4) 126–41.

Peet, R. (1969) The spatial expansion of commercial agriculture in the 19th century: a von Thünen interpretation. *Economic Geography* 45, 283–301.

Peet, R. (1972) Influences of the British market on agriculture and related economic development in Europe before 1860. *Trans., Inst. Brit. Geogr.* 56, 1–20.

Petrie, G. (1977) Orthophotomaps. *Trans., Inst. Brit. Geogr.* n.s. 2 (1) 49–70.

Pielou, E.C. (1965) The concept of randomness in the pattern of mosaics. *Biometrics* 21, 908–20.

Pocock, D.C.D. (1979) The novelist's image of the North. *Trans., Inst. Brit. Geogr.* n.s. 4 (1) 62–76.

Pocock, D.C.D. and Hudson, R. (1978) *Images of the Urban Environment.* London, Macmillan.

Pratt, W.K. (1978) *Digital Image Processing.* New York, Wiley.

Proudfoot, M.J. (1942) Sampling with traverse lines. *American Statistical Association Journal* 37, 265–70.

Quinn, J.A. (1939) The nature of human ecology: re-examination and redefinition. *Social Forces* 18.

Quinn, J.A. (1950) *Human Ecology.* Hamden, Conn., Shoe String Press.

Ratcliff, R.U. (1949) *Urban Land Economics* New York, McGraw-Hill.

Rhind, D.W. (1973a) Computer mapping of drift lithology from borehole records. *Rep. Inst. Geol. Sci.* 73/6, 12pp.

Rhind, D.W. (1973b) Generalisation and realism within automated cartographic systems. *Canadian Cartographer* 10, 51–62.

Rhind, D.W. (1974) An introduction to the digitising and editing of mapped data. In Dale, P.F. (ed.), *Automation in Cartography.* British Cartographers Society Special Publication 1.

Rhind, D.W. (1977) Computer-aided cartography. *Trans., Inst. Brit. Geogr.* n.s. 2 (1) 71–97.

Rhind, D.W. and Hudson, R. (1980) The Durham and Northumberland Land Use Surveys. *Occasional Paper*, Department of Geography, University of Durham.

Ricardo, D. (1817, repr. 1971) *Principles of Political Economy and Taxation.* Harmondsworth, Penguin.

Rice, P. (1978) Land use classification: a review of contemporary British sources. Informal Note 2, Transport Studies Group, University College, London.

Richardson, H.W. (1971) *Urban Economics.* Harmondsworth, Penguin.

Robertson, V.C. and Stoner, R.F. (1970) Land use surveying: a case for reducing the costs. In Cox, I.H. (ed.) *New Possibilities and Techniques for Land Use and Related Surveys,* pp. 3–16. Berkhamsted, Geographical Publications.

Robinson, A.H., Sale, R.D. and Morrison, J.L. (1978) *Elements of Cartography,* 4th edn. Chichester, Wiley.

Robson, B.T. (1969) *Urban Analysis: A Study of City Structure with Special Reference to Sunderland.* Cambridge, Cambridge University Press.

Rogers, A. and Dawson, J.A. (1979) Which digitiser? *Area* 11, 69–73; see also response by D. Rhind (1979) *Area* 11, 211–13 and reply by Rogers and Dawson.

Rogers, A.W. (ed.) (1978) Urban growth, farmland losses and planning. Rural Geography Study Group, Institute of British Geographers.

Rowley, R.L. (1978) Remote sensing and information. In *Proceedings of the European Seminar on Regional Planning and Remote Sensing,* Council of Europe, pp. 63–72 and subsequently.

Royaltey, H.H., Astrachan, E. and Sokal, R.R. (1975) Tests for patterns in geographic variation. *Geographical Analysis* 7, 369–95.

Rubinstein, J.M. (1978) *The French New Towns.* Baltimore, The Johns Hopkins University Press.

Rutherford, J., Logan, M.I. and Missen, G.J. (1966) *New Viewpoints in Economic Geography.* Sydney.

Rystedt, B. (1977) The Swedish Land Data Bank—a multipurpose information system. Cartographica Monograph 20. In Wastesson, O., Rystedt, B. and Taylor, D.R.F. (eds). *Computer Cartography in Sweden.*

Schaefer, K.H. and Sclar, E. (1975) *Access for All: Transportation and Urban Growth.* Harmondsworth, Penguin.

Schneider, D.M. with Amanullah, S. (1978) Computer-assisted land resources planning. Report No. 399, Planning Advisory Service, American Planning Association.

Schnore, L.F. (1965) On the spatial structure of cities in the two Americas. In Hauser, P.M. and Schnore, L.F. (eds) *The Study of Urbanisation,* ch. 10. New York, Wiley.

Sci-Tex (1979) *Response System for Cartography: Technical Description.* Bedford, Mass. Sci-Tex Corporation.

Scott, A.J. (1976) Land use and commodity production. *Regional Science and Urban Economics* 6, 147–60.

Seyfried, W.R. (1963) The centrality of urban land values. *Land Economics* 39 (3) 275–84.

Simmie, J.M. (1974) *Citizens in Conflict: the Sociology of Town Planning.* London, Hutchinson.

Simmons, J.W. (1971) Descriptive models of urban land use. In Bourne, L.S. (ed.) *Internal Structure of the City.* New York, Oxford University Press; also in *Canadian Geographer* (1965) **9** (3) 170–4.

Sinclair, R. (1967) Von Thünen and urban sprawl. *Annals, Assoc. Amer. Geogr.* **57**, 72–87.

Sjoberg, G. (1965) *The Pre-industrial City, Past and Present.* New York, Free Press of Glencoe.

Smith, P. (1962) Calgary: a study of urban patterns. *Economic Geography* **38**, 315–29.

Smith, T.F. (1978) Thematic cartography and remote sensing. In *Proceedings of European Seminar on Regional Planning and Remote Sensing,* pp. 154–71. Council of Europe, Ministers responsible for Regional Planning.

Smith, T.F., Van Genderen, J.L. and Holland, E.W. (1977) A land use survey of Developed Areas in England and Wales. *Cartographic Journal* **14** (1) 23–9.

Sneath, P.H.A. and Sokal, R.R. (1973) *Numerical Taxonomy.* San Francisco, Freeman.

Southard, R.B. (1978) Development of a digital cartographic capability in the National Mapping Program. Paper given to the 9th International Conference on Cartography, Maryland, USA.

Spicer, J. and members of the Joint Information System team (1979) *Information Systems for Government.* London, Department of the Environment.

Sraffa, P. (1960) *The Production of Commodities by Means of Commodities.* Cambridge, Cambridge University Press.

Stamp, L.D. (1931) The land utilisation of Britain. *Geographical Journal* **78**, 40–53.

Stamp, L.D. (1948) *The Land of Britain: Its Use and Misuse,* (3rd edn 1962). London, Longman.

Stamp, L.D. (ed.) (1961) *A History of Land Use in Arid Zones.* Paris, UNESCO.

Stamp, L.D. (1965) Land use statistics of the countries of Europe. *Occasional Paper* No. 3, World Land Use Survey.

Stamp, L.D. and Willatts, E.C. (1934) *The Land Utilisation Survey of Britain: An Outline Description of the First Twelve One-inch Maps.* London School of Economics.

Starkie, D.N.M. (1976) *Transportation Planning, Policy and Analysis,* Oxford, Pergamon.

Stevens, B.H. (1968) Location theory and programming models: the von Thünen case. *Papers Regional Science Association* **21**, 19–34.

Stoel, T.B. and Scherr, S.J. (1978) Experience with EIA in the United States. *Built Environment* **4** (2) 94–100.

Stringer, P. and Plumbridge, G. (1974) Publicity and communications media in structure planning. Linked research project in Public Participation in Structure Planning, Interim Paper No. 1, University of Sheffield.

Swain, P.H. (1978) Fundamentals of pattern recognition in remote sensing. In Swain P.H. and Davis, S.M. (eds) *Remote Sensing: The Quantitative Approach*, pp. 136–86 New York, McGraw-Hill.

Swain, P.H. and Davis, S.M. (1978) *Remote Sensing: The Quantitative Approach* New York, McGraw-Hill.

Taafe, E.J. and Gauthier, H.L. Jr. (1973) *Geography of Transportation*. Englewood Cliffs, New Jersey, Prentice-Hall.

Taylor, P.J. (1977) *Quantitative Methods in Geography*. Boston, Houghton Mifflin.

Thaman, R.R. (1974) Remote sensing of agricultural resources. In Estes, J.E. and Senger, L.W. (eds) *Remote Sensing: Techniques for Environmental Analysis*, pp. 189–223. Santa Barbara, Hamilton.

Thompson, C.J. (1978) Digital mapping in the Ordnance Survey 1968–78. Paper presented to International Society for Photogrammetry, Commission 4 meeting on 'New techniques for mapping', Ottawa, October 1978.

Thompson, L.L. (1979) Remote sensing using solid-state array technology. *Photogr. Engr. and Remote Sensing* **XLV** (1) 47–55.

Tobler, W. (1969) Satellite confirmation of settlement size coefficients. *Area* **3**, 30–3.

Tomlinson, R.F., Calkins, H.W. and Marble, D.F. (1976) *Computer Handling of Geographical Data*. Paris, UNESCO.

Turk, G. (1979) GT index: a measure of the success of prediction. *Remote Sensing of the Environment* **8**, 65–75.

Turner, D.M. (1977) *An Approach to Land Values*, Berkhamsted, Geographical Publications.

Unwin, D. (1979) Theoretical and quantitative geography in north-west Europe. *Area* **11** (2) 164–6.

van Genderen, J. and Lock, B.F. (1977) Testing land use map accuracy. *Photogrammetric Engineering and Remote Sensing* **43**, 1135–7.

van Genderen, J., Lock, B.F. and Vass, P.A. (1978) Remote sensing: statistical testing of thematic map accuracy. *Remote Sensing of the Environment* **7**, 3–14.

van Genderen, J., Vass, P.A. and Lock, B.F. (1976) Guidelines for using LANDSAT data for rural land use surveys in developing countries. *ITC Journal* **1**, 30–47.

von Neumann, J. and Morgenstern, O. (1944) *Theory of Games and Economic Behaviour*. Princeton, Princeton University Press.

von Thünen, J.H. (1826) *Der Isolierte Staat in Beziehung auf Landwirtschaft*, 1st edn. Rostock.

Waibel, L. (1958) *Capitulos de Geografía Tropical e do Brasil*. Rio de Janeiro.

Walker, P.A. and Davis, J.R., (1978) The Nelligen geographic processing system: system design. CSIRO, Division of Land Use Research Technical Memo 78/11, 25pp.

Walker, R.A. (1974) Urban ground rent: building a new conceptual theory. *Antipode* **6** (1) 51–78.

Walker, R.A. (1975) Contentious issues in marxian value and rent theory: a second and longer look. *Antipode* **7** (1) 31–53.

Watkins, T. (1978) The economics of remote sensing. *Photogrammetric Engineering and Remote Sensing* **44** (9) 1167–72.

Webster, R. (1977) *Quantitative and Numerical Methods in Soil Classification and Survey*. Oxford, Clarendon Press.

Wellar, B.S. (1969) The role of space photography in urban and transportation data series. In *Proceedings of the Sixth International Symposium on Remote Sensing of the Environment*, pp. 831–854, Ann Arbor University of Michigan.

Whitehand, J.W.R. (1972) Building cycles and the spatial pattern of urban growth. *Trans., Inst. Brit. Geogr.* **56**, 39–56.

Willatts, E.C. (1933) Change in land utilisation in the south-west of the London Basin, 1840–1932. *Geographical Journal* **82**, 515–28.

Willatts, E.C. (1937) *Middlesex and the London Region*. Report of the Land Utilisation Survey of Britain, Part 79.

Willatts, E.C. (1961) Contribution to discussion, following paper by Coleman, A. (1961). *Geographical Journal* **127**, 185.

Winch, K.L. (1978) *International Maps and Atlases in Print*, 2nd edn. Epping, Bowker.

Wise, M.J. (1951) On the evolution of the jewellery and gun quarter in Birmingham. *Trans., Inst. Brit. Geogr.* **15**, 59–72.

Wolpert, J. (1964) The decision process in the spatial context. *Annals, Assoc. Amer. Geogr.* **54**, 537–58.

Wood, W.F. (1955) Use of stratified random samples in a land use study. *Annals, Assoc. Amer. Geogr.* **45**, 350–67.

Wray, J.R. (1960) Photo interpretation in urban area analysis. In Colwell, R.N. (ed.) *Manual of Photographic Interpretation*, pp. 667–716. Washington D.C., American Society of Photogrammetry.

Yeates, M. (1965) Some factors affecting the spatial distribution of Chicago land values, 1910–60. *Economic Geography* **41**, 57–70.

Name index

Abler, R., 206, 210–12
Adams, T., 99
Aglietta, M., 179
AGRG, 5
Aldcroft, D., 216
Alexander, I. C., 114
Alexander, J. W., 162–3
Allan, J. A., 88
Alonso, W., 190, 196
Amanullah, S., 122, 124
Ambrose, P., 3, 6, 214, 221, 224, 231, 237–8
Ammer, U., 116
Anderson, J. R., 20, 31, 33, 38–9, 136
Anderson, K. E., 99
Anderson, M. A., 38, 51
Anderton, P., 131
Ash, M., 4

Baker, A. M., 20
Baker, W. S., 63
Balchin, W., 63
Barnbrock, J., 148
Barr, J., 4
Baver, M. E., 87
Baxter, R. S., 102, 110
Beard, J. S., 62
Berry, B. J. L., 20, 191, 196–8
Best, R. H., 7, 32, 49, 55–6, 131–3, 135, 139, 219
Betak, J. F., 115
Bigg, P. H., 131
Blenkinsop, A., 237
Blumenfeld, H., 183
Board, C., 62, 147
Boddy, M. J., 231
Bowler, I. R., 224
Boyce, R., 198, 200
Breugel, I., 235
Brooner, W., 51
Bruton, M. J., 4
Burgess, E. W., 161, 173–6, 178
Burley, T. M., 20
Burns, W., 219

Calvocoresses, A. P., 87
Carney, J. G., 216–17, 219, 224
Carter, H., 174, 183, 185, 189–90, 198
Carter, P., 65, 70–1, 82, 84
Castells, M., 186, 212–13
Catalano, A., 209
CCPD, 141–2
Chambers, M. J., 68
Champion, A. G., 13, 55–6
Chapin, S., 212–13
Chatterjee, L., 227
Chisholm, M. D. I., 147, 151–4, 160, 165–7
Civic Trust, 4
Clapp, J. L., 55
Clarke, G., 239
Clarke, S., 235
Clawson, M., 19
Cliff, A., 114
Cline, M. G., 39
Clout, H. P., 220–3, 236
Cocks, K. D., 120–1
Colby, C. C., 22

Coleman, A., 7, 13–14, 20, 36–7, 42, 50, 63, 132–3, 135, 139–40, 142
Colenutt, R., 214, 221, 224, 231, 237–8
Collins, W. G., 79
Colwell, R. N., 73, 75–7
Cooke, R. U., 72
County Council of Durham, 219
Coppock, J. T., 8, 16, 19, 24, 48, 53, 56, 122, 124, 129, 131, 139, 246
CSO, 6, 43, 142, 231
Curtis, L. F., 81

Dacey, M. F., 115
Dale, P. F., 55
Dantzig, G., 206
Darby, H. C., 4, 53–4
Davies, R. L., 198, 200–4
Davis, J. R., 105, 124
Davis, S. M., 105
Dawson, J. A., 98
Dear, M., 239
De Bruijn, C. A., 77–8
Denman, D. R., 6
Desai, M., 228, 240
Diamond, D., 8
Dickinson, G. C., 18–20, 25, 27, 29, 43, 75
DoE, 15–16, 22, 25, 39, 42, 50–1, 55, 65–6, 131, 134–5, 143
Doyle, F. J., 87
Duecker, K. J., 16
Duffield, B. S., 24, 124

ECU, 16, 55, 124
Edel, M., 235
Egbert, A. C., 206
El-Beik, A. H. A., 79
Elliott, B., 217, 236
Engels, F., 228
Epstein, B. J., 198
Estes, J., 69–70
Evans, I. S., 25
Everson, J. A., 177, 183, 185

Fegeas, R. G., 98
Field, E. E., 63
Firey, W., 205
Fitzgerald, B. P., 177, 183, 185
Fitzgerald-Lins, K., 68
Floyd, B. N., 7, 24, 125
Fordham, R. C., 57, 132, 135–7, 139
Form, W. H., 214
Found, W. C., 210
Frolov, Y. S., 20

GAG, 102
Gallagher, D. B., 5
Gardiner-Hill, R. C., 100–1
Gardner, W. E., 82
Garner, B. J., 191, 198–200
Garrison, W. L., 183
Gautam, N. C., 77, 143
Gauthier, H. L., 160
Gazzard, R., 4
Gebbett, L. F., 4, 19, 48, 53, 56, 129
Ginsburg, N., 235

Subject index

regional novels, 55
regional planning, 4, 42
remote sensing, 23, 25, 38, 42, 51, 65, 69–89
rent, 5, 174, 176–7, 190–7, 205, 215, 226, 231–4
  absolute, 233–5, 241
  capitalized, 194
  differential, 233–4, 236, 240
  ground, 224, 231
  maximization of, 209–10
  monopoly, 233–5, 238
Report on the Distribution of the Industrial
  Population, 1940 (the Barlow Report), 216–17
Royal Geographical Society, 7

sampling:
  non-random, 23
  point, 21–2, 25
  random, 20–1
  traverse, 22–3
  zones, 23–9
satellite imagery, 7–8, 20, 31–2, 49, 56, 69, 125,
  246
Scott Committee, 217, 221
Second Land Utilisation Survey of Great Britain,
  14, 35–7, 45, 49, 55, 63–5, 89, 130, 132, 139, 142
social process, 186, 188–9, 225, 226–7, 229
social relations, 150–1, 171, 189, 205, 229
socio-spatial structure, 213
  of city, 77, 172–4, 185
soil fertility, 151–3, 155, 158, 162, 164
spatial externalities, 226
Standard Industrial Classification (SIC), 37, 43
Standard Regions, 136
State intervention, 4, 180, 186–7, 214–25, 228,
  236–40
statistical analysis, 16
Structure Plans, 219–20, 237

suitcase farmers, 167–8
Swedish Land Data Bank, 120, 125

Thiessen polygons, 22
threshold, 197–8
Tithe Commutation Act, 1836, 59
Tithe Surveys, 59–62
Town and Country Planning Act, 1932, 216
Town and Country Planning Act, 1944, 224
Town and Country Planning Act, 1947, 32, 42, 49,
  216–20, 238
Town and Country Planning Act, 1968, 42, 219–20
Town and Country Planning Act, 1971, 45, 219
Town Development Act, 1952, 223
Town Map, 136, 218–19
Town Planning Act, 1909, 216
transport costs, 151, 153–4, 160–4, 168, 190–3,
  196, 233, 236
Tyne and Wear Joint Information System, 92, 94,
  101, 110, 117, 125

urbanization, 5–6, 176, 186, 214–16
US Geological Survey Classification, 37–41
US Standard Land Use Code (SLUS), 39–41
utility, 191, 196, 204, 236
Utthwatt Committee, 217–18

value, 232, 235, 240
  exchange, 227–31
  land, *see* land value
  surplus, 232–3, 240
  use, 228–31

wasteland, 4, 54
windfall gains, 3, 218, 237–8
Wisconsin Land Economic Inventory, 62
World Land Use Survey (WLUS), 13, 35–7, 45

Location index